Beyond 'Present

Beyond 'Presentism'

Re-Imagining the Historical, Personal, and Social Places of Curriculum

James Nahachewsky
University of Victoria, Canada

Ingrid Johnston
University of Alberta, Canada

SENSE PUBLISHERS
ROTTERDAM/BOSTON/TAIPEI

A C.I.P. record for this book is available from the Library of Congress.

ISBN 978-90-8790-998-7 (paperback)
ISBN 978-90-8790-999-4 (hardback)
ISBN 978-90-8790-001-2 (e-book)

Published by: Sense Publishers,
P.O. Box 21858, 3001 AW
Rotterdam, The Netherlands
http://www.sensepublishers.com

Printed on acid-free paper

Cover photo was taken by Bronwen Strembiski

TABLE OF CONTENTS

INTRODUCTION

Spaces can be real or imagined. Spaces can tell stories and unfold histories. Spaces can be interrupted, appropriated, and transformed through artistic and literary practices. (hooks, 1992, p. 153)

The curriculum task becomes the recovery of memory and history in ways that psychologically allow individuals to re-enter politically the public sphere in privately meaningful and ethically committed ways. (Pinar, 2004, pp. 240–241)

In recent years, place and history have emerged as key concepts in the effort to understand curriculum—what "curriculum" contains and what it could possibly signify. Pinar (2004) shows the deep connection of place and history to our own experiences of education and curriculum, and the deep necessity to avoid the condition of what he terms "presentism" by rethinking and reimagining our relationship to place and time. hooks (1992) also privileges the historical spaces of curriculum and pedagogy, suggesting the potential of remembered and imagined stories and histories to interrupt and transform how we live and learn together in today's society. Chambers (1999) points out that memory and history, both individual and collective, are located in particular places. She challenges curricular scholars and educators to write from a sense of place, "to find and write in a curricular language of our own, to seek and create interpretive tools that are our own, and to use all of this to map a topography for Canadian curriculum theory, one that is begun at home but works on behalf of everyone" (p. 11).

Yet curriculum, and its study, are not easily located or mapped in an ever-emergent era/culture of "posts," such as postmodernism, postcolonialism, poststructuralism, postfeminism. Societal and educational projects seem to be moving from past to present, unity to fragmentation, representation to a constant deferral of meaning, nationalism to global capitalism, and nature to text (Chambers, 2003). Smith (2003) believes that this can be a time and place of hope for Western societies and education, though. As modernism and its hold on education fluctuates, postmodernism makes possible a "motility of meaning . . . [that] works in favour of a deep relationalism," a possibility that is "relational, ecological, modest, conversational and somewhat mysterious" (p. 35). We need not be blindly submerged in the present—curricular studies should also create spaces to investigate the personal and social past as well as the future. It is this ability to engage in that which is "recollected forward" (Kierkegaard 1983, p. 131) that invites an understanding of the 'historical' and 'places' that inform curriculum theorizing and avoids the entrapment of presentism (Pinar, 2004).

The space of this book strives to expand, rather than contain, the plurality of curricular studies in Canada and throughout North America today. Each of the authors in this book's 12 chapters draws upon diverse personal, social, and geographical experiences to address a shared question of how remembered and imagined cultural histories and places interrupt, and possibly transform, teachers' and students' learning. Interruptions metaphorically open possibilities for seeing what Hershel (1955) calls "the past in the present tense" (p. 211). This book's edited collection of writings encourages educators to think broadly about the potential of historical personal and social places as concrete experience and metaphor to understand curriculum, in part, as the "yet-unnameable-which-is-constantly-proclaiming-itself" (Smith, 2003, p. 53).

Metaphor is used to challenge educational and curricular grand narrative through Blades's, Johnston and Tupper's, Donald's, and Naqvi's chapters. Blades explores how the Old Testament life of Serah—or her song—is an archetype for how the past provides a way to understand curriculum in the present, organized around three interrelated themes: announcing hope, remembering promise, and sharing witness. Johnston and Tupper relate Bakhtin's (1981) idea of "chronotope" to an educational context. Time and place in the school chronotope are synonymous, indicating the placement of self in a social world of particular making in relation to dominant cultural and social influences. The school chronotope thus naturally supports an exploration of the processes of identity formation and the constraints imposed by society on individuals as they grow up. Donald uses concepts of "fort" and "frontier" to reveal a colonial past and the present social/spatial divides that separate Aboriginal peoples and Canadians; how these ideas have deeply influenced the assumptions educators hold about knowledge, classroom culture, subject disciplines, and the purposes of education and schooling. Naqvi focuses on a discourse of how languages can serve as a bridge to create an imaginary space that can provide a present hybrid generation of students with a means to reflect upon identity, roots, and notions of ancestry.

Autobiography, history, and place mix throughout Garramone's, Callaghan's, Nellis's, and Ng-A-Fook's examinations of contradictions in curricular structure and experience. Garramone situates an autobiographical story of working as a tree planter in the clear-cuts of northern Ontario, a summer job for many Canadian youth, within a discussion of how space and place reveals a racial curriculum. Callaghan draws upon Michel Foucault's (1975/1995) notion of surveillance, Antonio Gramsci's (1971) idea of hegemony, as well as her own personal experience within Catholic schools, to illuminate the ways in which homophobia functions as an organizational structure within those schools. The film Farewell Oak Street is a touchstone in Nellis's understanding of his mother's and his own lives in Toronto. His chapter argues that curriculum is inseparable from place and mobilizes a knowledge/place relationship, creating an ethical obligation to these places and to what he calls their "hauntings." Ng-a-Fook's autobiographical writing maps his search for a method of understanding Derrida's curriculum on inhabiting and being inhabited by languages of the "other." Through his autobiographical writing, he demonstrates how reflecting critically on the historical significance of one's past helps to challenge the shadows of White colonialism perpetuated within the spaces of many Canadian classrooms.

In the book's final four chapters, curricular and classroom response to the many challenges and complexities of teaching today are examined. Richardson's chapter examines the degree to which Canadian education, particularly the social studies and history curriculum, plays a role in creating symbolic, internal borders between identity communities in Canada. The chapter reveals the failure of a regional curriculum initiative. Beck inquires into the internationalization of campuses across North America and its accompanying call for the internationalization of curriculum. Hers is a nuanced critique and analysis of internationalization employing concepts of "third space," "contact zones," and "inter" as transformative resistance. De Froy takes up the spatial possibilities offered by certain approaches to understanding in the classroom, and considers how one establishes movement from the periphery to the center of the literacy domain. By listening to struggling adolescents in an alternative high school setting, engagement in critical learning is recast through "imaging" before print is privileged. In the book's final chapter, Nahachewsky and Slomp explore the "sound and fury" of changing perspectives and practices in contemporary literacy education. Through two case studies—one in an online senior high language and literacy course and the other located in the brick and mortar spaces of a senior language and literacy classroom—they examine the emergent challenges educators and students face as they strive to understand what curriculum contains, and what it can possibly signify through a re-imagination of the personal, social, and historical places beyond presentism.

REFERENCES

Bakhtin, M. (1981). *The dialogic imagination*. Austin, TX: University of Texas Press.

Chambers, C. (1999). A topography for Canadian curriculum theory. *Canadian Journal of Education, 24*(2), 137–150.

Chambers, C. (2003). As Canadian as possible under the circumstances: A view of contemporary curricular discourses in Canada. In W. Pinar (Ed.), *The new international handbook of curriculum studies* (pp. 221–252). Mahwah, NJ: Lawrence Erlbaum.

Foucault, M. (1995). *Discipline and punish: The birth of the prison* (A. M. S. Smith, Trans.). New York: Vintage Books. (Original work published 1975).

Gramsci, A. (1971). *Selections from the prison notebooks*. New York: International.

Heschel, A. J. (1955). *God in search of man: A philosophy of Judaism*. New York: Farrar, Straus and Giroux.

hooks, b. (1992). *Black looks: Race and representation*. Boston: South End Press.

Kierkegaard. S. (1983). *Fear and trembling/Repetition* (H. V. Hong & E. H. Hong, Trans.). Princeton, NJ: Princeton University Press.

Pinar, W. F. (2004). *What is curriculum theory?* Mahwah, NJ: Lawrence Erlbaum.

Smith, D. (1998). *Pedagon: Interdisciplinary essays in the human sciences, pedagogy and culture*. New York: Peter Lang.

Smith, D. (2003). Curriculum and teaching face globalization. In W. Pinar (Ed.), *The new international handbook of curriculum studies* (pp. 35–51). Mahwah, NJ: Lawrence Erlbaum.

DAVID BLADES

1. SERAH'S SONG: LESSONS FOR DANCING WITH HISTORY AND CULTURE IN CURRICULUM STUDIES

History presents a beautiful vista—until you begin to traverse the land before you. At that moment, it immediately becomes clear that in certain places you might wish to go the ground is soft, wet, and dangerously unmarked. There is quicksand out there, but you have little advice to guide you, other than to stay on the well-worn, hardened paths that beckon. But we are tired of these routes and rightly suspicious of their destinations. It's those other spaces and places that call to us; it's their promise of discovery and insight into how we came to arrive at our present situation, and what we might do next, that gives us hope, that gives us a pedagogy of the past. Before you have hardly set out, however, it is easy to become bogged down, as I discovered when I set out to learn about my great-grandfather. What remains for my education are fragments already invested in the form and styles of their time, a time I don't live in and can't truly appreciate. There are letters, sure, but the ones written by my great-grandfather focus on different events and people than those written by my great-grandmother. There are pictures and objects. I can look at his tractor—that one-cylinder machine that shook like an out-of-balance washing machine—or try to imagine the dreams and hopes in his face, in those pictures of a face that is disturbingly like mine, only to be distracted and disenchanted by the hunting rifle he is carrying as he tries to live the life of an English country gentleman, whatever that is, in Canada.

Culture loves to dance, like the Dervish movements of intrigue and sophistication that invite breathless participation. Just as you consider what familiar tunes would make for a comfortable engagement, just as you find the courage to step out onto that polished, wooden floor to join in the dance, culture swings by already embraced in the arms of race. The two form a stunning pair. Their intoxicating, compelling waltz calls to us, like the sirens, to join in. But we are still wisely tied to our chairs, fettered by an evolving horror of their movement, and as the evening goes on we become increasingly convinced that if ever there were dancers who should be divorced, it's these two. The night is young, though, and we persist in the hope of having at least one dance with culture, excited by the possibility that if we can only hold our arms in the right positions, our feet will find the ability to learn new steps. But it's a tedious wait, for culture always seems to find new partners: first race, now religion, then economics, and finally, the most beautiful of all, history.

How do we come between these whirling bodies, cut into the dance, and choose a partner with whom we can start our own dance of curriculum studies? Standing at the brink of possibility, it is easy to be entranced by the complexity of the

J. Nahachewsky and I. Johnston (eds.), Beyond 'Presentism': Re-Imagining the Historical, Personal, and Social Places of Curriculum, 1–9.

movements required, our confidence shattered by the understood and well-appreciated challenge of resisting the seductive flirtations of the spaces and places that culture, dancing with colonial delight, would take us. History is an equally domineering partner, and there are better partners if we want to find new ways to dance, for, all too often, the caretakers of history—and they are everywhere, especially within the machinery of government—have chosen the spaces and places to explore. It's as if, stepping forward to begin the dance, a certain shyness takes over, justified by the haunting of poststructural voices over our shoulders, telling us that the minute we take the hand of culture or history or both the dance is already compromised by a strong partner determined to lead.

As for me, just when shyness was giving way to that kind of paralysis that entertains despair, an odd disjuncture in the form of a footnote appeared in the curriculum of my life. An exploration of a character from the past seemed to offer hope and the possibility of insight into how one can approach the spaces and places of culture and history in curriculum studies—or, at least, some useful dancing lessons.

Recently I learned of an odd reference in that collection of ancient narratives that Jews, Christians, and Muslims call the Bible, a small anomaly that became a mystery that became an education. According to the textual context, the patriarch Jacob had 53 grandsons. In accordance with the ancient patriarchal tradition of listing the names of sons only, the text identifies every one of those 53, but then inexplicably breaks with tradition and names one of Jacob's granddaughters: "Serah[1] the daughter of Asher." Although it is inconceivable that Jacob had only one granddaughter, no others are mentioned. A little research revealed, not surprisingly, that commentators, both ancient and modern, had also noticed this anomaly.

The mystery deepens considerably, for the commentators alerted me to the fact that Serah's name also appears much later in the Bible as the only woman listed by name within the extensive census taken of the Hebrew people who left Egypt (Numbers 26:46; I Chronicles 7:30). There is little doubt that this is the same person since her full name is provided, but this doesn't make sense, at least to our modern mind, for, according to the evidence interpreted by modern archaeology (Unger, 1954), the exodus from Egypt occurred at least 430 years after Jacob took his family there in the first place! Indeed, according to Jewish legend, Serah also appears in several other biblical accounts, intimating that she lived an exceptionally long life, either as a legend or, as the text suggests, a woman who experienced a type of immortality.

Who was this person? Given the considerable discussion about Serah in the *Midrashim*, the stories from the Jewish oral tradition that elaborate biblical accounts, this question seems to have intrigued ancient biblical scholars. These scholars consider Serah, the "living memory" of the descendants of Jacob, a woman blessed or cursed—and there is some debate about this—with a long life that enabled her to serve her people as both witness and repository of wisdom and story. She seems to appear at least three times in the history of her people (Bregman, 1998), each time providing that interruption to the discourses of culture that Heschel (1955) calls "seeing the past in the present tense" (pp. 211–212). Serah's timely voice at each moment seems to enable Jacob's children to "recollect forward," to use Kierkegaard's lovely phrase (Kierkegaard, 1983, pp. 131–132), the hopes and promises of a people in ways that encourage the realization of possibilities. Her subtle, timely enactment offers us lessons today on how those of us committed to understanding curriculum might walk right up to history and culture and ask them to dance. We already know that we should take the lead. What Serah's life offers us, I believe, is advice on *how* we might lead this dance, an intervention characteristic of Serah's life in our own curriculum theorising that reveals how we might invent new steps if we are willing and able to hold our strong, determined partners in new ways.

ANNOUNCING HOPE

We first encounter Serah by way of 16th-century Midrashic writings about Jacob's sons. These men sold their brother Joseph into slavery and then lied to their father, Jacob, telling him that wild beasts had killed his son. It was a loss Jacob never ceased to mourn. Yet the Bible records that Joseph not only survives his enslavement but through a series of events becomes the Minister of Agriculture for Egypt. With poetic irony and justice, Joseph becomes the person his brothers must meet and beg for help during a time of famine.

Returning from their travels with the news that Joseph is alive, the brothers now face a dilemma: How do they break the news to their father? Jacob has a weak heart, and the joyous news that his lost son is alive may be more than he can survive. He also is not known for his understanding temperament: The revelation of his sons' treachery is sure to invoke his considerable wrath. According to the legend, the brothers "decided to employ Asher's daughter, Serah, [to break the news] since she knew how to play the harp in a soothing manner" (Bregman, 1998, p. 4). As legend declares, Serah sat near Jacob while he was in prayer and repeatedly sang, "Joseph my uncle is alive and rules over the land of Egypt." In a moment of deep, personal revelation, Jacob realized that the message of his granddaughter was true. At this point Jacob, reinspired by hope, blesses Serah, saying, "My child, may death never rule over you for you brought my spirit back to life" (p. 4).

As messenger for her undeserving uncles, Serah enters into the history of Jacob's children as one willing and able to announce hope during a time of darkness. This suggests a direction in our calling—to engage in the project of what Pinar (2004) calls the "social and subjective reconstruction" of curriculum (p. 8). In the same way that Pinar offers help without necessarily giving advice, a poststructural strategy we all appreciate, Serah's song offers help by example, in this case in the form of a difficult question: How do we dance with the spaces and places of culture and history in ways that announce hope?

It is certainly easier to dance in the other direction, to explore curriculum theorising by travelling down the familiar pathways of those dark, insidious, offensive practices and beliefs of the past that are always threatening to resurface, albeit camouflaged in clichés that seem to be new. We justifiably recoil at accounts of the lives of Aboriginal children as lived within the residential schools of Canada, the systemic racism and sexism evident in former school textbooks, texts that pretended neutrality, and the science curriculum implemented in prairie schools during the 1930s that encouraged children to grow and use tobacco. There is something almost sexy about these endless dark educational histories and cultural practices, lurid, like the way our eyes are drawn to automobile accidents. And scholarship in these areas lays bare for us how the past and culture continue the dances we see today. This is absolutely important work, essential discovering and deconstruction of the assumptions and givens that rule educational practice today and the origins of these discourses in culture and history.

But Serah sings a new song, invites us to a new dance, a curve in our trajectory that is most difficult to follow, yet also, I believe, most needed. In a quiet voice, her song calls us to embrace hope, to approach history and culture in the *expectation* of finding spaces and places of hope, and then to announce these spaces and places to the world.

Spending some time recently thinking about hope, I find there is much to announce. I find hope in the playful yet poignant poetry of curriculum scholar Carl Leggo. There's an agenda of hope in the works of Ted Aoki in his call to explore those spaces in between the mandated and lived curriculum. There is hope in remembering teachers who profoundly influenced our thinking, wise people who demonstrate that is possible to live, think, and be in the world differently—like my mentor, Terry Carson. There is hope in our schools. I'm thinking of the full-scale model of a humpback whale I recently saw at Strawberry Vale School, and the Grade 5 students who, as we crawled into the belly of this whale, were there to greet us with an informative presentation about these gentle giants, complete with a reminder that we can do more to protect them.

There is hope in history, in the journals and narratives of people and communities who refused to bow to an agenda of intolerance, hatred, and despair. The Dutch Mennonites of 17th-century Europe, for example, refused even on point of death to compromise their belief in the importance of creating living examples of how all humankind can live in peace. I wonder about the hope in the great spiritual traditions of cultures around the world—for example, the thoughtful advice given by the Buddha as he lay dying: Inner harmony is possible as we learn to give into the flow of events but only as we learn the wisdom of when to intervene. And consider the hope found in the languages of the world, those oral and written expressions with delightful sounds that, thank God, cannot be translated into English. There seems to me to be an infinite number of Josephs, alive and well, out there in the world. If we look for them, we will find those hope-full historical and cultural spaces waiting for the announcements of curriculum scholars.

REMEMBERING PROMISE

On his deathbed, Serah's uncle, Joseph, asked his extended family to promise to take his remains out of Egypt so that he might someday be properly buried in the land settled by the descendants of Jacob, Rachael, and Leah. That day arrived 430 years later. But the liberator named Moses faced a problem, for although the promise remained alive in the memory of the Hebrew people, the exact location of Joseph's bones was long since lost. The *Midrashim* asks, "But how did Moses know where Joseph was buried?" and responds with,

It is said: Serah daughter of Asher, who was of Joseph's generation, was still living. Moses went to her and asked, "Do you know where Joseph is buried?" She replied, "The Egyptians made a metal coffin for him, which they sank into the Nile, in order that its waters might be blessed thereby." (Bialik & Ravnitzky, 1992, p. 70)

The *Midrashim* then goes on to explain how, with Serah's guidance, Moses was able to retrieve the coffin, thereby enabling the descendants of Jacob to fulfil a promise made centuries earlier: restoring Joseph to his family (Bialik & Ravnitzky, 1992, p. 71).

Once again, Serah intervenes to restore relationships in a way that allows movement, in this case the exodus of Jacob's descendants and the fulfilment of the promise they made to Joseph. Serah not only remembered the promise, she acted at the appropriate moment to ensure that this promise was kept.

A few months ago, I had the privilege of seeing a promise kept as 17 students in a First Nations teacher education programme completed the first step of their educational journey: certification as language teachers. Thirty years earlier, the Elders of four nations began the process to save the ancestral languages of their communities through educational programmes, and it was an honour, decades later, to be part of the ceremony, as I recognized that this promise had not been forgotten. After the ceremony, one of the students asked me why my Faculty was willing to spend so much time, so much effort, and so much money on such a small group of students. My answer: "It's a matter of justice," for it's the least we can do to begin to make amends for an imposed education system that put these communities in their situation in the first place.

How many of the spaces and places of history and culture contain promises where curriculum studies can, like Serah, play a role in the fulfilment of past commitments? I think, for example, of the energy and work in the 1960s and 1970s in developing the public awareness of ecology and global systems, those books like *Silent Spring* and the work of Jacques Cousteau that awoke us from our cultural slumber and the naïve assumption that humanity could dump into our aquatic and atmospheric systems whatever we wanted without consequence. The promise of awareness leading to action has not been achieved; take, for example, how the federal government of Canada has followed the lead of the United States, in our case by reneging on the commitment of the previous government to the Kyoto Protocol. Who should remember the promises of industrial countries to clean up their act? How might we, in our examination of the spaces and places of culture— our culture, for example—and our history remind the upcoming generation of voters that we have a promise to keep?

We have buried skeletons to consider as well. In the 1970s a group of curriculum scholars broke with the rather technical approach to change embedded in Ralph Tyler's too popular four-step approach to curriculum change by calling into question the rationality of Tyler's thinking. These reconceptualists were, and still are, an exciting bunch, and their works have enabled a rebirth in curriculum studies that challenged J. J. Schwab's famous diagnosis of the curricular field as moribund. Encouraged and animated by philosophical works in the areas of neo-

5

Marxism, literary criticism, poststructuralism, deep ecology, and other forms of social criticism, these new scholars have teased education for decades with the promise of significant change in how we think about and enact change in the systems that educate our children. But our collective critique, so cleverly and expertly accomplished, has not been able to realize the promise to actually make a change in the social realities of schooling.

Take senior high school chemistry as a case in point. My frequent visits to schools confirm that there has been absolutely no change in the pedagogy or subject content of this secondary school course since the time, over 2 decades ago, when I taught chemistry, or even when I first took it as a high school student. This is not a case of "if it's not broken, then don't fix it." This course is a direct result of the post-Sputnik reforms in science education that were implemented—and I mean this word in the etymological sense of "being tooled"—into secondary schools by noneducators determined to produce more scientists and engineers. Not only did this social engineering prove to be a disaster of epic proportions as *more* students turned away from studies in science, the course now stands as an immoral waste of time when students could be studying aspects of science that would enable them to be more active, informed, and engaged citizens, say, for example, studies in "environmental chemistry." In curriculum studies we have yet to keep our promise that reconceptualisation will make a difference; our Joseph is still under water. Meanwhile, educational systems continue to go about their absurd business as humanity rushes along a path of self-destruction. It is time for our scholarship to remember the promises of our reconceptualisation, to engage history and culture in conversation as we dance, to move through the curves of spaces and places in search for actions that we can take *now* to enable radical, sustained difference in what we are doing in the name of education so that our children, at least, may have a chance.

SHARING WITNESS

The *Midrashim* reports that in the first century C. E., Rabbi Yochanan ben Zak-kai was one day teaching his students that when the descendants of Jacob crossed the sea of reeds, fleeing the Egyptian army, the waters had parted and the water resembled a wall of bushes just sprouting leaves. The *Midrashim* reports that suddenly,

> A voice came through an open window in the back of the beit midrash [school or house of midrash—a traditional educational setting]: "No. That's not right." All the students turned around and saw an old lady peering through the window. "I am Serah bat Asher. I know what the walls looked like because I was there! They looked like mirrors, mirrors in which every man, woman and child was reflected so it seemed as though even more people crossed there, not only those who were present, but their descendants and the descendants of their descendants!" (Bacher & Broydé, 2002, p. 2).

The Rabbi, in this case, assumed the mantle of authority granted a highly respected teacher claiming, as fact, his account of events, even though there was no possible way that he could have know for certain what the waters looked like. The *Midrashim* notes Serah's correction as a reminder not only of what happened during the event, but also of how eyewitness accounts are critical in helping us understand history and culture, warning us as well to be especially humble in our dance with these partners.

We are called by Serah's example to find witnesses to events, those who can say, "I was there; it was like this . . ." so that our exploration of the spaces and places of curriculum avoids what Bill Pinar calls the entrapment of presentism (Pinar, 2004). We are also called to *be* witnesses ourselves. For example, I have seen tremendous changes in educational technology during my years as an educator. I remember vividly in my teacher education compelling investigations of the mysteries of the 16 mm movie projector and long discussions about our concerns pertaining to the newest technological wonder, the overhead projector. This tool, we felt, introduced danger of a teaching style emphasizing the endless presentation of notes for students to copy. It is important to remember that these conversations centred on how to keep teaching more humane and more invested in personal relationships at a time when machines that threatened to minimalise such connections had begun to appear. We need to bear witness to the relentless march of technology, to listen to Heidegger's warnings that technology is no mere means (Heidegger, 1970), to listen with respectful attention to the voices of those who remember when teaching employed different technologies so that we can appreciate what is gained and what is lost with each invention.

As scholars of curriculum, we are also historians of the present, each of us a living memory of events that we now explain to our children and grandchildren. How can we engage in the reimagination and rethinking of the present, to re-present the present through our curriculum scholarship? For example, George Richardson and I have discovered, while talking with high school students in Japan and Canada, that these school students *already* think as global citizens, ready and willing to interact with their peers internationally (Blades & Richardson, 2006). This discovery surely has implications for how we might imagine history unfolding before us and how we might now act.

But this dance of research is the hardest of all, for we are immersed in our cultural situation and historical development and can hardly step outside to gain the perspective that would make new steps possible. This is why the voices able to bear witness to the recent past, or to cultural and historical experiences in other places and spaces, are so essential to our ability to engage in a scholarship of new imagination. These voices change the music in the middle of our dances with culture and history; they keep us alert to new rhythms and songs. We are called by Serah's example to intervene in teaching as well as to bear witness to what we have seen and learned. I recall, for example, getting to know my Egyptian neighbour while living in student housing. One day as we travelled the bus together, he asked me my opinion of the *Satanic Verses*, which he had just read. I was surprised that he had been reading this book, my reaction exposing some stereotypical views of religiously observant Muslim men that were thoroughly destroyed as I developed a relationship with my neighbour.

Stereotypes and their subsequent dismantling provide amazing opportunities for learning new steps in this dance and, subsequently, testify to new possibilities. I recall meeting the CEO of Imperial Oil and discussing with board members their educational policy and vision of corporate responsibility. I was frankly surprised by their attitude and concerns. I'm not praising this corporation, but I am admitting that my view that such corporations are the true "axis of evil" bent on world domination have suffered a radical setback. I can cite one example: In my quest to have Imperial Oil fund science education in Canada, I ensured that the president of their donations program knew that the funding would go to support programmes in action-related environmental education. The response of the corporation shocked me: They not only encouraged such a plan but also suggested I go further in promoting this sort of activism! The point of my witness to this experience is that I have come to realize that we are all enmeshed in discourses that promote an "us versus them" mentality, an adversarial stance that oversimplifies the issues and neglects to consider possibilities that do exist for responsible corporations, if we can only begin to imagine such an entity. And it is exactly this type of witness, a brave, dangerous, and likely unpopular testimony that is needed if we are to step into the arms of history and culture with the confidence to lead, and not follow, their predetermined patterns.

We don't know what happened to Serah or how her long life unfolded. According to some legends, she perished in a fire in 1133 C.E. Some legends say that she still lives among us. It's the latter possibility that delights me, for I'd love to meet this mysterious woman and ask her to share the wisdom and experience she has acquired from thousands of years of living. Even so, I must remember that Serah offers only one perspective; today, we have the opportunity to share and consider a broad set of voices and views, inspired, I hope, by Serah's dancing lessons: announcing hope, remembering promise, and bearing witness. She challenges us to join in a new dance with history and culture, to lead others into those spaces and places of an educational imagination that enables us to realize new possibilities for education. It is to that never-ending challenge that we now stand up from our chairs, walk across the floor in confidence, and ask either History or Culture, or perhaps both at the same time, to come and dance with us. And as we lead one or both off into a new dance, we can respond to their surprised query, "Where are you taking us?" With a smile of hope, promise and witness, we can say, "It's a surprise."

NOTES

[1] Genesis 46:17; Serah is pronounced "Ser-ach" where the ch is the same as "loch." Her name is an unusual amalgam of two Hebrew words, Sarah, or "princess," and Chai, or "life."

REFERENCES

Bacher, W., & Broydé, I. (2002). *Serah*. Retrieved January 21, 2006, from http://www.jewishencyclopedia.com

Bialik, H. N., & Ravnitzky, Y. H. (Eds.). (1992). *The book of legends: Sefer Ha-Aggadah* (W. G. Braude, Trans.). New York: Schocken Books.

Blades, D., & Richardson, G. (2006). Restarting the interrupted discourse of the public good: Global citizenship education as a moral imperative. In G. Richardson & D. Blades (Eds.), *Troubling the canon of citizenship education* (pp. 115–123). New York: Peter Lang.

Bregman, M. (1998). *A lady of legend: Serah Bat Asher*. Retrieved February 1, 2006, from http://www. huc.edu/faculty/pubs/pbregman.html

Carson, T. (2005, October 7). *Help without giving advice: Pinar, curriculum studies and Canada*. Paper presented at the William Pinar Retrospective Panel, American Association for Teaching and Curriculum, Austin, TX.

Heidegger, M. (1970). The question concerning technology. In D. Krell (Ed.), *Heidegger: Basic writings* (pp. 283–318). New York: Harper & Row.

Heschel, A. J. (1955). *God in search of man: A philosophy of Judaism*. New York: Farrar, Straus and Giroux.

Kierkegaard, S. (1983). *Fear and trembling/Repetition* (H. V. Hong & E. H. Hong, Trans.). Princeton, NJ: Princeton University Press.

Pinar, W. F. (2004). *What is curriculum theory?* Mahwah, NJ: Lawrence Erlbaum.

Serach. (2006). Retrieved February 1, 2006, from: http://www.geocities.com/m_lock_2000/serach.htm

Unger, M. F. (1954). *Archaeology and the old testament*. Grand Rapids, MI: Zondervan.

David Blades
University of Victoria

INGRID JOHNSTON AND JENNIFER TUPPER

2. THE CHRONOTOPE OF SCHOOL: STUDENTS NEGOTIATING IDENTITIES IN THE SOCIAL AND CULTURAL TIME/SPACE OF AN URBAN HIGH SCHOOL

RESEARCHING IDENTITIES IN THE CHRONOTOPE OF SCHOOL

In this chapter, we use Bakhtin's (1981) notion of chronotope to consider how students negotiate identities in the social and cultural time/space of a large urban high school. Bakhtin gives the name chronotope (literally, time-space) to the intrinsic connectedness of temporal and spatial relationships. He reminds us that all contexts are shaped fundamentally by the kind of time and space that operate within them. His crucial point is that time and space vary in qualities; different social activities and representations of those activities presume different kinds of time and space. In their book on Bakhtin, Morson and Emerson (1990) explained, "In...culture generally, time is always in one way or another historical and biographical, and space is always social; thus the chronotope in culture could be described as a 'field of historical, biographical and social relations'" (p. 371).

A school chronotope is a specific instance of representation of historical time and human experiences as these occur in a particular historical period and cultural environment. Time and place in the school chronotope are synonymous, indicating the placement of "self" in a social world related to dominant cultural and social influences. We consider this notion of a school chronotope through the lens of a 3-year study that explored the relationships between schooling, spatial practices, and identity formation in a large public high school in Western Canada with an ethno-culturally diverse school population. The study built on previous research that linked curriculum to identity construction. Hwu (1998) explained that "identity formation is subject-positioned, context-situated and discursively-located" (p. 23). Theorists such as Chambers (1999), Hurren (2000), Pinar, Reynolds, Slattery, and Taubman (1995), and Goodson (1998) suggested the importance of "investigating and promoting more contextual and intertextual studies of the process of identity" (Goodson, p. 3). Benko and Strohmayer (1997) showed how space and spatial practices play a constitutive role in the construction of individual and group identities.

In our study, we considered the space of school both as observable space, with measurable and boundable aspects, and as culturally coded space that is "characterized by specific social activities with a culturally given name and image"

J. Nahachewsky and I. Johnston (eds.), Beyond 'Presentism': Re-Imagining the Historical, Personal, and Social Places of Curriculum, 11–22.

(Shields, 1997, p. 188). We recognized that spatial practices are deeply embedded within curricular practices and that space cannot be separated from the lived experiences of curriculum. While students learn the required curriculum in certain designated spaces, covertly they learn that "certain spaces = certain identities" (Natter, 1997, p. 152).

The study was conducted at a public high school in a Western Canadian city with a growing ethno-culturally diverse school population. At the time of the study, there were approximately 2,200 students in attendance at the school, representing over 60 language groups. Our goals for the study were to further understanding regarding spatial and temporal aspects of educational theory and practice, specifically in the areas of curriculum and identity formation, and to consider how students from a range of ethno-cultural backgrounds are able to negotiate identities in the out-of-classroom spaces of school. We invited students in three Grade 10 social studies classes in the school to participate in the study. These classes ranged across the spectrum of the academic streams offered by the school. In addition, two teachers, an administrator, a counsellor, a secretary, and the school police resource officer agreed to be interviewed about their perceptions of students' spatial practices in the school.

The following methods were used to gather data:
- A survey of participant populations regarding use of school spaces. The survey gathered demographic information about participants and asked respondents to rank-order a list of school spaces from most to least preferred, and most to least frequented. An open-ended question was included, in which students were able to include anecdotal information on school locations that were significant to them, and to provide reasons for the significance.
- Student-produced photos of school spaces. A few student volunteers were provided with digital cameras and invited to take a collection of photos of significant spaces in the school. For ethical reasons, students were asked to take photos with few or no people in them or to blur or obscure the faces.
- Individual interviews with student participants to explore their understandings of the significance of the photos they had taken for negotiating identities in the out-of-classroom spaces of the school.
- Interviews with school staff to provide their perceptions and insights on how students negotiated spatial and temporal relationships in the school.

The data were interpreted in order to draw connections between time, space, and student identities. As part of the interpretive process, we noted how students described and categorized particular school spaces, how spaces were socially coded, and ways in which students accepted or transgressed common spatial practices within the school. We were particularly interested in the reasons students cited for feeling comfortable or uncomfortable in particular out-of-classroom spaces and how they identified certain areas of the school in relation to particular student identities. Our own observations of students' interactions and conversations in the hallways between classes also informed our understandings of spatial practices and ethno-cultural diversity.

OCCUPYING SCHOOL SPACES THROUGH PARTICULAR AFFILIATIONS

Demographic information from the surveys of Grade 10 students revealed the heterogeneous nature of student participants' cultural backgrounds and linguistic affiliations. A number of participants were immigrants from China, India, Vietnam, Thailand, Eastern Europe, and countries in Africa and South America; others were children of immigrants. Many were bilingual or multilingual. In their anecdotal responses to the survey, students articulated their understandings of how school spaces are occupied through specific categories, including social, academic, ethno-cultural, and religious affiliations and gender. The following categories emerged as significant in students' identifications of spatial practices in their school:

– Social identifications. Student respondents categorized themselves and others through particular labels such as "preps," "jocks and cheerleaders," "gangsters," "skaters."
– Academic and social hierarchies. Many of the labels addressed particular hierarchies related to academic standing or social status. These included "geeks," "nerds," "the library group," and "druggies," "smokers," "partiers."
– Gender and sexuality. Several labels referred specifically to gendered identities, for example "hoochies," "the very popular girls," "prissy, all about looks," "rough guys."
– Race and ethnicity. Many students used notions of race or ethnic identity to label others in the schools. The most common designations were: "the Korean group," "the Asians," "the Brown group," "Chinese," "people of Indian background," "racial outcasts."
– Religion. This affiliation, used particularly in relation to "the Mormons," appeared many times as an identity marker in the survey.

In individual interviews, student participants elaborated on how they thought these particular group affiliations developed. They indicated that peer groups were selected for a variety of reasons. These included friendships established in junior high school, religious affiliation, extracurricular interests, and similar circumstances such as being new to the school. Most of the students interviewed in the study observed that there were many ethnically homogeneous and religious peer groupings in the school, but they were unwilling to identify their own affiliations along ethnic, racial, or religious lines. It seemed easier for students to articulate a group identity for others than for themselves. Among their own peer group they could see the individual similarities and differences that created friendships. One student commented,

> I don't know if there's actually a said thing like, you don't hang out with them because they're a different race than you, I mean I'm just naive but I don't think anyone actually thinks about that when they're hanging out with them. Because the Brown group will hang out next to the people of the Asian group.

Staff members at the school were less tentative about identifying student affiliations along racial and religious lines. The school guidance counsellor commented that "cultural ethnic groups tend to kind of hang together." A secretary who had been in the school for many years discussed the changing demographics of the student population; she noted that "certain groups from diverse cultural backgrounds group together during breaks." Similarly, one of the school administrators suggested,

> You start to see groupings taking place and as the year progresses those groupings get to be more and more solid. . . . a lot of the students have made their friends outside of school . . . either in their community grouping, their church grouping, their cultural grouping, their linguistic grouping. We have between 70 and 80 international students. Many of them come from Korea; that group likes to have their breaks together so they can touch base a bit with the Korean element. . . . We also have a large South Asian population. I mean, that's their background and they're all Canadians, they're all born here but because of their religious affiliations, their family connections, and the like, we have quite large groups coming together that way. . . . you go with people you're comfortable with.

These friendship groupings in the school appeared to be reinforced through the historical conditions of the school, specifically, physical structures such as lockers and hallways. Lockers as permanent features of school space also served social functions through the process of student locker selection. Lockers were located in hallways throughout the school and groups of students could select lockers together at the start of each school year. Depending upon where these lockers were located, certain hallways became designated as the domain of particular social groupings.

Several students indicated that they frequented certain hallways with other students based upon common ethnic characteristics. For one participant, this meant that he chose to "hang out" in a particular hallway with primarily Chinese or

Korean students. In addition to ethnicity, religion seemed to inform students' spatial practices. Several students identified one hallway in the school as the "Mormon hallway," and this was supported by the comments of staff. The school guidance counsellor stated, "We have a Mormon group which is kind of interesting. We actually have a large population of Mormons in our school. And they kind of have a Mormon hall they staked out . . . and that seems to be their place." Sikhs and Muslims also were identified as distinct religious groups in the school.

SCHOOL SPACES OF COMFORT AND DISCOMFORT

While particular social, ethnic, and religious groupings in the school appeared to inform students' spatial practices, the physicality of certain spaces also emerged as significant. Student-produced images of the school revealed a particular spatial physicality that either attracted students to certain areas of the school or deterred them from spending time there. In discussing their photographs of school spaces, students reflected on their feelings of comfort or discomfort with particular areas. Certain hallways were cited as places of discomfort because they were dark with no natural lighting. One student explained,

> This is a photo up by the automotives hall. That's the hallway there. And it's really dark and loud because of the boiler room and just dark and gross. I just don't like that hallway. It's really dark and it, it's just, like it's really long and the only light is the window on the other end.

In contrast, places of light and colour were frequently photographed as spaces of comfort.

> This one is the library. I took a picture of it because it's really bright and it's really colourful and it's really open and big. I took a picture of the skylight. Because that's the only place in the school really with natural light.

Other areas were designated as places of comfort or discomfort because they were crowded or empty. For example, the cafeteria was described as a pleasant "active" space to spend time:

> We have made our cafeteria a nicer place. It used to just be a big empty room with square tables and the like; now we've gone to round tables, put a sound board around the outside so the noise in there is a lot less. And so, that has become a much more pleasant place to be. So at lunch time our cafeteria is very active.

Certain hallways were also identified as places to avoid because they were "crowded and loud" or places where there were "people on phones all the time." Others were described as "hallways and corners where I feel comfortable in and exits that I like."

Gruenewald (2003) reminded us that "places are social constructions filled with ideologies, and the experience of places . . . shapes cultural identities" (p. 5). The students we interviewed spent a great deal of time discussing the relationship between social experience and the experience of place. While many different areas of the school were mentioned as gathering areas for various student groups, the central rotunda was identified by students as the most socially active space in the school. The rotunda appeared to function as a site where students negotiated their social and civic interactions, positioning themselves to see and to be seen and to conduct much of the informal business of school. One student described the rotunda as "just a big open space where everyone gets together." Another said, "It's the centre of everything and you can get to any place from there."

In reflecting on how groups congregate and interact in the rotunda, student participants in the study focused on the hierarchies established by particular groups and on the tensions and unspoken rules that governed how students should behave in this central space. One student commented,

> In the rotunda they all sit around, on the edge and that way you can kind of feel like you can keep an eye on everyone. And you have your own section, whereas if you're in the middle everyone's just looking at you. And you're not looking at everyone else. That's why doing activities in the rotunda is so hard because you have to get the people into the middle. But then when there is an activity or something, you kind of get the adrenaline to go in the middle and do it.

Another explained,

> I can also see how some people wouldn't feel comfortable in the rotunda.
> Because there are groups and because going in the middle is so forbidden and
> some people think, like, if you fall on the stairs you'll be criticized for the
> rest of your high school career.

The rotunda in the school could be seen as an informal platform for civic
participation, reflecting the changing demographics of the larger society and
enabling students to "try out" various identifications and affiliations within the
safety of their selected groupings. Students considered the rotunda as their own
democratic space in which to negotiate a burgeoning sense of citizenship. As Hall,
Coffey, and Williamson (1999) suggested, places such as town centres, or in this
case the rotunda of the school, "seek to provide young people with the opportunity
to establish themselves locally: to make their presence felt and to publicly affirm
(collective) identities through the conspicuous occupation of territory" (p. 506).
Students' sense of ownership, however, is ambivalent and somewhat illusory.
While they have the right to decide on informal rules of group ownership and
behaviour, students are still performing within the imperatives of school which
sees its role *in loco parentis* as one of control and management. Students have the
right to make certain decisions and to perform certain behaviours in the social
spaces of the school; at the same time, they operate under a shared responsibility
with the administrators and teachers in the school who make the formal rules that
govern how students will live within its open spaces.

PERFORMING IDENTITIES "UNDER THE GAZE"

In the *in-between* spaces of school, behaviour is regulated and controlled through a highly complex system of formal and informal rules. Many rules, particularly surrounding the use of space, are often enforced through the strategic use of video surveillance cameras and closed circuit television and through the presence of school resource officers. These themes of surveillance and control surfaced unexpectedly through our conversations with participants. What is most significant is that the themes were more apparent in discussions with school staff members than with students, suggesting that surveillance and control may have become somewhat normalized in the lives of young people.

At several entrances to the school, signs remind both visitors and students that "these premises are monitored by video surveillance cameras." We asked one of the teachers about these signs, and she indicated that indeed there were cameras positioned throughout the school to monitor student behaviour. She seemed to feel that they were effective without being overly obtrusive, that students might easily forget the cameras were there. This teacher indicated that the cameras and closed-circuit television exist as a precautionary measure, not because the behaviour of students was already out of control.

When we asked one of the school administrators about the surveillance equipment, he suggested that they were intended not to monitor student behaviour but to monitor the behaviour of visitors to the school. Despite this initial assertion, he went on to indicate that the equipment was installed the previous school year and that "it has an impact on the students because I notice they'll look up and they'll see that there's a camera." He also maintained that these cameras "made all the students aware that they are more accountable for what's going on in the hallways," and even though they are used "surprisingly little," having them in the school "tells the students that they need to be responsible for what they're doing."

The students we spoke with expressed little concern for the use of the surveillance equipment. One student commented, "It's a big school so they might just need those [cameras] to know what's happening." When asked if she felt she was being watched, she responded, "No, not really. I've never actually thought about them. I sort of just see the sign and I'm like, oh, okay." Her matter-of-fact attitude towards the cameras was echoed by many of her peers. Pitsula (2003) suggested that "the person who is constantly fixed in the gaze of the supervisor begins to internalize the mechanism of power to which [she] is subjected" (p. 386). Such power, however, can be understood only as relation (Foucault, 1975). The lack of resistance cannot be taken to mean the lack of an ability to resist. We are actively involved in accepting or resisting the normative constraints placed upon us. So our student's lack of concern does not necessarily denote a lack of agency, nor does it imply that she is not in some way resisting or subverting these constraints. It is possible that while students do not appear concerned about being watched, they may be exerting an ironic or "efficacious resistance" (Katzenstein, 1996) to the surveillance by exaggerating behaviour in view of the camera, or alternatively choosing not to change their behaviour at all as a result of being watched.

Several student participants indicated a degree of self-regulation in their spatial practices as a result of the presence of surveillance cameras. One Grade 11 student told us that at her previous school there had been no signs informing students of the use of cameras for surveillance. She said she was unsure whether there should be signs indicating the presence of cameras. When asked why she thought that, she replied,

'Cause people are going to be careful. I guess that's a good thing, but I mean they're going to try and stay out of the way of where the camera's pointing. If you don't know there's a camera then you'll do it and get caught.

These comments suggest that the students are very aware of the purpose of the surveillance cameras, and while they do not know if they are being observed "at any given moment," they are "always sure that [they] may be so" (Pitsula, 2001, p. 386).

Another student participant reinforced this notion:

I heard about [the video cameras] before I came, that they would have cameras at school, but I mean as long as I can go in the washroom without cameras, it doesn't matter (laughing). I mean it doesn't really matter to me if it's not people constantly watching you or something. I mean they don't listen to you. So it's not that they would hear what you say.

This student articulates a distinction between the "me" that is heard and the "I" that is seen, expressing a distinction between inside (the personal) and outside (related to social, historical, and cultural factors). Lacasa, Del Castillo, and Garcia-Varela (2005) discussed this in the context of identity construction within "specific historical, social and cultural contexts" (p. 287). The student's comments illustrate how she perceives words to be more important than actions in the spaces of the school—so as long as she is not heard, she is not troubled by being seen. We could argue that this extends to relationships in the school as well: Students are aware that they will be seen and adjust their actions accordingly (as in their occupation of the rotunda) but may not do the same with speech because they perceive it as a more private act.

FINAL REFLECTIONS

The role of institutions turns out to be very significant in the negotiating of identities, particularly in relation to two major properties. First, the structure and organization of institutions constrain people to organize their relationships according to particular rules and norms. Second, institutions can be related to the obligations of actors to their own groups (Lacasa et al., 2005, p. 289). In our study, we saw how students negotiated their identities within the physical time-space of the school through particular relationships constructed within categories such as gender, race, ethnicity, and religion. While students performed these identities under the gaze of surveillance cameras, administrators, and their peers, they maintained a sense of agency through subtle subversions of the controls they encountered in the school.

We recognize that a school's out-of-classroom spaces are not monolithic or static; rather, they are dynamic contexts within which social worlds are negotiated and enacted. As Gee (2000) suggested,

Situations (contexts) do not just exist. Situations are rarely static or uniform, they are actively created, sustained, negotiated, resisted, and transformed moment-by-moment through ongoing work. . . . This type of work I will call enactive and recognition work. (p. 191)

School-related discourse is an important means of "discursively producing identity, agency, and power relations" (Leander, 2001, p. 1). Relating such discourse to Bakhtin's notion of time-space, we see how "chronotopes are not so much visibly present in activity as they are the ground for activity" (Morson & Emerson, 1990, p. 369). The particular school setting in our study provided a rich time-space context for the production and negotiation of student identities and curricular practices within specific historical, biographical, and social relations. Such identities and practices were never static but constantly being reproduced, renegotiated, and transformed within the social contexts of school places and spaces.

Note: This research was part of a 3-year study that was funded by the Social Sciences Research Council of Canada and the Prairie Centre for Excellence on Research in Immigration and Integration. Principal researcher was Dr. Wanda Hurren, and coinvestigators were Dr. Ingrid Johnston, Dr. Terry Carson, Dr. Jennifer Tupper, and Jyoti Mangat.

REFERENCES

Arnot, M. (1997). "Gendered citizenry": New feminist perspectives on education and citizenship. *British Educational Research Journal, 23*(3), 275–295.

Bakhtin, M. (1981). *The dialogic imagination: Four essays* (C. Emerson & M. Holquist, Trans.). In M. Holquist (Ed.), Austin, TX: University of Texas Press.

Benko, G., & Strohmayer, U. (1997). *Space and social theory: Interpreting modernity and postmodernity.* Oxford, UK: Blackwell.

Chambers, C. (1999). A topography for Canadian curriculum theory. *Canadian Journal of Education, 24*(2), 137–150.

Delamont, S., & Galton, M. (1986). *Inside the secondary classroom.* London: Routledge.

Foucault, M. (1975). *Discipline and punishment.* New York: Vintage Books.

Gee, J. P. (2000). The new literacy studies: From "socially situated" to the work of the social. In D. Barton, M. Hamilton, & R. Ivanic (Eds.), *Situated literacies: Reading and writing in context* (pp. 180–196). New York: Routledge.

Giroux, H. (1998). The politics of insurgent multiculturalism in the era of the Los Angeles uprising. In H. Shapiro & D. Purpel (Eds.), *Critical social issues in American education: Transformation in a postmodern world* (2nd ed., pp. 181–198). Mahwah, NJ: Lawrence Erlbaum Associates.

Goodson, I. (1998). Storying the self: Life politics and the study of the teachers' life and work. In W. F. Pinar (Ed.), *Curriculum: Towards new identities* (pp. 3–20). New York: Garland.

Gordon, T., Holland, J., & Lahelma, E. (2000). *Making spaces: Citizenship and difference in schools.* London: Macmillan.

Gruenewald, D. (2003). Foundations of place: A multidisciplinary framework for place-conscious education. *American Educational Research Journal, 40*(3), 619–654.

Hall, T., Coffey, A., & Williamson, H. (1999). Self, space and place: Youth identities and citizenship. *British Journal of Education, 20*(4), 506.

Harris, S. (1994). Entitled to what? Control and autonomy in school: A student perspective. *International Studies in Sociology of Education, 4*(1), 57–76.

Hurren, W. (2000). *Line dancing: An atlas of geography curriculum and poetic possibilities.* New York: Peter Lang.

Hwu, W.-S. (1998). Curriculum, transcendence, and Zen/Taoism: Critical ontology of the self. In W. F. Pinar (Ed.), *Curriculum: Toward new identities* (pp. 21–39). New York: Garland.

Katzenstein, P. (Ed.). (1996). *The culture of national security.* New York: Columbia University Press.

Lacasa, P., Del Castillo, H., & Garcia-Varela, A. B. (2005). A Bakhtinian approach to identity in the context of institutional practices. *Culture and Psychology, 11*(3), 287–308.

Leander, K. M. (2001). "This is our freedom bus going home right now": Producing and hybridizing space-time contexts in pedagogical discourse. *Journal of Literacy Research, 33*(4), 637–679.

McCarthy, C. (1998). *The uses of culture: Education and the limits of ethnic affiliation.* New York: Routledge.

McLaren, P. (1989). *Life in schools.* Toronto, ON: Irwin.

Morson, G. S., & Emerson, C. (1990). *Mikhail Bakhtin: Creation of a prosaics.* Evanston, IL: Northwestern University Press.

Natter, W. (1997). Identity, space and other uncertainties. In G. Benko & U. Strohmayer (Eds.), *Space and social theory: Interpreting modernity and postmodernity* (pp. 141–161). Oxford, UK: Blackwell.

Noddings, N. (1992). Social studies and feminism. *Theory and Research in Social Education, 20*(3), 230–241.

Pinar, W., Reynolds, W., Slattery, P., & Taubman, P. (1995). *Understanding curriculum.* New York: Peter Lang.

Pitsula, J. (2003). Unlikely allies: Hilda Neatby, Michel Foucault, and the critic of progressive education. *Canadian Journal of Education, 26*(4), 383–400.

Schutz, A. (1999). Creating local "public spaces" in schools: Insights from Hannah Arendt and Maxine Greene. *Curriculum Inquiry, 29*(1), 77–98.

Shields, R. (1997). Spatial stress and resistance: Social meanings of spatialization. In G. Benko & U. Strohmayer (Eds.), *Space and social theory: Interpreting modernity and postmodernity* (pp. 186–202). Oxford, UK: Blackwell.

Ingrid Johnston
University of Alberta

Jennifer Tupper
University of Regina

DWAYNE TREVOR DONALD

3. THE CURRICULAR PROBLEM
OF INDIGENOUSNESS: COLONIAL FRONTIER
LOGICS, TEACHER RESISTANCES, AND THE
ACKNOWLEDGMENT OF ETHICAL SPACE

The colonial past and the social and spatial divides that separate Aboriginal peoples and Canadians haunt contemporary Canadian society.[1] This problem of separateness has manifested itself in the form of civilizational frontiers that effectively demarcate social and cultural boundaries which reinforce these divides. This colonial frontier logic conceptualizes historic and current realities as separate and distinct. Historical, social, and cultural understandings of the concepts of fort and frontier have become conflated with ways of organizing and separating people according to race, culture, and civilization; as a result, Aboriginal peoples and their ways have been reduced to an existence *outside* Euro-Western civilization.

The socio-spatial separation of Canadian (insiders) and Aboriginal (outsiders) is a naturalized idiosyncrasy of Canadian society that has been passed down generation by generation in the form of an authoritative national historical narrative. Unquestioned, these ideas have deeply influenced the assumptions educators hold about knowledge, classroom culture, subject disciplines, the purposes of education and schooling, and have perpetuated a logic that divides the world in troubling ways (Willinsky, 1998). These influences leave many educators unable to comprehend historic and ongoing Aboriginal presence and participation within Canadian society.

Colonial frontier logics have also been perpetuated curricularly in the form of stories of nation and nationality that children have been told in Canadian schools for decades. Increasingly, however, Aboriginal educators who wish to demonstrate the presence and participation of their people are contesting this curricular logic. The perspectives being shared are very much related to the exclusion or isolation of Aboriginal ways of knowing and the processes of colonialism through which Aboriginal people and communities were relegated to the sidelines as the nation of Canada was developed.

Governments and educational jurisdictions across Canada have .heard these critiques and developed curricular initiatives that focus on reimagining the roles that Aboriginal people, communities, and their diverse perspectives can and will play in the future of Canadian society. Such acknowledgements and resultant initiatives suggest the need for trans-cultural understanding. On what terms should this be done? In curricular terms, the tepees and costumes approach has been tried for many years, but leaves teachers and young people with the unfortunate impression that Indians have not done much since the buffalo were eradicated.

J. Nahachewsky and I. Johnston (eds.), Beyond 'Presentism': Re-Imagining the Historical, Personal, and Social Places of Curriculum, 23–41.

Attempts at the so-called *inclusion* of Aboriginal perspectives have usually meant that an anachronistic study of Aboriginal people is offered as a *possibility* in classrooms only if there is time and people are still interested. More recently, Aboriginal educators have forwarded curricular initiatives specifically designed for Aboriginal students that focus on the revitalization of Aboriginal cultures and languages. Despite some successes with these initiatives, I note that colonial frontier logics are recapitulated in curricular forms and a troubling form of civilizational separation is maintained. What is needed is a decolonizing form of curriculum theorising that conceptualizes Aboriginal and Canadian perspectives as relational, inter-referential, and mutually implicative.

Such a shift will only be possible, however, if the field of curriculum studies can eschew received colonial and neocolonial renditions of Indigenousness and instead accept Indigenous knowledge systems as viable expressions of culture that require a respectful place within public contexts.[2]

This chapter focuses on the conceptual problem posed by Indigenousness for practitioners in the field of education and on how and why this problem persists in the current context of identity politics. In addition, this chapter argues that respectful recognition of Indigenous knowledge systems constitutes an important opportunity for academics and educators to engage with Indigenous peoples and their wisdom traditions in ethical ways.

This argument is developed around reflective comments from preservice teachers studying at the University of Alberta who resist, in various ways, the integration of Aboriginal perspectives in the Social Studies curriculum that they are expected to teach. This resistance is rooted in colonial frontier logics that have reductively portrayed Indigenousness as a primeval cultural and sociological condition anthropologically categorized as an example of how people live before they become civilized. Indigenousness has thus been considered a condition to be overcome through education rather than a perspective worthy of curricular inquiry.

This is why many educators today still view the idea of Aboriginal curriculum perspectives as a strange aberration that works at cross purposes—mixing insider notions of education with outsider cultural beliefs and practices. Settler societies like Canada are slowly beginning to come to terms with this intellectual legacy. An important starting point for this process is public recognition that Indigenousness is a viable subject position in the world today that does not require congruence to Euro-Western standards.

IDENTITY POLITICS AND THE PROBLEM OF INDIGENOUSNESS

Over the past several decades, it has become fashionable for academics and theorists to use the prefix *post* to designate advances in thinking and corrections to earlier misinformed theories of culture, identity, language, and knowledge. When using terms like postmodern, postcolonial, or poststructural, for example, the common perception is that critical progress has been made in thinking. These *new* theories, as post, imply a temporal quality to these advances, as though the project of human enlightenment will move forward with time as the error of past ways is revealed and critiqued.

These post theories have had a profound effect in conceptions of identity. Post theorists dispute the possibility of a coherent and unified identity, arguing instead that each of us, from birth to death, has a contingent sense of self that will be subsequently altered as we age, experience the world differently, and affiliate ourselves with various people, contexts, and ideas. Identity, in this view, is considered conflicted, fluid, and constantly shifting.

Some minority groups, however, have rejected these post theories of identity and countered that there is much more at stake with identity when the social context is rife with oppression, systemic violence, market logic, and institutionalized injustice. In such conflicted and conflictual situations, identity becomes a means for making a political statement and the grounds from which one can stand in opposition to common-sense societal norms. This identity politics involves consciousness of one's personal and inherited history—identity—and sustained efforts to assert and reiterate this consciousness via public discourse as a way to strategically remind listeners of difference (Bromley, 1989, p. 210). Thus, identity claims that post theorists dismiss as impossible fantasies are deemed as necessary to the sociopolitical struggles of marginalized groups.

In light of these critiques, how is it possible to claim Indigenousness? It is perhaps best to begin with an understanding of who is Indigenous and how such an identity claim can be viewed as directly tied to wisdom traditions. Indigenous peoples can be considered members of communities who have lived in particular locations for a very long time (Dei, 2000, p. 114; McLeod, 1999–2000, p. 39). This long-term habitation has supported and perpetuated deeply rooted spiritual and metaphysical relationships with the land (and other entities) that thoroughly inform and infuse the specific cultural practices and linguistic conventions of the people. Indigenous communities are considered unique, in relation to other distinct communities, because these venerable connections to land and place have been maintained and continue to find expression in communities today.

In this sense, then, Indigenous peoples, as descendents of the original inhabitants, are seen as the holders and practitioners of a sui generis sovereignty in their traditional lands. The inherited traditions, although certainly altered and adjusted in response to changing times, connect the people to cosmological, epistemological, and ontological insights that foster the maintenance of a unique form of citizenship. Politically, and on a global scale, Indigenous peoples are seen as united in a common struggle to defend their cultures, languages, and lands from further damage and erosion brought under the guise of economic progress and development.

Thus, Indigenousness, as a subject position, is less of a constrained and essential burden and more of a personalized responsibility to honour inherited wisdom traditions. To properly grasp this important difference, we must remember that most Indigenous societies do not conceptualize individuality in ways congruent with European liberal democratic assumptions. For many Indigenous peoples, an individual's sense of self grows out of how he or she fits into the community. The community itself stands at the centre of a much larger whole, and the role of the individual is always to give back to the community. In general, "Indigenous societies are *synecdochic* (part-to-whole) rather than the more Western conception that is *metonymic* (part-to-part)" (Weaver, 2000, p. 227). Little Bear (2000) illuminates this distinction by emphasizing the value placed on holism in Indigenous wisdom traditions:

> The value of wholeness speaks to the totality of creation, the group as opposed to the individual, the forest as opposed to the trees. It focuses on the value of the constant flux rather than on individual patterns. . . . If a person is whole and balanced, then he or she is in a position to fulfill his or her responsibilities to the whole. (p. 79)

Ideally, then, an Indigenous person would see his or her identity as intimately connected to inherited wisdom traditions and the vitality of the community as a whole.

Unfortunately, the political economy of being Indigenous does not always allow individuals to operate in the realm of the ideal. Indigenousness is also often evoked to inspire opposition to colonial and neocolonial logics. From the perspectives of many Indigenous scholars, what needs to be opposed are current post theories that discount the beliefs of their communities, unilaterally proclaiming the end of subjectivity just at the time Indigenous communities are beginning to recover from colonial legacies and assert their ways.

The ironic flip-flop wherein Indigenousness is declared a romantic fantasy in the wake of an intense, centuries-long studying and theorising of Indigenous *difference* is not lost on Indigenous scholars. Quite naturally, there is suspicion that someone else is, once again, exercising a self-proclaimed intellectual authority to determine Indigenous identity and delimit its expression in the world. The shifting post academic field fails to acknowledge the viability of a pointed, critical, and Indigenous reply rooted in subjective "communitist" experience (Weaver, 1998, p. 22). Such replies insist that Indigenous wisdom traditions offer a viable way out of the trap created by neo-liberal market logics and vivify the possibility that we can live differently in the world today (Alfred, 2005; Battiste & Henderson, 2000; Smith, 1999; Stewart-Harawira, 2005).

The key point here is that the assertion of Indigenous identity does not necessitate a negation or discounting of other perspectives, as though Indigenousness can only be properly considered in isolation from other commitments. It is possible to simultaneously promote Indigenousness while also recognizing that Indigenous and Euro-Western knowledge systems exist simultaneously, in context and in relation to each other, and that the quality and character of those relationships is unpredictable (Nakata, 2002). Thus, the form of Indigenous identity being promoted here is relational rather than hermetic.

Take the concept of Aboriginality in Canada as an example of this. The Canadian concept of Aboriginal, as a nationalized interpretation of Indigenousness, has legal and constitutional purposes and is used to denote, as a distinct minority group, the modern-day descendents of the original inhabitants of the place now called Canada. Uniting these diverse peoples as Aboriginal are two general identity assertions: Aboriginal people are inheritors of Indigenous wisdom traditions *and* victims of oppression and disenfranchisement stemming from colonial policies.

However, many Indigenous groups reject the label Aboriginal as a colonial term itself, see it as only convenient for the needs of governments, and repudiate it as too generic and dismissive of the cultural and linguistic distinctiveness of various Indigenous communities (Alfred, 2005). Despite these critiques, the categorical definition of Aboriginal still applies in Canada, and it encompasses, for the most part, First Nations peoples, Status Indians (with and without specific Treaty rights), Non-Status Indians, and Métis; people defined as such live in various regions of the country in urban or rural (reserve or settlement) settings with huge disparities in terms of access to economic, political, and social resources.[3] This undeniable diversity of Aboriginal experience in Canada makes it seem blatantly contradictory to claim any fixed form of Indigenous identity.

The emphasis on legal and political definitions of Indianness coupled with the intense social and cultural ramifications of the Imaginary Indian (Francis, 1992) have created a situation in which many Indigenous people, still reeling from the devastating effects of colonization, yearn for an authentic understanding of who they are and what such an identity claim might mean. This complex and ambiguous situation is a natural reaction to tremendous change in a relatively short period of time.

Ontologically speaking, what these identity conflicts indicate is that many Indigenous people desire some foundational philosophies to provide them with guidance and direction in confusing times. In many Indigenous communities, these foundational cosmologies, ontologies, and epistemologies, though certainly not understood and expressed as they were in precolonial times, have nonetheless survived much tumultuous change. These then inform identity statements and are the basis for revitalization movements in many Indigenous communities today. However, rather than striving for some form of unattainable authenticity, I argue that Indigenous peoples should instead be concerning themselves with the ways in which their inherited wisdom traditions and spiritual principles can provide guidance on how to engage and teach the dominant society about balance, justice, peace, and living well on the land. Such a focus does not require denial of the diverse, complex, and contradictory influences that shape Indigenous subjectivity today. It does, however, call on Indigenous peoples to frame their own understandings of wisdom traditions in ways that honour and sustain their practice in Indigenous communities *and* demonstrate their relevance to Canadian public policy. After all, as *Kainai* Elder Andy Black Water advises, our tepees are all held down by the same pegs now (Blood & Chambers, 2008).

POSITIONING THE TEACHER: RESISTANCE, AMBIGUITY, AND BIOGRAPHICAL CRISIS

This message of shared reality and relationships connecting Aboriginal and Canadian has become a rising public policy priority. Across Canada, curricular initiatives have been introduced that acknowledge Aboriginal perspectives and integrate them into Programs of Study across subject areas and grade levels. Alberta Education, the branch of government responsible for education in my home province of Alberta, has been a curricular leader in these initiatives. These policy shifts are guided by the *First Nations, Métis and Inuit Education Policy Framework* (Alberta Learning, 2002) that specifically identifies the need to increase the knowledge and understanding of Aboriginal cultures and knowledge systems by all Albertans as a major educational goal.

Following these directives, program leaders from Alberta Education have had extensive consultations with Aboriginal leaders, educators, and community members regarding curriculum reorientation to these new policies. Social Studies is the first major subject discipline in Alberta in which new Programs of Study are being gradually implemented by teachers in the classroom. While most curriculum change creates anxiety for teachers, especially when there is high expectation that teaching practice will be significantly altered, the new Social Studies program in Alberta has caused a particularly high level of stress for Social Studies educators. Most noted among the changes to this curriculum is a shift to an emphasis on issues-focused and inquiry-based approaches, as well as the explicit statement that an understanding of Aboriginal perspectives and experiences is an integral part of Canadian citizenship and identity (Alberta Education, 2005, p. 4).

As these policies have been translated into Programs of Study from Kindergarten to Grade 12, educators across Alberta have been confronted with two realities. First, the new Social Studies curriculum demands that teachers embrace the issues-focused and inquiry-based approach which means, for many, a significant shift in their pedagogical practices. Second, the writers of the new Social Studies curriculum documents did an admirable job of linking Aboriginal perspectives with larger topical issues like globalization, nationalism, democracy, ideologies, and Canadian history.

The significance of this shift is that Aboriginal perspectives cannot be treated as separate special interest topics of inclusion somehow supplemental to more rigorous issues. Teachers are expected to engage their students in explorations of Aboriginal perspectives on a wide variety of topics as a regular part of their classroom inquiry processes, in association with other considerations (such as immigration, multiculturalism, globalization, or environmentalism), and this practice obviously requires significant background knowledge on the part of teachers. Most teachers in Alberta find themselves woefully unprepared to engage with Aboriginal perspectives in these ways. Few of these teachers have taken a single university or college course connected to Aboriginal perspectives, and fewer still have ever actually met an Aboriginal person in their private lives. Although many teachers are themselves highly educated, there is a huge informational gap when it comes to Aboriginal knowledge systems and perspectives on, for example, history, politics, economics, and citizenship.

Given that Alberta's teaching population is overwhelmingly Euro-Canadian, and given also that this demographic reality is unlikely to change any time soon, we can expect that the success of these critical curricular initiatives will ultimately depend on educators who have little or no experience with Aboriginal perspectives. This seems a rather daunting challenge that places the teacher in the awkward and unconventional position of the learner rather than the expert who possesses all necessary knowledge. Yet, the complex tasks of rethinking the role of the teacher in the classroom, reconsidering what counts as knowledge, and challenging some of the common-sense and normalizing discourses of teacher education is precisely what is at stake in this curriculum shift. If this curriculum is to be successfully implemented, I believe that it will be as a result of teachers' ability to resist the normalizing assumption that everything that occurs in the classroom depends on the teacher as expert and reframe their task as an opportunity to learn *from* Aboriginal perspectives rather than as a government-imposed requirement to learn *about* Aboriginal peoples:

> Whereas learning about an event or experience focuses upon the acquisition of qualities, attributes, and facts, so that it presupposes a distance (or, one might even say, a detachment) between the learner and what is to be learned, learning from an event or experience is of a different order, that of insight. (Britzman, 1998, p. 117)

The implication here is that regarding Aboriginal perspectives, in a teacherly manner, as yet another set of facts to be added to one's burgeoning teaching informational repertoire replicates the very same colonial frontier logics that the new curriculum has been designed to contest. The desire to externalize knowledge of Aboriginal peoples is coextensive with the need to regard Aboriginal reality as separate and distinct from Canadian reality. A separate culturalist interpretation of Aboriginal reality permits a rendition of lovely knowledge—studying their traditional culture in culturally appropriate ways will improve their self-esteem—to stand in place of the need to interrogate the difficult knowledge of colonial frontier logics that condition and propagate common-sense myths about history, identity, and human relationality (Britzman, 2003). Here we also see the deep influence of anthropology, exhibition pedagogy, and representational epistemology (Biesta & Osberg, 2007, pp. 16–17) in relation to Indigenousness, in that knowing *about* Indians through lectures, textbooks, history books, and films still has more intellectual authority than sustained social, political, and ethical engagement (Deloria, 1998, p. 189).

To see oneself implicated in discussions of difficult knowledge regarding the history of Aboriginal peoples in Canada is to experience a certain biographical crisis (Britzman, 1991, p. 8). "New knowledge is first confronted as a criticism toward and loss of the learner's present knowledge if the knowledge offered is felt as discontinuous with the self, if it seems to threaten the ways the world has been perceived" (Britzman, 1998, p. 128).

In such engagements, teacher resistance to such knowledge is natural and to be expected (Carson, 2005 p. 6). When we consider that so much of teacher education is predicated on the need for the individual who wants to be a teacher to conform to a predetermined identity role that suits institutional needs, demonstrate normalized competence in these contexts, and unconsciously conflate teacher thinking with teacher identity, we begin to understand the intense postcultural dynamics that are invested in the creation of a teacher.

As Smits (1997) points out, this predetermined role of the teacher plays out as a storyline that parallels, and often displaces, a person's own history, and the difficult task of the teacher becomes one of conciliating the teacher story with the personal story in ways that maintain fidelity to some meaningful moral orientation (p. 284).

This moral orientation is most often informed by common-sense notions of citizenship and the characteristics of a good person and how these are, in turn, conditioned through the process of education in various contexts. These influential forces interact to create a powerful conception of identity that is often seen as cultureless, that is, shaped by common-sense naturalized ways of doing things rather than by specific historical and cultural assumptions and prejudices that can be genealogically traced.

Such conceptions of identity are resistant to reflexive auto-critique done in the interest of understanding personal and professional presuppositions and priorities more intimately. This explains, in part, why the possibility of new curricular knowledge, like Indigenous knowledge, is resisted by many teachers. Most do not see their personal or professional selves, which are often difficult to distinguish, implicated in such knowledge. Instead, the knowledge, as new, is perceived by many educators as foreign and thus outside accepted educational practice, usually only included at the behest of government officials pandering to special interest groups, and therefore a malignant threat to the professional integrity of the teacher to properly deliver meaningful lessons and prepare their students for continued study of more worthwhile forms of knowledge.

Thanks, in part, to the long-lasting influence of the writings of Herbert Spencer, Euro-Western conceptions of scientific knowledge have been considered the most worthwhile curricularly (Banks, 1980). An education focused on the teaching of science as a subject discipline and general scientific thinking throughout the curriculum, Spencer contends, would properly prepare young people for complete living (Deering, 2001, p. 147). This idea of useful curriculum "appealed to politicians and the administrators of the great institutions of modern states because it made the schools very largely into agencies of socialization" (Egan, 2002, p. 117). Such emphasis on scientific principles as the guiding purposes for education would obviously exclude Indigenous perspectives from serious consideration. Rather, Indigenousness, in anthropological terms, was interpreted as scientific evidence and confirmation of Euro-Western civilization and ascendancy (p. 28). This insight helps us better understand how common-sense educational talk came to classify curriculum as a developmental and scientific exercise undertaken to get the topics of study accurately sequenced, organized, and delivered.

I have had the unique opportunity to investigate these conceptions of curriculum as an invited presenter to preservice teachers studying and preparing to teach Secondary Social Studies during their Advanced Professional Term (APT) at the University of Alberta. Course instructors would typically request, in nonspecific terms, a 2-hour session for their students on Aboriginal perspectives in Social Studies as seen in the new curriculum. After doing several of these invited presentations, I became critically aware of the problematic position I was placed in when I parachuted into the classroom unaware of the context or previous discussions, delivered the necessary information on Aboriginal perspectives, and left without eliciting much response from the students.

In my presentations, I used texts and images to contest and interrupt the official history of Canada with the experiences, memories, and stories of Aboriginal peoples, some of which included the memories of my own extended family. Mixed in with this were digressions into extended explanations of contemporary issues of Aboriginal identity, stereotypes, accepted identity terms, and some philosophical thoughts regarding Aboriginal perspectives and the need to reframe our understandings of curricula. I thought it was an interesting and provocative presentation. However, the students rarely engaged with these issues in ways that would indicate that they felt the same. Silence was the most common response, although some students would ask informational-type questions to clarify or correct their previous understandings. Obviously, there are many ways to interpret these responses (one of which might be that I am not a very effective presenter!), but during my time with the students I discerned a strange externalization of Aboriginal perspectives—as though the information I shared with them needed to be kept at a cautious distance. In light of the current context of identity politics, this should not be surprising. Still, deep consideration of the ways in which preservice teachers reacted to the presentation of Aboriginal curriculum perspectives led to a related preoccupation with the terms according to which I spoke to them. How could I speak in ways that would foster deep listening and engagement?

In the effort to gain more insight on this question, I decided to ask students from two different Social Studies APT classes at the University of Alberta to provide a written reflective response to my presentation. Most respondents expressed appreciation for the presentation, and many suggested that the presentation had more accurately reinforced or confirmed much of their previous thinking about Canadian history and Aboriginal perspectives. These findings are consistent with general observations that I have made during previous and subsequent interactions with preservice teachers. For the most part, these students recognize that formal education systems have marginalized Aboriginal peoples and their knowledge systems in the past, and they express a related desire to critique accepted teaching practices and discuss new ideas and approaches.

While the responses are interesting and useful in some ways, I find most of them uncritical in the sense that the respondents simply repeated or confirmed their agreement with statements they heard from me during the presentation. I believe that most students choose to respond in these uncritical ways because they perceive it as safer and easier to simply tell a researcher what they believe he wants to hear.

I am much more interested in critical statements from respondents and interpreting the significance of those statements to the larger project of better understanding the deep influence that colonial frontier logics continue to have on the field of curriculum studies. Below, I share selected excerpts of critical written responses from students that will be interpreted with these issues in mind. I present the statements in groupings based on their subtle commonalities:

> I think I require more training on how to present a lesson in an aboriginal context before I attempt one and claim that it is authentically aboriginal. Perhaps more examples on how to do this would have helped.

I am interested in Aboriginal history, but with my limited knowledge at this point in the subject am not confident in how I will present the Aboriginal views properly.

It seems like a very logical approach, but I think it would be very difficult to engrain a way of thinking into one's process of instruction that they do not know inside and out. This may be a reason why this dichotomy between curriculum and aboriginal education exists. You would have to be an internal element of a particular society in order to perpetuate their corresponding views. Such views would, at that point, flow freely and uncandidly to illustrate indigenous perspectives in the many facets of the instructional and educational processes.

These three statements demonstrate a reliance on the notion of cultural disqualification as a form of resistance to new teacher knowledge. The current context of identity politics has fostered a conceptualization of cultural difference as a imposing rift that works to restrict membership, and its related authority to speak and re-present, to those deemed most culturally authentic. The preservice teachers who authored the statements express a self-conscious awareness of Aboriginal identity politics (in relation to themselves as outside that culture), and a cautiousness in discussing such issues. At some point in their education, privately and publicly, they have come to believe that discussing Aboriginal issues can be extremely contentious, emotionally unsettling, and fraught with danger of being accused of cultural insensitivity, closed mindedness, or even racism. When confronted with these tensions, these preservice teachers retreat behind a comforting shelter of real or passive ignorance that effectively disqualifies them from participation.

The pedagogical logic implied here is that teachers are only allowed to teach about their own cultures—a logic that the field of education has never upheld. In accepting this ignorance and disqualification, these teacher candidates dismiss the opportunity to interrogate the constructs that shape group identifications and better understand how their responses are conditioned by common-sense answers to the problematic question of cultural difference. The unfortunate result of this disengagement is that the boundaries of inside/outside are maintained and reinforced. In so doing, however, the integrity of the individual identity is also stabilized, a phenomenon that has also been noted in another recent study: "Ensuring, therefore, that there is the continued separation of the ideological sets enables the candidates to provide justifications for their ideas, while simultaneously limiting the degree of dissonance that they experience" (Solomon, Portelli, Daniel, & Campbell, 2005, p. 156).

Kanu (2005), in her study of Manitoba teachers' perceptions of the inclusion of Aboriginal culture in curriculum, also suggests that teacher disengagement from the curriculum based on lack of knowledge of Aboriginal perspectives may be understood as an active resistance to difficult and dissonant knowledge. Resistance to this knowledge, and the feelings of estrangement, discomfort, guilt, and defensiveness it foments, is performed through the "ideal of ignorance," disqualification, and the denial of self-implication (p. 58). These "contradictory positions are a manifestation of a whiteness striving to maintain its distance and legitimacy against an unstable social network" (Levine-Rasky, 2000, p. 265).

It seems worthwhile, in light of these teacher resistances, to consider the ways in which common notions of knowledge, knowing, teaching, and learning also become problematic when new curricular knowledge is confronted by the teacher.

In the three responses, there is a palpable concern with the new knowledge of Aboriginal perspectives as a perceived threat to the respondent's abilities to be competent teachers. This concern reveals a certain mindset regarding a teacher's relationship to knowledge that has deep roots in Euro-Western culture and formal structures of education. There is a common-sense perception that the teacher must be an expert in control of the knowledge that will be presented and represented to the students. This perception is built on the notion that the world is ultimately knowable. Knowledge, in this sense, is considered measurable, quantifiable, calculable, and an accurate representation of a preexisting reality independent from the school context (Biesta & Osberg, 2007, p. 16). True knowledge is considered accurate and dependable according to how well it represents an independent reality.

This understanding of knowledge is connected to the modernist assumption that preexisting epistemological truths are out there in the world to be uncovered if the proper mental habits are employed. The accumulation of knowledge parallels human progress and forges a linear teleological path. Colonial renditions of Indigenousness have been represented in the Euro-Western academy as knowable, in a reductive cultural sense, when appropriately positioned on this human evolutionary path. However, recent decolonized assertions of Indigenousness that contest and belie colonial logics are increasingly considered outside Euro-Western knowability and thus incomprehensible.

For a teacher to attempt to teach something that is perceived as unknowable is a fundamental contradiction of basic pedagogical tenets that are foundational to institutionalized understandings of teaching, education, and knowledge (Jones, 2001, p. 283). Linked to this contradiction, and the ambiguousness it causes for those trying to teach, is the psychoanalytic possibility that the comprehension of Indigenousness has the potential to so thoroughly disrupt and destabilize fundamental Euro-Western economic, historical, and postcultural assumptions that the regular citizen cannot tolerate *knowing* such things subjectively.

> Ignorance [or professing not to know] is thus no longer simply *opposed* to knowledge; it is itself a radical condition, an integral part of the very *structure* of knowledge . . . . Ignorance, in other words, is not a passive state of absence—a simple lack of information: it is an active dynamic of negation, an active refusal of information. Ignorance . . . is nothing more than a *desire to ignore*. (Felman, 1982, pp. 29–30)

I believe that the admission of ignorance of Aboriginal perspectives evidenced in the statements from the preservice teachers is indicative of a biographical crisis on their part precipitated by their inability to comprehend Indigenousness and ameliorate the implications of this to their growing challenge of becoming a teacher. The curricular mixing of insider and outsider knowledge subverts more established forms of knowledge and challenges the notion that everything can be known, and thus controlled, by the teacher.

From the perspectives of these student teachers, the imposition of Aboriginal perspectives in the school context amounts to changing the subject and context because formal schooling has never before considered Indigenousness in these ways. "Ignorance . . . 'grows' only in someone when knowledge and context no longer fit each other" (Vitebsky, 1993, p. 107). Ignorance, in this example, is a form of resistance and a strategy of self-preservation on the part of the preservice teachers.

The admission and acknowledgement of Indigenous knowledge systems in institutionalized settings has the potential to so thoroughly destabilize common-sense assumptions of knowledge, teaching, and learning that this disruption must be resisted and externalized. Engagement with Aboriginal perspectives is forestalled until knowledge and expertise arise. This teacherly preoccupation with guaranteed meaning is a significant impediment to their necessary engagement with Aboriginal curriculum perspectives. If educators could come to see that they, as Canadian citizens, have a personal and family history that already intimately implicates them in Aboriginal issues, then the realization and interpretation of these inherited relationships could begin to break down these resistances. Implicative knowledge of Aboriginal perspectives will emerge through their sustained engagement with those topics. In this educational context, Aboriginal perspectives are reframed as an opportunity to learn rather than a threat to existing knowledge.

Active ignorance of Aboriginal perspectives and resistance to its implications is linked to the belief that the imposition of Aboriginal curriculum initiatives in school settings is a moral threat to the character of schools and schooling. Note the following statements from two preservice teachers:

> Curriculum is scary! Unfortunately this presentation has not eased any fears regarding my impending "doom/awaking" and the mini-revolution that is about to occur in Alberta.

> I know it is important for my students to understand the history and how the cultures are different, but I still feel like I would be cheating my students if I focused on aboriginal studies and ignored everything else. My students come from many backgrounds and I don't think it would be fair to teach one perspective if we can't teach them all.

A commonality discerned in these statements is the perception that the integration of Aboriginal perspectives into the new Social Studies curriculum is considered a disorienting disruption of the regular business of school. These respondents view this disruption as a significant threat to the philosophical and moral integrity of the education system and thus themselves as future teachers. These perceived threats of Aboriginality in educational contexts are linked to larger societal concerns regarding Canadian public policy and the future of Aboriginal peoples in Canada. In general, there is a pervasive belief that Aboriginal peoples are a thorn in the side of Canadian society. Although many Canadians will readily admit that Aboriginal peoples and communities have been victims of historical injustices, this admission is tempered with the conviction that civilization has brought more good than bad to them. Historical injustices are thus justified on these grounds.

For many Canadians, the cult of victimization surrounding Aboriginal peoples today is a trap that can only produce anger, frustration, dysfunction, animosity, dependence, and victimhood for those caught in it. The suggested solution to this problem is that Aboriginal peoples get over their past, shed their communal role as special status victims, and live in Canadian society with the same rights, privileges, and responsibilities as individual Canadians. That this solution has never really been seriously considered as a viable option to Canada's Aboriginal *problem* seriously irks many Canadians.[4] Coupled with the irksome reactions to these public debates is resentment over the ways in which Aboriginal peoples are literally and figuratively regarded as obstacles or barricades to social harmony in Canada. Such resentment stems from the belief that Aboriginal peoples in Canada frequently extort economic resources and political attention to selfishly get what they want from the Canadian government. Morality, in the sense of accepted standards of goodness and badness in public contexts, informs and fuels this resentment.

Aboriginal perspectives are perceived as a moral threat to Canadian society when they are experienced as an unwelcome imposition foisted upon Canadians to placate someone's demand for recognition of historical wrong-doing. Many Canadians believe that their right, as citizens, to follow their own moral guidelines is in danger of being co-opted by a constrained morality that typifies the Aboriginal agenda. What is considered at stake in these debates, then, is the right of the large majority of Canadian citizens to maintain their own standards of moral correctness. The postspatial configuration of insiders and outsiders reappears in yet another context.

The contentiousness of statements of moral correctness in Canadian public contexts can be seen in the speech given by Assembly of First Nations Grand Chief Phil Fontaine to the Canadian Club of Ottawa in May 2007. Fontaine, in his efforts to raise awareness of the devastating effects of poverty, crime, and unemployment in Aboriginal communities across Canada, warned the audience that they could see an increase in peaceful protests and blockades if significant efforts were not immediately undertaken to improve the shameful living conditions of Aboriginal peoples. In his warning, Fontaine emphasized that the anger and frustration levels of Aboriginal peoples were palpable, and he feared that these feelings could reach a breaking point and threaten public safety and well-being.[5] In this case, Aboriginality is framed as a very real threat to the existing social order *if things do not improve.* How might this message be heard by Canadians? The image of the recalcitrant and threatening Indian man has certainly played a prominent role in popular media for many generations. The natives are expected to be restless and pose a moral threat to the lifestyle of the insiders—this is the mythical story, based on fort logics, which Canadians have been told for many generations.

More recently, however, the spectre of Aboriginal unrest has been expressed as an impending crisis to Canadian social order. Aboriginal policy has been informed by this idea of crisis as moral threat. Rather than driven to respond to the low quality-of-life crisis lived daily by many Aboriginal people, this spectre of impending crisis has influenced Canadian public policy makers as a looming disruption of the social good. So, while Aboriginal leaders describe the living conditions of their people as unacceptable and *im*moral, average Canadians insist that conformance to accepted moral standards is precisely what will help Aboriginal peoples climb out of the debilitating political and postcultural morass that deforms their lives.

As with most issues of conflictual social concern, these contentious debates eventually find controversial expression in educational contexts. The "moral panic that stages education" has been a significant force in the attempted reconciliation of Indigenousness to Canadian curricular standards (Britzman, 1998, p. 58). Consciousness of the impending crisis of Aboriginal dissatisfaction has influenced curriculum thought by encouraging "crisis policy-making" (Tomkins, 1981, p. 163). This insight suggests that curriculum initiatives involving Aboriginal peoples in Canada, such as the one under consideration here, are not necessarily motivated by some ideal of social good, but rather by a need to address, through policy, an impending social crisis. In this conception, curriculum is a policy tool that can be used to anticipate possible disruptions to the social order and stabilize the status quo. Gradual change is desirable as long as it conforms to the moral model supported by the curriculum.

When the moral character of debates surrounding Aboriginal policy and curriculum initiatives are considered in their fullness, it becomes easier to understand how Aboriginal curriculum perspectives can be perceived as "scary," fearful, an "impending doom/awaking" and "mini-revolution" by some preservice teachers. The perceived scariness of Aboriginal curriculum perspectives is directly linked to the widespread incomprehensibility of Aboriginal presence and participation in Canada today.

While many educators would readily support the teaching of Aboriginal perspectives to Aboriginal students, they have a much more difficult time accepting a policy decision requiring them to teach Aboriginal perspectives to all students. Two things make this notion scary. First, there is the historical, cultural, and moral baggage associated with Aboriginal peoples that constructs them and their ways as outside Euro-Western knowledge systems, unknowable to insiders, and thus incommensurate with any formal public education endeavours. The second is the realization that acceptance of Aboriginal perspectives in education will necessarily call into question many of the common-sense assumptions associated with knowledge and schooling. For example, the acknowledgment of Aboriginal perspectives as they relate to official versions of Canadian history will necessitate critical reflection on the many civilizational myths that have shaped the story of the nation. To call into question such institutions is to also question one's own identity as socially constituted and regulated by them:

> The point is that sociality is governed by relations of power, and relations of power govern the self. A central dilemma, then, of the slippery and shifting meanings of equity and difference concerns how individual and collective perspectives on these terms become implicated in larger discourses of

social regulation. (Britzman, Santiago-Válles, Jiménez-Múñoz, & Lamash, 1993, p. 190)

Such subjective disruptions are indeed potentially quite scary. One way to resist such scariness is to invoke transcendent values both as a way to withdraw from and resist personal implication and instead take a moral stand. One respondent asserts resistance to Aboriginal curriculum perspectives through a declaration of allegiance to universalized values of Canadian multicultural equality and fairness. Adherence to such transcendent values can be understood as one way to attempt to stabilize meaning when faced with an ambiguous teacherly dilemma such as this (Britzman, 1994, p. 67). The desire is to rise above the ambiguity and locate one's position through the logic of accepted and moralized social standards. However, in taking such a stance, the respondent reveals a grave misunderstanding of the Aboriginal perspectives curriculum initiatives in Social Studies in Alberta. The teacher is not required to teach Aboriginal studies or ignore "everything else," but is expected to help students understand how the various perspectives on issues (one of which is Aboriginal perspectives) are connected.

Problematic, too, is the respondent's concerns over the fairness of teaching "one perspective if we can't teach them all." This statement expresses equality as a moral compass to aid in the deflection of the various claims made by cultural groups for special recognition and attention. The multicultural rhetoric of equality has particular currency as a public policy logic: "The *Canadian*-Canadian model of nationhood, which has 'citizenship,' civil and legal rights, political rights and duties, and socioeconomic rights as ideals, is a Western liberal model that places the notion of equality at its centre" (Mackey, 2002, p. 157).

What needs to be unpacked and interpreted with the respondent's statement and its implications for teacher education are the ways in which regular or normal curriculum is perceived as free of specific perspectives while curriculum initiatives that emphasize particular perspectives are dismissed as overly biased. Previous curricula were not regarded as perspectives-based because they were presented as culturally neutral and based on supposedly universal social, economic, and democratic values. Ironically, while the equality argument has powerful pull associated with multicultural rhetoric, it is precisely in the ways such idealized democratic qualities are constructed as "*not cultural* (in that it is not presented as the project of one cultural or ethnic group)" that requires sustained critique in teacher education (Mackey, 2002, p. 162, italics original).

CONCLUSION

The argument that frames this chapter is that Euro-Western interpretations of Indigenousness have fostered the creation of a colonial frontier logic that supports the isolation of Indigenous peoples within settler societies and excludes them from serious consideration on public matters like educational policy and curriculum. In recent years, this logic has been challenged in the form of curricular initiatives that forward Indigenous perspectives as a necessary part of the process of improving the relationships linking Indigenous peoples with the peoples who have come to live on their lands. These initiatives need to be interpreted and understood according to de-colonial goals and in accordance with the concept of "ethical space" between Aboriginal and Canadian in order to instigate the processes of understanding necessary to traverse received colonial divides (Ermine, 2004).

How can the creation of an ethical space be fostered in educational settings? One of the most important ways is through ethical interpretive work by educators that forwards human connectivity as a critical starting point for working through the tension-filled terrain of cultural politics today. Following insights from Indigenous wisdom traditions, I see ethics as a shared public project that fosters respectful engagement and more critical understandings of culture. Understanding culture more critically requires recognition that cultures are not insular things, but rather that cultures embody process-oriented theories of the world that are recursively renewed through interactions with others.

While the significance of contextually-specific cultural practices and beliefs cannot be discounted, it must be remembered that culture is a frame through which we understand ourselves as different *and* in relation to others, the Creator, and the Earth. The challenge is to balance these relationships in sustainable ways. In this conceptualization, then, culture is not an oppositional problem of Inside versus Outside that must be overcome through assimilation and incorporation. Instead, and at its heart, cultural practice is an organic theory of renewal and relationality. We can understand ethical interpretive work and ethical space in the same ways.

Simple informational answers concerning identity, culture, and history will not suffice here. What needs to be recursively worked out, in the form of temporary answers, are the terms according to which ethical space can constitute the character of Aboriginal and Canadian relations in Canada. The guiding vision of this reeducation project will not be to forward Aboriginal perspectives in place of all else, but rather to help Canadians realize that their formal education and socialization has, both subtly and overtly, presented them with a theory of Indigenousness that has shaped and conditioned their ability to respond to Aboriginal presence and participation encountered in their daily lives.

To facilitate this reeducation process, Indigenous teachers and scholars, on behalf of the families and communities that they come from, have a responsibility to promote their values, perspectives, and priorities *as matters of common public concern and consideration.* This requires cordial and respectful engagement beginning with building relationships with those outside of one's own identifiable group. This is how decolonization on a societal level will occur. To clarify this point, I lean on Martin Nakata, an Australian Indigenous scholar who has "attempted to theorise the Indigenous position as an interface position, rather than an oppositional position" (McConaghy, 2000, pp. ix–x). He writes,

> Our position is one of intersection in the first instance, however we are geographically, historically, socially, or economically located. Our position— historic, cultural, social and economic—has been discursively circumscribed for us and governmentally enacted upon us . . . . Unless we begin to understand our position in terms of the (often shifting) discursive regimes that produce that position we will continue to have difficulty articulating the

complexity of our position. Until we do we are bound to reify the very categories of race and culture that have historically constituted our position as inferior, as secondary, as marginal, as different, as other. (p. x)

Taking up Nakata's challenge, then, as well as the commonly heard Aboriginal spiritual invocation *All My Relations*, I wish to assert relationality and inter-referentiality as ethical curricular and pedagogic positions from which to interpret the conflictual cultural terrain and publicly address the tensions that arise there. Resisting the temptation to frame Indigenousness in isolated and exclusionary ways is the first step toward decolonization.

NOTES

[1] These labels were chosen after much deliberation. The term Aboriginal is meant to refer to all people living in Canada who are of Aboriginal descent and identify themselves as such. Canadian is meant to denote those people living in Canada who are not Aboriginal, mostly Euro-Canadians, but also people from all over the world who have come to live in Canada. For the purposes of discussions like this, it is necessary to label different groups according to descent and genealogy, but I am also mindful of the ways that such labeling can unintentionally separate and split people. In using these labels, I also wish to acknowledge that people come from diverse contexts, and their experiences and frames of reference have much to do with how they participate in discussions such as this. These contexts, experiences, and frames of reference often overlap. Aboriginal people are obviously also Canadian, though being Canadian is often only a circumstantial concern. Aboriginal connections to the land are usually considered more important than allegiances to the Canadian nation.

[2] The switch in terminology from *Aboriginal* to *Indigenous* is meant to denote broader and more global concerns regarding the intersection of knowledge systems and intellectual traditions that often traverse arbitrary political boundaries. I use *Aboriginal* when considering specific Canadian concerns and *Indigenous* when referring to issues of common concern to Indigenous people throughout the world.

[3] This definition does not include Inuit peoples, themselves Indigenous to their traditional territories in northern Canada, because their individual and collective experiences with colonial governments are markedly different from those termed Aboriginal.

[4] The Trudeau government did introduce the infamous White Paper in 1969 that suggested the removal of special status for Aboriginal peoples, but this suggestion instigated a widespread political uprising in Aboriginal communities that is still being felt today. The reaction against the White Paper was so vociferous that it was soon removed from the political agenda as a workable option.

[5] Media coverage of Fontaine's speech can be found at: http://www.cbc.ca/canada/story/2007/05/15/fontaine.html?ref=rss

REFERENCES

Alberta Education. (2005). *Program rationale and philosophy: Social studies kindergarten to grade 12*. Edmonton, AB: Alberta Education. Retrieved from http://www.education.gov.ab.ca/k_12/curriculum/bySubject/social/sockto3.pdf

Alberta Learning. (2002). *First Nations, Métis and Inuit education policy framework*. Edmonton, AB: Alberta Learning.

Alfred, T. (2005). *Wasáse: Indigenous pathways of action and freedom*. Peterborough, ON: Broadview Press.

Banks, P. (1980). Herbert Spencer: Victorian curriculum theorist. *Journal of Curriculum Studies, 12*(2), 123–135.

Battiste, M., & Henderson, J. (2000). *Protecting indigenous knowledge and heritage: A global challenge*. Saskatoon, SK: Purich.

Biesta, G., & Osberg, D. (2007). Beyond re/presentation: The case for updating the epistemology of schooling. *Interchange, 38*(1), 15–29.

Blood, N., & Chambers, C. (2008). *Love thy neighbour: Repatriating precarious blackfoot sites.* Retrieved from http://www.learnalberta.ca/content/ssmc/html/lovethyneighbor.html

Britzman, D. (1991). *Practice makes practice: A critical study of learning to teach*. Albany, NY: State University of New York Press.

Britzman, D. (1994). Is there a problem with knowing thyself? Towards a post-structuralist view of teacher identity. In T. Shanahan (Ed.), *Teachers thinking, teachers knowing: Reflections on literacy and language education* (pp. 53–75). Urbana, IL: National Council of Teachers of English (NCTE).

Britzman, D. (1998). *Lost subjects, contested objects: Toward a psychoanalytic inquiry of learning*. Albany, NY: State University of New York Press.

Britzman, D. (2003). Speculations on qualities of difficult knowledge in teaching and learning: An experiment in psychoanalytic research. *International Journal of Qualitative Studies in Education, 16*(6), 755–776.

Britzman, D., Santiago-Válles, K., Jiménez-Múñoz, G., & Lamash, L. (1988). Slips that show and tell: Fashioning multiculture as a problem of representation. In C. McCarthy & W. Crichlow (Eds.), *Race identity and representation in education* (pp. 188–200). New York and London: Routledge.

Bromley, H. (1989). Identity politics and critical pedagogy. *Educational Theory, 39*(3), 207–223.

Carson, T. (2005). Beyond instrumentalism: The significance of teacher identity in educational change. *Journal of the Canadian Association for Curriculum Studies, 3*(2), 1–8.

Deering, T. (2001). The utilitarianism of Herbert Spencer. In T. Deering (Ed.), *Essays in history & philosophy of education* (pp. 145–158). Dubuque, IA: Kendall/Hunt.

Dei, G. (2000). Rethinking the role of indigenous knowledges in the academy. *International Journal of Inclusive Education, 1*(2), 111–132.

Deloria, V. (1998). *Playing Indian*. New Haven, CT: Yale University Press.

Egan, K. (2002). *Getting it wrong from the beginning: Our progressivist inheritance from Herbert Spencer, John Dewey, and Jean Piaget*. New Haven, CT, and London: Yale University Press.

Ermine, W. (2004). *Ethical space: Transforming relations*. Retrieved from http://www.traditions.gc.ca/docs/docs_disc_ermine_e.cfm

Felman, S. (1982). Psychoanalysis and education: Teaching terminable and interminable. *Yale French Studies, 63*, 21–44.

Francis, D. (1992). *The imaginary Indian: The image of the Indian in Canadian culture*. Vancouver, BC: Arsenal Pulp Press.

Jones, A. (2001). Cross-cultural pedagogy and the passion for ignorance. *Feminism & Psychology, 11*(3), 279–292.

Kanu, Y. (2005). Teachers' perceptions of the integration of aboriginal culture into the high school curriculum. *Alberta Journal of Educational Research, 51*(1), 50–68.

Levine-Rasky, C. (2000). The practice of whiteness among teacher candidates. *International Studies in Sociology of Education, 10*(3), 263–284.

Little Bear, L. (2000). Jagged worldviews colliding. In M. Battiste (Ed.), *Reclaiming indigenous voice and vision* (pp. 77–85). Vancouver, BC: University of British Columbia Press.

Mackey, E. (2002). *The house of difference: Cultural politics and national identity in Canada*. Toronto, ON: University of Toronto Press.

McConaghy, C. (2000). *Rethinking indigenous education: Culturalism, colonialism, and the politics of knowing*. Flaxton, Queensland: Post Pressed.

McLeod, N. (1999–2000). Cree narrative memory. *Oral History Forum, 19–20*, 37–61.

Nakata, M. (2002). Indigenous knowledge and the cultural interface: Underlying issues at the intersection of knowledge and information systems. *International Federation of Library Associations and Institutions Journal, 28*(5/6), 281–291.

Smith, L. (1999). *Decolonizing methodologies: Research and indigenous peoples.* Dunedin: University of Otago Press.

Smits, J. (1997). Living within the space of practice: Action research inspired by hermeneutics. In T. Carson & D. Sumara (Eds.), *Action research as living practice* (pp. 281–297). New York: Peter Lang.

Solomon, R., Portelli, J., Daniel, B.-J., & Campbell, A. (2005). The discourse of denial: How white teacher candidates construct race, racism and "white privilege." *Race, Ethnicity and Education, 8*(2), 147–169.

Stewart-Harawira, M. (2005). *The new imperial order: Indigenous responses to globalization.* New York and London: Zed Books.

Tomkins, G. (1981). Foreign influences on curriculum and curriculum policy making in Canada: Some impressions in historical and contemporary perspective. *Curriculum Inquiry, 11*(2), 157–166.

Vitebsky, P. (1993). Is death the same everywhere? Context of knowing and doubting. In M. Hobart (Ed.), *An anthropological critique of development: The growth of ignorance* (pp. 100–115). New York: Routledge.

Weaver, J. (1998). From I-hermeneutics to we-hermeneutics: Native Americans and the post-colonial. In J. Weaver (Ed.), *Native American religious identity: Unforgotten gods* (pp. 1–25). Maryknoll, NY: Orbis.

Weaver, J. (2000). Indigenousness and indigeneity. In H. Schwarz & S. Ray (Eds.), *A companion to postcolonial studies* (pp. 221–235). Oxford, UK: Blackwell.

Willinsky, J. (1998). *Learning to divide the world: Education at empire's end.* Minneapolis, MN: University of Minnesota Press.

Dwayne Trevor Donald
University of Alberta

RAHAT NAQVI

4. MIRRORS AND WINDOWS: SEEING OURSELVES AND OTHERS THROUGH DUAL-LANGUAGE READING

This chapter will focus on a discourse on how languages can serve as a bridge to create an imaginary space that will provide our hybrid generation of students with a means to reflect upon identity, roots, and notions of ancestry. Too often, languages have been reduced to the acquisition of grammatical, phonetic, and oral mechanisms. Using dual-language books for children, I will focus on how this space, identified by Pinar (2004) and others, can in fact become a medium to reimagine who we are as individuals, to go back and fetch what we have forgotten, and to understand identity, history, and culture in the context of our present day world. Languages, scripts, and stories have the power to transform that space in our classrooms that too often seems to be overshadowed by questions of curriculum and classroom strategies. I understand children's multilingual literature as an opening, allowing us various possibilities and interpretations entry points in this quest for identity.

The heightened migration induced by the current processes of globalization has necessitated social realities such as multilingualism and multiculturalism. Due to the fact that immigrant students often have diverse linguistic backgrounds, it has become increasingly important to seek modes of validation of this and other forms of diversity within the classroom. Traditionally, teachers and administrators alike have applied low academic expectations to English as a second language (ESL) and second-language learners and have collectively failed to both appreciate and acknowledge nondominant language knowledge and skills. Not only does this negatively affect immigrant children's academic achievement, it translates into other social inequalities, which combine to serve as an impetus for negative individual and group identity formation strategies. Knowing this, the educational system can now endeavour to develop and support the cultural competence of its teachers to better meet the needs of its diverse student population.

There currently exists a resultant sense of immediacy for dual-language curriculum and multicultural education ignited by findings from recent studies. Through dual-language initiatives in early literacy programs, it might be possible to begin to bridge the ever-widening gap between marginalized students' achievement and their respective capabilities. Such initiatives are equipped to achieve a number of results—a heightened awareness of the experiences of the "other" around us; a more appropriate understanding of the experience of the "Third Space" of these students in their home languages (private) and their school language (public) (Ruiz, 1984); more recognition and acknowledgement of these students in the realm of

J. Nahachewsky and I. Johnston (eds.), Beyond 'Presentism': Re-Imagining the Historical, Personal, and Social Places of Curriculum, 43–53.
© 2009 Sense Publishers. All rights reserved.

public education; a broader appreciation of culture; and a more genuine and authentic spirit of multiculturalism in Canadian education. This chapter will focus on examples drawn from my current research on the incorporation of dual-language books in early literacy programs. This study illustrates how ethnography clarifies the nuanced, contextualized processes that operate in a school and classrooms, particularly those inhabited by students of color. It provides a window on the school and classroom contexts of immigrant students of color, and it helps readers to recognize how culture and identity become implicated in the learning process. It is simply not enough to acknowledge the cultural and familial frames of reference that students bring with them to school. Schools must attempt to infuse these perspectives into both the social and academic fabric, while remaining ever vigilant to protect against the ways that larger social discourse of "us" and "them" may serve to isolate and marginalize students.

In her 1988 essay "Curriculum as Window and Mirror," educator Emily Style suggests that the curriculum [in schools] can be seen as an architectural structure that schools build around students. Often it provides windows revealing the experiences of others but few mirrors reflecting the students' own reality and validity. Given better balance, it can provide mirrors that reflect and validate students' various identities and multiple ways of making meaning, as well as windows into the experiences of others and into ways of making meaning and being that are not part of a student's own cultural repertoire. A curricular balance of windows and mirrors helps the young [and adults] to participate in society with both assertiveness and respectfulness.

Many students new to Canada enter schools without a strong sense of identity. They often do not speak English very well or at all and feel a sense of loss between leaving their first culture behind and yet a pressure to maintain it, all the while trying to fit into mainstream Canadian culture. In many Canadian schools, a multi-cultural approach to teaching and an awareness of what each student brings to the classroom is paramount, and it begins as early as kindergarten. This diversity often includes a variety of cultures represented within a single school and even within a single classroom. The teacher, thus, is called upon to administer a multicultural education.

According to Banks (2005), multicultural education can be defined as a "total school reform effort designed to increase education equity for a range of cultural, ethnic and economic groups" (p. 233). This is, in essence, what the Falconridge study has attempted to examine: how one classroom could contribute to a sense of total school reform and raise awareness of the issues and concerns within a multicultural/lingual classroom.

Mirrors and Windows: Seeing Ourselves and Others Through Dual Language Reading is a multiphase research project that investigates the use of dual-language books in the classroom as a support to literacy, diversity, self-esteem, and community-building in elementary schools in Calgary, Alberta, Canada.

These demographic shifts are changing the face of Canada, where it is projected that 20% of the population will be a visible minority by 2016 (City of Calgary, 2003). In Calgary, these numbers are even more striking as the visible minority population has increased to 25% in 2003 from 16% in 1996 (City of Calgary,

2003). These demographic transformations have generated unique challenges in K-12 education, where mainstream generalist or subject-specialist teachers are encountering students and families with increasingly diverse language, literacy and cultural backgrounds, expectations and needs. This challenge is pronounced for primary teachers entrusted with helping children negotiate the juncture from home to school environments.

The current research has a four-pronged goal. Firstly, the study attempts to determine the effect a dual-language reading program will have on kindergarten children's literacy acquisition within a multilingual/cultural school environment. (Dual-language books are defined as readers incorporating English on one page and another language on the facing page.)

Secondly, with an increased multilingual and multicultural makeup in school classrooms also comes the necessity to examine and research the role of the (unilingual) teacher and what best practices enable him/her to create the most notable climate in which to help the students acquire literacy skills. Such linguistic diversity within today's classrooms has raised questions and presented challenges to teachers that this research hopes to address in a concrete manner. This is particularly prevalent in the northeast quadrant of the city where children of diverse language and cultural backgrounds form a major part of many northeast Calgary school populations. Because children of immigrant or visible minority backgrounds are "not blank slates" (August & Shanahan, 2006); and they bring a variety of proficiencies into the classroom setting. Educators, therefore, need to be made aware of the potential impact different languages and cultures bring to the classroom, and how they can be integrated positively into the learning experience of all their pupils.

Within areas where the immigrant and visible minority populations are highest, Grade 3 children have produced some of the lowest scores on written achievement tests (The Fraser Institute, 2006). Popular opinion is that socioeconomic indicators along with language diversity of this sector are the reason these students do not succeed. However, the Fraser Institute states that "the more effective schools enable all their students to succeed, the weaker will be the relationship between the home characteristics of students and their academic success. Thus, socioeconomic indicators should not be used as an excuse for poor school performance" (p. 9), nor should a first language other than English.

The study also demonstrates how teachers can capitalize on dual-language books while creating a positive and challenging climate in which to help students on their way to literacy. Dual-language reading programs constitute an approach that connects a child's previous literacy steps to their current learning situation.

While dual-language books have existed in libraries for many years already, very few attempts have been made to use them in a proactive manner. The third facet of the study highlights a comprehensive database that will delineate the characteristics of quality dual-language books and categorize them according to appropriate age and grade level. As participants incorporate the books into the study, further guidelines will enable future interested parties to best utilize them within the classroom.

The research also suggests a theoretical framework that draws on the inquiry of leading scholars, thus providing a research mandate for stakeholders and furthering the understanding of the role minority languages can play in improving literacy in the dominant language.

The ongoing study of a dual-language reading program in Calgary has resulted in the development and production of a dual-language book database. Over 2,300 hundred dual-language books have been identified and catalogued for this database. These books are available through the Calgary Public Library System, as well as through many major publishers.

There is much evidence to indicate a strong correlation between first-language literacy and literacy development in English, including word and pseudo-word reading, reading comprehension, reading strategies, and writing (August & Shanahan, 2006). Acknowledgement of children's first languages must be brought forward in the classroom.

Currently, the awareness of dual-language curriculum and multicultural education has been ignited by findings from recent studies (Cummins, 2001; Gagné, 2005; Taylor & Berhard, 2005). Through dual-language initiatives in early literacy programs, multicultural classrooms are able to assist those students whose language and culture prevents them from achieving their full potential. Although dual-language books exist in several Calgary school libraries, teachers are often at a loss as to what to do with them and how to incorporate them into their multicultural classrooms (Naqvi, 2007).

Research of family literacies (Taylor, 1983) and cultural capital (Bourdieu, 1973) reiterate that the core issue is to create an approach that accommodates and capitalizes on this wide range of linguistic and cultural diversity in the classroom.

Language minority students enter classrooms with varying degrees of oral proficiency and literacy in their first language. Specifically, evidence indicates that English-language learners with a different first language are able to utilize higher order vocabulary skills from their first language, such as the ability to provide formal definitions and interpret metaphors, when speaking a second language. Additionally, studies indicate that ESL students have the ability to make connections between their first language and English to better understand English words, important to comprehension. It is therefore important to consider the transferability of some literacy skills when planning and providing second-language literacy instruction to multilingual students. Results of tested theoretical models of the development of print concepts and word reading indicate that children expand their knowledge in each of the following print components with age: print, graphic awareness, phonemic awareness, grapheme-phoneme correspondence knowledge, and word reading components (Lomax, West, Harmon, Viator, & Madaus, 1995; McGee, 2005).

Cummins (2001) believed that teachers' attitudes and expectations of their students affected students' educational performance. When language minority students have the opportunity to utilize their first language(s), teachers learn more about the students' previous literacy experiences. In other words, they see that the slate is far from blank. As the teachers gain a deeper and fuller understanding of their students, they can better select teaching materials and strategies to benefit the student.

Cummins (2001) attempted to address these issues through his Expertise Model, which highlighted the use of dual-language books within a multilingual school in Toronto. A dual-language book is defined as a book written both in English and another language such as Punjabi, French, or Spanish. His study emphasized the importance of being acquainted with students' previous literacy experiences by involving their parents in the school. The parents provided a link between home and school and thus allowed the teachers to better comprehend their students' literacies. Parents were often in the classrooms reading dual-language books to the students. The study also described various strategies for incorporating these books through show and tell, show and read, diaries written by the students, taped versions of the books, and learning centers.

Although elementary teachers are generally aware of the importance of incorporating strategies such as those highlighted by Cummins and others, little has been done to define a framework that will help them to adequately address the needs of their individual classrooms, particularly, any linguistic challenges that may exist. Defined details and criteria for effective dual-language book use and their contribution to literacy acquisition is required.

A Mirrors and Windows pilot study has been underway at Falconridge School in the northeast quadrant of Calgary for over a year. The project explores the issues and evaluates the experiences of kindergarten students (including immigrant and ESL children) through the use of dual-language books. The school services a large and densely-populated community that boasts an 80% to 90% ESL population and is represented by over 25 different home languages. The sample population consisted of 60 students within two classrooms representing rich and wide-ranging linguistic and cultural backgrounds and two teachers. Dual-language books were read to students in Kindergarten and Grade 1 classrooms in videotaped sessions. The books in this project were used as a medium to help students and teachers develop a common link through language and culture and break down barriers between the cultures represented within the classroom and the school.

THEORETICAL FRAMEWORK

Ayers (2004) reflected on what it means to be a teacher and what lies behind teaching with "justice and care." Ayer states that a "model teacher" is a person who, rather than focusing on the problems of the profession, tries to find solutions through various practices. The teacher is also a person who is aware and awake, who rethinks and who links consciousness to conduct. Ayer connects this definition to the following: "Teaching as an ethical enterprise is teaching that arouses students, engages them in a quest to identify obstacles to their full humanity and the life chances of others, to their freedom, and then to drive, to move against those obstacles" (p. 13).

Banks et al. (2005) added to this dimension by stating that teachers must be prepared to teach a diverse population of students and must further "take into account the different experiences and academic needs of a wide range of students" (p. 233). Thus, a multicultural approach to teaching and an awareness of what each student brings to the classroom is paramount in many Canadian schools, and it begins as early as the kindergarten level.

Mody (2005) suggested that the most difficult meanings to share across cultural boundaries are those associated with the moral, ethical, or religious domain. Often, family wishes to retain cultural and linguistic traditions, while school does not know how or where to begin to address the inevitable need for a solution to the needs these students will have in trying to reduce the polarization between home and school, cultural identity, and cultural amalgamation.

THE THEORY OF DUAL-LANGUAGE BOOKS

Although (beginning) teachers are being made aware of these challenges, little has been done to incorporate strategies into the classroom. One approach that is making its way to the forefront, however, is the utilization of dual-language books. These books, used as tools to encourage the multicultural perspective and vision of the school community, are an important tool to help develop a sense of diversity awareness amongst young children. In addition, dual-language books attempt to embrace the notion of acceptance and tolerance, that through differences can be found the path to find similarities. By combining dual-language books as a preliteracy activity, teachers almost inadvertently contribute to the ongoing learning regarding the children's literacy, as will be pointed out in the results.

Since 1940, the use of multicultural picture books has increased steadily, indicating the growing awareness of the value this type of book can bring to the (multicultural) classroom (Mendoza & Reese, 2001).

THE DUAL-LANGUAGE READING PROGRAM

The dual-language reading program incorporates a guest reader who reads with the teacher from a book written in two languages. The storybooks are printed with English and a second language on facing pages, and the readers take turns, alternating the languages, with the classroom teacher reading in English and the guest reading in the second language. The 12 books to be used for this program will be chosen on the basis of the pilot data analysis.

The study examined the role dual-language books can play in various components of today's education system. Dual-language books were incorporated into multilingual/ multicultural classrooms through a variety of preliteracy activities to showcase best practices. The focused areas included the importance dual-language books can have in literacy acquisition, especially amongst language-minority students, and the role these books have in affirming the language and culture of these students, as well as the role of the monolingual teacher within a multilingual setting. In addition, the books were categorized as to those most conducive to meeting the objectives of the study.

Results of the study highlight the significant impact of preliteracy activities on postcultural attitudes. The study also contributed to the development of strategies for inclusive pedagogy using dual-language texts among monolingual teachers working within a multilingual class. This research has a significant impact on how minority languages and cultures are dealt with and perceived within school boards, and its relevance is very timely within the global context. From a research perspective, the research has shed light on how languages and cultures intersect in schools and communities and how such activities can impact literacy acquisition. It has also given solid and innovative direction to future initiatives regarding children's multilingual literature.

Teachers who bring a multicultural perspective into their classrooms (as well as administrators who do so in their schools) encourage appreciation and understanding of other cultures as well as one's own. Teaching with a multicultural/multilingual perspective (e.g., using dual-language books) promotes children's sense of uniqueness of their own culture and language. In addition, it provides opportunities for them to accept the uniqueness of other cultures and languages as well as to learn that these other cultures and languages have similarities to their own. Teaching about and promoting the various cultures and languages represented in a school and classroom can encourage positive attitudes in young children, which, hopefully, will continue to flourish as they grow up.

Mendoza & Reese (2001) cite Rosenblatt's continuum of reading from aesthetic (the user of the book is drawn into the story by identifying with its characters and is entertained by the book) to efferent (reading for information). In a Kindergarten or Grade 1 class, books will be employed anywhere along this continuum. By incorporating dual-language books, children can identify with the different characters and also consider their own actions, beliefs, and emotions. Examining what the world may look like through someone else's eyes, children can also learn to construct their own values and opinions of self and the world.

RESULTS

Teachers' Perspectives

At the outset, the teachers involved in the project were sceptical of what they were getting involved in and did not understand the goal of the study. In their videotaped interviews, they stated that they were at a loss as to how to begin using the dual-language books and to what end these books would serve with reference to the goal presented initially. Ayers's (2004) definition of what it means to be a teacher helped them. This definition involves understanding that teaching is an activity aimed at creating an atmosphere in which students are alert, engaged, and eager to learn. It embraces the humanity and the life opportunities and provides skills to overcome obstacles therein.

The teachers involved in the Falconridge School study needed to be reminded of the challenges they faced within their educational community and the various manners with which they could meet these challenges. The dual-language project helped solidify many issues for them.

This study also demonstrated a valuable strategy to help monolingual teachers work best with multilingual/multicultural students. It also afforded them the occasion to discover the rich qualities these types of classrooms can teach them in return.

Students' Perspectives

The narratives provided by the researchers helped put together a perspective from the students' point of view. Students demonstrated typical behaviour for the most part, including body language such as fidgeting, riveted attention span, talking, and giggling. The interesting note, however, was that as the project unfolded, some themes began to emerge as they pertained to the various perspectives the students manifested. They included the following themes:

1. Acceptance of the "routine" of dual-language books: Students' preliminary reaction to the reading of dual-language books was scepticism, even mistrust. They were not sure they would enjoy this novel activity, especially because they often did not understand what was being read and needed to acquire an ear for that particular second language. As the study progressed, however, and as with all kindergarten routines, the 15 minutes at the end of the day gradually were accepted as being part of the ritual of their class, and they began to look forward to that time. One of the teachers described a session in Urdu for the story *The Very Hungry Caterpillar*.

> The mother who read this story works at the local day care, and has experience with children. She was the first parent who came to me asking to read in Urdu, at her child's request. Her child attends the morning class, but the mother could only come in the afternoon, so returned at the end of the day with her daughter. The mother also offered to read the story in both English and Urdu (a first). At lunch time prior to her visit, she asked which story she was reading and if she could look at it. I let her take the story, asking her to bring it back with her at the end of the day.

> The story was one for which I had props: a puppet and cardboard pictures. As the mother read in both English and Urdu, I used the props to act out the story. The children were very attentive and engaged in the story. Most of the time, they focused on Mrs. X reading, and the rest of the time they watched me act out the story. Mrs. X read with fluency and expression and showed pictures on the page after reading each page. Nobody giggled or was fidgety, as they had been on other occasions. Interestingly, the three children who speak Urdu sat up front almost on Mrs. X's feet! This was where the children chose to sit, without any prompting from me. The three Urdu speaking children were wide-eyed and very attentive. One little boy, who speaks Urdu, tends to have problems focusing on the carpet; however, he sat very still, very quiet, and was leaning forward with his body. The child whose mother was reading had a look of pride on her face and was grinning from ear to ear the whole time. At the end of the story, Mrs. X taught the kids to say caterpillar

and then the title in Urdu. This story time was a big success and I attribute it to the following factors: the story was high quality and age appropriate, the children were familiar with the story, the reader was fluent, and there were props.

2. Improved linguistic awareness: The narratives produced by the researchers indicated a shift in linguistic attitudes as the study progressed. Students whose language was being represented in a particular book began to demonstrate a willingness to recognize and vocally acknowledge that the language in question was "their language." By the end of the study, many of these students both inside the observational groups and in the larger groups were deviating from the original feelings of denial of their language and increasingly manifesting public displays of it. For example, several of the Punjabi-speaking students increasingly referred to their language in the classroom. Some of the non-Punjabi speakers expressed a willingness to claim this language. Overall, the teachers were pleasantly surprised at the reaction to how the language attitudes had changed throughout the course of the study.

3. Improved cultural awareness: As a natural consequence of increased linguistic awareness, the narratives revealed an increased cultural awareness as well. Some of the dual-language books incorporated interaction between the reader and the student, and it was noted that a few of them in the class discussions would make comments. As an example, a Spanish child taught the class how to count from 1 to 10 in Spanish. One of the researchers commented on a reading in Spanish.

The first class had the little guy in it who spoke Spanish. He was very excited about knowing so much—his delight, so it seemed to me, was of something familiar being brought into his school (presumably the two had not coexisted before!). Other children seemed to know some of the words too. At one point a little fellow went up on his knees and asked that the reader teach them all Spanish words. His spontaneity was echoed by many other students—it was delightful to see the children respond so genuinely to another language/ culture. The students do have the curiosity and the ability to learn so much at this age. Could it reduce prejudice and stereotypes?

The observer recorded, "As the reader went through numbers and colors with the children they listened so carefully. They all listened so carefully—in a sense it was as though they were listening to music and wanting to be part of the song."

Towards the end of the reading, the Spanish child was invited to the front of the class and became the Spanish expert. The reader whispered the words to him and he said them aloud. A safe presumption would be that the participants enjoyed the dual-language sessions and were quite interactive, especially when the second language in question was part of their lexical experience.

4. Improved literacy awareness: Towards the end of the project some of the participants were taking the books to "reading centers," pronouncing some of the languages in the way they had remembered, and were undertaking some literacy activities based on what they had heard in the classroom.

51

Stakeholders' Perspective

The parents who participated in the study as readers were very supportive of the endeavor. Those who were unable to participate could not do so because of varying reasons, specific to the posteconomic and cultural nature of the school.

Other students at the Grade 3 level were also incorporated into the study, and their presence in the classroom, using dual-language books they had written themselves, was a very positive one.

The most important point to consider towards the end of this study, however, is the implication it has for the school as a whole (the teacher who participated in the study this year will be teaching a Grade 1 class next year and hopes to continue the tradition in her class), and the excitement and enthusiasm generated within the Board of Education amongst administrators and the bureaucracy.

CONCLUSION

– The use of dual-language books at the kindergarten level has increased the appreciation of a variety of languages other than English.
– Dual-language books were incorporated into a multilingual/multicultural classroom through a variety of preliteracy activities to showcase best practices.
– Results of the study highlight the significant impact of preliteracy activities on postcultural attitudes.
– The study demonstrates how monolingual teachers working within a multilingual class can develop strategies for inclusive pedagogy using dual-language texts.
– Overview of some practical strategies as to how to incorporate dual-language books within the classroom.
– It will also give direction as to what type of book renders the most success in terms of language and other features.
– As the study continues to grow to more schools within Calgary, it is apparent that incorporating literacy strategies into dual-language reading will provide opportunities for all children, regardless of language or race, to participate in a very comprehensive reading program. Strong communities are built on strong citizens and creating an awareness of those around us helps society build strong citizens.
– Further research continues to explore exciting avenues that open up a world of cutting edge research in language and literacy.
– The research continues to be community-based, which enables the children to build bridges between the past and the present and between the minority language and culture and the majority language and culture.

REFERENCES

August, D., & Shanahan, T. (Eds.). (2006). *Executive summary: Developing literacy in second-language learners.* Report of the National Literacy Panel on Language-Minority Children and Youth. Retrieved August 29, 2006, from http://www.cal.org/nat-lit-panel/reports/Executive_Summary.pdf

Ayers, W. (2004). *Teaching toward freedom: Moral commitment and ethical action in the classroom.* Boston: Beacon Press.

Banks, J. (1993). Multicultural education: Historical development, dimensions, and practice. *Review of Research in Education, 19*, 3–49.

Banks, J., Cochran-Smith, M., Moll, L., Richert, A., Zeichner, K. M., LePage, P., et al. (2005). Teaching diverse learners. In L. Darling-Hammond & J. Bransford (Eds.), *Preparing teachers for a changing world* (pp. 232–274). San Francisco: Jossey-Bass.

Bourdieu, P. (1973). Cultural reproduction and social reproduction. In R. Brown (Ed.), *Knowledge, education, and cultural change* (pp. 71–112). London: Tavistock.

Canadian Council on Learning. (2006, May 12). *First language not necessarily linked to reading proficiency.* Retrieved August 29, 2006, from http://www.ccl-cca.ca/CCL/Reports/LessonsInLearning/LiL12May.htm?Style=Print&LAnguage=EN

Calgary Board of Education. (2007). *Quick Facts. 2006–2007 school year facts, figures, questions and answers about the CBE.* Retrieved October 1, 2007, from http://www.cbe.ab.ca/media/facts.asp

Cummins, J. (2001). *The dual language showcase: Valuing multilingualism and multiculturalism.* Retrieved August 29, 2006, http://thornwood.peelschools.org/Dual/about.htm

Gagné, A. (2005). *Growing new roots.* Retrieved August 30, 2006, from http://eslinfusion.oise.utoronto.ca/

Lomax, R., West, M., Harmon, M., Viator, K., & Madaus, G. (1995, Spring). The impact of mandated standardized testing on minority students. *Journal of Negro Education.* Retrieved August 30, 2006, from http://www.findarticles.com/p/articles/mi_qa3626 /is_199504/ai_n8718747

McGee, M., & Morrow, L. (2005). *Teaching literacy in kindergarten.* New York: Guilford Press.

Mendoza, J., & Reese, D. (2001, Fall). Examining multi-cultural picture books for the early childhood classroom: possibilities and pitfalls. *Early Childhood Research and Practice, 3*(2). Retrieved March 5, 2006, from http://ecrp.vivc.edu/v3n2/mendoza.html

Mody, S. (2005). *Cultural identity in kindergarten. A study of Asian Indian children in New Jersey.* New York and London: Routledge.

Naqvi, R. (2007). Expérience de lecture croisée en littérature jeunesse. *Français dans le monde, 350,* 26–28.

Pinar, W. (2004). *What is curriculum theory?* Mahwah, NJ: Lawrence Erlbaum Associates.

Style, E. (1988). *Curriculum as window & mirror.* National seeking educational equity & diversity project, Wellesley centers for women. Retrieved May 5, 2007, from http://www.wcwonline.org/joomla/index.php?option=com_content&task =view&id=652&Itemid=127&Itemid=54

Taylor, D. (1983). *Family literacy: Young children learning to read and write.* Portsmouth, NH: Heinemann.

Taylor, L., & Berhard, J. (2005). *Transforming identity relations through expanded multiliteracies curriculum: Designing learning environments for knowledge generation within the new economy.* Retrieved March 20, 2006, http://www.toronto.ca/metropolis .metroplistoronto2005/english/workshoips_oct.20.html

The Fraser Institute. (2006, June). *Report card on Alberta's elementary schools: Studies in education policy.* Vancouver, BC: Author.

Rahat Naqvi
University of Calgary

PARISS GARRAMONE

5. GETTING TO THE ROOTS: RETHINKING CANADIAN FORESTS AS CURRICULUM

We sit in the dining tent. The wood stove at the back glows red. Wet clothes hang on every available tent beam, a forest within a forest. A tangle of wet boots—propped up, bent over or layered on top of each other to catch the warmth of the stove—root these trees to the floor of our tent. We are the remaining few still sitting here. We savour our last bites of dinner, our tea, our coffee. Some read. All of us lingering, postponing that moment when we must return to our damp tents, our sleeping bags, where we will quickly fall asleep, only to wake to another long day of planting trees in the clear-cut.

I've done this for too long, I think to myself. This is my twelfth season of working in this so-called "forest." I have worked in the same area—three hours north of Thunder Bay—for most of those 12 years. Each summer I have returned: first, as a young tree planter working for a two-month stretch, and now, as an old hand living and working in the community six to seven months a year. A white, privileged university student, a girl from southern Ontario who had never before seen a small northern community, let alone a clear-cut, now, as a 12-year veteran, I return to familiar, smiling faces, genial conversations about the winter now past, and laughter-infused exchanges about family members. These are my co-workers and friends, people who live and work in the community and, at times, on the Clearwater reserve. They have lived and worked here with their families far longer than I. I feel connected to these people, and this community. I wonder . . . do I think that I am now an expert? That the experience can be somehow knowable by virtue of having relived it each year?

As I sip my tea, I begin to listen to a first-year tree planter recounting his day.

"I realized today—that where I was planting—well, I was walking where no one has ever walked!" A seasoned planter nodded his head in understanding.

I felt my heart beating fast. I blurted, "What do you mean, no one has ever walked there? All of the Clearwater crew grew up on this land."

The first-timer glanced nervously towards the seasoned planter who said, "Not on the 'block'—they didn't live there."

As workers, we often talk about the clear-cut as "the block," and often as "your block." We use the phrase to refer to the small sectioned-off area of clear-cut assigned to each planter.

I continued, "It wasn't always a clear-cut. John Senior was born about 20 km from our camp on his family's trap line, when this was actually a forest."

J. Nahachewsky and I. Johnston (eds.), Beyond 'Presentism': Re-Imagining the Historical, Personal, and Social Places of Curriculum, 55–60.

Silence. I looked around the dining tent. At the far end of the last table sat Joseph, a local tree planter who lives on the Clearwater First Nation. I didn't know Joseph very well. I wondered how long he had worked as a planter, and how long he had lived in the community.

In the weeks that followed, I looked for Joseph, intending to speak with him; but I never did get the chance. I wonder what he made of the first-timer's comment? I wonder what he made of my response? I remember that he was often silent.

Stories are complex entities. They complicate, implicate, and haunt. I begin this paper with my own story, one version of what happened that evening in the dining tent. This is an autobiographical story set within autobiographical time—a complication of 'fictions' and 'forgettings' crafted by me in the *now*, reflecting a *then*, which was once another *now*, another present moment. My story offers no transparent window onto the past, but it does offer a doorway through which I can pass as I begin to think my way into the difficult ordinary space of forestry work. This story caused a rupture for me; as I reflected upon the past and the events of that day I returned to a time when the complicatedness of my taken-for-granted everyday work became, as Ellsworth (2005) might say, a "place of learning." I want now to tease out a few moments of insight—not all, only a few. In this chapter, I link the ideas of curriculum as school-based text and curriculum as it is "in the making" within environments outside of schools. Next, I consider this linkage as I develop the idea of forests as curriculum. I extend this idea to include the ways in which national identity links to curriculum. And finally, I want to suggest how this story can become a site for excavating the reproduction of the imperial conquering narratives, and fertile ground for exploring the always complicated though compelling character of story.

CURRICULUM

I want to begin by situating this discussion within curriculum discourse. I am aware of the tangle involving pedagogy—critical, feminist, radical—and current curriculum discourses. Why discuss forests as curriculum and not as pedagogy? In this instance, I choose to think about curriculum because historically curriculum has subsumed pedagogy. What might happen if we think curriculum in ways that diminish the hierarchy that stratifies curriculum and pedagogy, if we take up Ellsworth's (2005) challenge "to think [curriculum] in ways that make [curriculum] encompassed by [pedagogy]" (p. 12)? Thinking curriculum differently has a rich history. It is not my intention here to sketch this long and winding road, but only to map some important terrain that we need to navigate.

OUTSIDE SCHOOLS

What is curriculum? Egan (1978) defines curriculum as the way "Children are initiated into particular modes of making sense of their experience and the world around them, and also into the norms, knowledge and skills which the society requires for its continuance" (p. 66). Yet, we must ask of Egan, What and whose norms, knowledge, and skills? What society and what type of continuance?

Curriculum has also been described as "what every Canadian needs to know." But again—who decides what matters? Who decides not only what and whose knowledge will matter, and *be* matter, but also what and whose *needs* matter? More troubling is the notion of "every Canadian." It is not simply that the phrase "every Canadian" begs the question (for it fails to ask, What do we mean by *Canadian*? What criteria do we use in judging whether or not one is Canadian? and Who is inevitably left out?). It also implies that we can ask and find the answer to the question, Who am I? before we ask and discover, Where is here? and What matter(s)?

By uprooting the curriculum and shaking off the loose soil, one can begin to see the colonizing aspects of schooling that have dictated what knowledge is of value and what knowledge matters. As Willinsky (1998) argues, the curriculum is implicated in the creation of particular types of "subjects" for the empire, and, as Egan indicates, the dominant curriculum reconstructs a particular society and attempts to ensure its continuance through ongoing practices of marginalization. Many have begun to re-place curriculum, finding within the discourse spaces for remembering the work of silences and absences. By rethinking curriculum in this way, we cannot only renegotiate what matters and what needs to become matter for curriculum, but also challenge and expand the places of learning to involve the materiality of learning/ teaching bodies.

Returning to curriculum as "what every Canadian needs to know," the questions of Who am I? and Where is here? are important questions that must be addressed. As Pinar (1993) argues, curriculum debates are now also "debates over who we perceive ourselves to be and how we will represent that identity, including what remains 'left over' as 'difference'" (p. 2). Pinar adds that "curriculum is one highly significant form of representation, and arguments over the curriculum are also arguments over who we are as [Canadians], including how we wish to represent ourselves to our children" (p. 2).

At this point, I want to consider curriculum as representation by engaging with Stuart Hall's (1997) discussion of representation (see pp. 3–7). According to Hall, one experiences reality only through the complex lens of culture, that is, through representation, or the stories we tell about the world in which we live. Hall argues that culture is about shared meanings and that it is through language that we collectively make meaning. I want to complicate this by introducing the idea of discourse. What I am suggesting is that discourse is not a synonym for language. Foucault himself speaks of discourse, and not language. Discourse frames discussion and constructs particular types of knowledge. It limits alternative ways of constructing knowledge around a topic and alternative ways of relating to that topic. Knowledge, power, and history are very important to Foucault's ideas of discourse. Meaning is always shaped by history and fixed by power. Discursive practices produce subjects and objects of knowledge practices. The idea of text is also significant in this context. Pinar (1993) understands text as pieces or moments of social reality. A text, he claims, can be "social practices, cultural products . . . anything that is created as a result of human action and reflection" (p. 2). I want to think about the curriculum of forests as a text we can read both from this story and by thinking differently about forests.

What happens when I uproot one common representational practice—the making and telling of stories of our experiences with the land? To excavate this site we need to keep in mind how representation operates and what meanings are reproduced and fixed through the representation. Also, how might our ways of thinking about curriculum change when we move curriculum outside of schools? What lies outside schools is the imagined nation—in our case, Canada. Rethinking curriculum in this way means addressing not only the question of Who am I? but also the question, Where is here? In my rethinking of curriculum I address the tangle of national identity, the self, and the nation as imagined.

FORESTS

When I retell the story with which I began this chapter, I often highlight only this comment made by the first-year tree planter: "Where I was planting trees, I was walking where no one has ever walked!" His words and his narrative suggest a reconstruction of the land into a *terra nullius*, an empty place waiting to be "discovered" by a tree planter. How was my co-worker able to see the land in this way?

As Willinsky (1998) reminds us, education in the colonies evolved as part of a history of empire building. Education—and with it curriculum—has played a significant role in the construction of particular fictions that have served to erase a land already named, populated, organized, governed, mapped, and measured, leaving instead a *terra nullius*, an empty no man's land. Erasure was and continues to be a complicated endeavour, one that requires ongoing and time-intensive maintenance. Only in such a context is it possible for this perception of the land to become naturalized and subsequently integrated into the dominant (read nonindigenous) national imaginary.

What is this national imaginary? Lloyd (2000) sees the national imaginary through the organization of fictions that structure collective imagining for nonindigenous Australians. She identifies two key structuring fictions in the Australian imaginary. First, the fiction of a *terra nullius,* a land free of inhabitants and therefore free to be occupied. Within such a fiction, occupation becomes naturalized and deemed legitimate. Second, the creation of a national fiction of the Indigenous population as "an inferior and doomed race." Again, the myth has been maintained, naturalized, and integrated into the national imaginary. I suggest that similar fictions haunt the national imaginings of Canada.

How does a society structure, reinforce, and maintain these types of fictions so that they become naturalized and accepted? This is the work of schooling, specifically curriculum. Curriculum has been exported to the colony for the purpose of shaping a particular type of imperial subject. This has been the Canadian story. These collective fictions of the land have not only silenced the stories of conflict and negotiation among people living in a land that had already become a well-developed nation, but have also called into question the humanness of the Indigenous peoples of the Americas. Education has played a central role in this violent "clear-cutting" of history. The story told by the first-year tree planter conjures a familiar ghost from the past, a dominant white-settler narrative fiction used to naturalize the collective imagining of a *terra nullius.*

Many writers, among them Willinsky (1998), have traced the construction of these myths and the evolution of imperial practices established on the basis of their authority. Such practices are still evident throughout much of the curriculum as it is taught and lived in the schools of today. Willinsky and others have argued that these fictions have been a way of imagining the empire, and with it the nation of Canada. In this dominant white-settler narrative, it is the white settler who braves the savage land and changeable climate to "find" Canada. The fictional narrative persists, though much effort has been expended to construct alternative, multi-cultural narratives to replace it.

The white settler within this no man's land is a myth that continues to lurk in the curriculum (even in current discourse about teacher training) to haunt our imaginings of a nation. We also find it permeating the stories we continue to tell about our experiences with the land. These vestiges of the past are profoundly consequential. As Code (2001) notes, "No repetition is a mere re-using of the old: it is simultaneously a making of the new, reinforcing the dominant imaginary or unsettling it" (p. 190).

One can see in this first-year planter's remark evidence of the collective imaginings of a nation. This storyteller was only able to name his new relationship with the forest and construct his new experience with the land by calling upon the myths of the past. In the act of telling his story, naturalized fictions were once again reenacted, past narratives brought forth into the present to become the sextant by which he will navigate both his present and his future. Could the use of these old stories of the land by the first-year tree planter signal a disruption of a presumably unified self? As Code (2001) argues, it is the unimaginable everyday ordinary events of violence, those specifically of human origin, that destabilize the self. Could it be argued that the violence we inflict on the land, once witnessed and experienced as ordinary, could provoke such an "undoing of the self"? (p. 273). Many writers have taken up this question. Where is here? as a question of relation—a "here" is constructed by a "there." This question evokes both the places from which one speaks and the identity of the speaker; they speak to the intertwining of epistemologies and ontologies. This suggests for me a sense of "home" and a way to conjure Barad's (2003) ontoepistimology, being visible in bodies that are at the same time locations of knowing practices.

In the story that I told at the outset of this paper, I wrote, "I have done this for far too long." I also tell of returning each year to a place, once unfamiliar, now recognizable, to people once cool and distant, now warm and friendly. This was a place once unknown, and now, perhaps, is known to be unknowable. I describe this place in many ways: first as "a so-called forest," then an "area," and finally, a "small northern community." My feelings of comfort with this place may be a sense of being at "home," of being "here." This feeling of being "at home anywhere" comes from having others "see" or "read" us as undeniably Canadian. I am never asked, "But where are you really from?" or "Sorry, I mean, what is your heritage?" The white settler fiction might well be read alongside my enactment of "being Canadian."

One of the many difficulties of this story is that I create a narrative landscape made up of many locales, spaces that merge and shift in and out of each other as the story unfolds: the camp site, the small northern Ontario town, the Clearwater reserve, southern Ontario, a university campus, a dining tent, and a clear-cut. The clear-cut itself becomes, euphemistically, both the forest it once was and the community "block" that is our home. All of these spaces are created in relation to each other. Similar to the identities that they represent, they become meaningful only in their relations to each other. In a sense, these spaces are performed into places through the telling of the story.

It is the impossibility of this story to keep things "straight" that, for me, makes it a pedagogical place. The story could be rewritten, but that is not the point—the difficulty of the story would remain. Where is this place? Where is the forest in this story? I wonder, Where are the forests so central to the images/imaginings of this Canada? I think of the people-less forests in the Group of Seven's paintings in conjunction with the discourse of forests as out there, outside the city, pristine, wild, and savage. The forest described in this story could easily be imagined as a tree farm. But what does seeing forests allow us to maintain?

Returning to the idea of forests *as* curriculum—I want to suggest that it is by seeing forests as constructed by knowledge/power and history that we are able to read forests as a curriculum text. Possibly in this reading we can uproot the myths of a nation, the dominant national imaginary that prevents other stories of the land from taking root. We might also begin to think about the materiality of forests and the scars on bodies/land that are marks of how knowledge/power and history have shaped a nation.

REFERENCES

Barad, K. (2003). Posthumanist performativity: Toward an understanding of how matter comes to matter. *Sings: Journal of Women in Culture and Society, 28*(3), 801–831.
Code, L. (2000). Statements of fact: Whose? Where? When? Moral epistemology naturalized. *Canadian Journal of Philosophy Supplementary, 26*, 175–208.
Code, L. (2001). Rational imaginings, responsible knowings: How far can you see from here? In N. Tuana & S. Morgen (Eds.), *Engendering rationalities* (pp. 261–282). New York: State University of New York Press.
Egan, K. (1978). What is curriculum? *Curriculum Inquiry, 8*(1), 65–72.
Egan, K. (2003). Retrospective on "What is curriculum?" *Journal of the Canadian Association for Curriculum Studies, 1*(1), 17–24.
Ellsworth, E. A. (2005). *Places of learning: Media, architecture, pedagogy.* New York: Routledge.
Hall, S. (1997). The work of representation. In S. Hall (Ed.), *Representation: Cultural representation and signifying practices* (pp. 15–64). London: Sage.
Lloyd, G. (2000). No one's land: Australia and the philosophical imagination. *Hypatia: A Journal of Feminist Philosophy, 15*(2), 26–39.
Pinar, W. F. (1993). Notes on understanding curriculum as a racial text. In C. McCarthy & W. Crichlow (Eds.), *Race, identity and representation in education* (pp. 60–70). New York: Routledge.
Willinsky, J. (1998). *Learning to divide the world: Education at empire's end.* Minneapolis, MN: University of Minnesota.

Pariss Garramone
York University

TONYA D. CALLAGHAN

6. THE HISTORICAL, PHILOSOPHICAL AND SOCIOLOGICAL FOUNDATIONS THAT CONTRIBUTE TO THE INSTITUTIONALIZATION OF HOMOPHOBIA IN CANADIAN CATHOLIC SCHOOLS

In a discussion with Paul Rabinow (2003) on the topic of the subject and power, Michel Foucault (1926-84) commented on the importance of beginning an analysis with a *how* question. He specified "How?" not in the sense of "How does it manifest itself?" but "How is it exercised?" In this way, he underscored the importance of undertaking a critical investigation of the thematic of power. It is within this tradition that I explore how homophobia operates in Canadian Catholic schools. My questions are two. First, how do the historical and philosophical foundations of Canadian Catholic schools contribute to the institutionalization of homophobia? Second, how does homophobia function as a structure?

Michel Foucault's (1975/1995) notion of surveillance and Antonio Gramsci's (1971) idea of hegemony provide a double lens through which I direct my investigation. Two texts in particular underpin my analysis: Foucault's chapter entitled "The Means of Correct Training" in his book, *Discipline and Punish: The Birth of the Prison* (first published in 1975 as *Surveiller et Punir: Naissance de la Prison*), and Gramsci's notes on education, which he wrote while imprisoned in Mussolini's gaols from 1929–35 and which are now compiled as Chapter Two "On Education" in *Selections from the Prison Notebooks*. I apply this theoretical framework in seeking to understand the how of the homophobic structure that currently exists within Canadian Catholic schools.

In order to determine how the Church contributes to the institutionalization of homophobia, one must begin by critically examining the historical and philosophical foundations of Catholic schools in Canada. The historical construction of an educational state in 19th-century Canada was born out of a need on the part of the ruling elites to maintain social order by controlling the working classes. The Catholic hierarchy of early Canada capitalized on the need for social order by arguing for the establishment of a separate school system. As a minority faith under siege by a Protestant majority, Canadian Catholic officials recognized that they could strengthen their claim for a separate school system by demonstrating their ability to maintain social order through public schooling. Early Catholic school officials were able to facilitate the control of citizens by emphasizing the traditional hierarchical, patriarchal, and authoritarian philosophical ideals of the

J. Nahachewsky and I. Johnston (eds.), Beyond 'Presentism': Re-Imagining the Historical, Personal, and Social Places of Curriculum, 61–72.

Church. Although the historical establishment of separate schools in Canada ultimately hinged on the protection of a Catholic faith minority from a strong Protestant majority, today Catholic school boards in Canada actively ignore the rights of certain minority groups—namely, nonheterosexual students and staff.

When I examine my own experiences in Canadian Catholic schools, both as a student and as a teacher, I easily recognize surveillance and hegemony at work. The Catholic schools of my experience maintain an historic distrust of the Rousseauean approach to education that attends to the spontaneous, natural creativity of the child and instead adopt a Platonic respect for reason and authority coupled with a Durkheimian desire to socialize students to fulfill the perceived needs of society. Thus, by employing a critical theoretical lens in my analysis of homophobia within Catholic schools, supported by an examination of my own experiences with homophobic attitudes and behaviours within the Catholic school system, I argue that the historical and philosophical foundations of Canadian Catholic schools have facilitated the institutionalization of homophobia in Canadian Catholic schools today.

THE ROLE OF EDUCATION IN STATE FORMATION

In 19th-century Canada, the ruling classes recognized that education could play a central role in maintaining social order. Indeed, Katz (1976) argued that the notion of public education came not from altruistic impulses but from a perceived need on the part of the ruling classes to control and mould the masses. Canadian society at this time was becoming increasingly divided along the lines of class. Bourgeois educational reformers saw the systematic construction of an educational state as essential for the direct socialization of the masses and for the training of men of modest property in representative government through the management of local government. As Curtis (1988) observed, "schooling produced character and thus its organizational principles were of great importance to social order" (p. 29). Consequently, Canada West (referred to as Upper Canada until 1840, and Ontario after 1867) began the "practical construction of an educational state" (Curtis, 1988).

Green (1990), drawing on the ideas of Karl Marx (1818–83) and Antonio Gramsci (1891–1937), offered a theory about the development of state-run public education that emphasizes not the advantages for the ruling class but rather the emancipatory benefits for the working class. Green posited state-formation as a cultural revolution with education at its heart, arguing that public education was as much a means for liberation as it was for control. Green noted that Marx, a fervent believer in the educational potential of the working class, supported demands for a system of public education funded directly by the state (p. 90), and that Gramsci stressed both the coercive force and the emancipatory potential of the school. For Gramsci, education was a weapon in the struggle for hegemony, and the school was a vital agency in the process of state formation (Green, p. 99).

Katz (1976) offered another theory explaining the birth of the public school system. According to Katz, members of the ruling class eventually came to regard the state-run institution as a solution to common social ills. Clearly, public schooling did usher in a number of diverse social improvements. Curtis (1988) noted that the School Act of 1850, developed by the Reverend Egerton Ryerson (1803–82), contained some progressive elements that were radical for the time: notably a focus on social mobility, some new rights for women, and the idea of the *pleasure* of pedagogical matters. However, the underlying tone of the School Act revealed a fundamental belief in education as the means by which the state could produce citizens who were duly subordinated to God, the state, and the structure of worldly authority (also known as a class system).

THE ESTABLISHMENT OF SEPARATE SCHOOLS AS A PROTECTION OF MINORITY RIGHTS

The Reverend Egerton Ryerson's conceptions of a "universal" public and a "common Christianity" (Curtis, 1988, p. 176, note 22) were put to the test by several members of the hierarchy of the Catholic church who would only support public education if separate school clauses were written in to various school acts. Conservative Catholics, writing in the late 19th century, emphasized one persistent theme: "Education is worthless without morality, and morality impossible without religion" (cited in Ognibene & Paulli, 2002, p. 41). Religious schools, they argued, would "reduce crime and vice and produce orderly citizens" and provide "the greatest school of respect the world has ever seen" (cited in Ognibene & Paulli, 2002, p. 41).

Reverend Ryerson, for his part, contended that "Separate Schools cannot be claimed as a right" (Hodgins, 1897, p. 201), but it was precisely the argument of minority rights that finally enabled the various Catholic bishops to win their repeated debates in parliament after several years of dispute. The final agitation in 1866 resulted in the passing of a separate school bill, which was written to "extend to the Roman Catholic minority in Upper Canada similar and equal privileges with those granted by the Legislature to the Protestant minority in Lower Canada" (cited in Hodgins, 1897, p. 195). The Catholic hierarchy in Upper Canada continued to campaign vigorously for a virtually autonomous system of Catholic education, setting a pattern not only for that part of the country but also for the rest of Canada generally (Carney, 1992).

DISRESPECT FOR MINORITY RIGHTS WITHIN THE SEPARATE SCHOOL SYSTEM

Ironically, separate schools in Canada, born of the perceived need to protect faith minorities from a hostile Protestant majority, are now often culpable of the same hostility once directed towards them. There are many instances of Canadian Catholic school boards actively ignoring the rights of certain minority groups in their care. A case in point is the 2002 legal hearing in Whitby, Ontario, regarding high school student Marc Hall's right to take his boyfriend to his high school prom in the Durham Catholic School District. In their discussion of the Hall case, Grace and Wells (2005) argued that churches have no business in the publicly funded classrooms of the nation. The authors cited churches as being among "the most invasive cultural forces in making certain that there are consequences for living queer" (p. 1). Churches and their cousin, the denominational school, create "consequences" for queer (nonheterosexual) youth and staff by demeaning, dismissing, and deserting the Catholic queer youth who are also under their charge and who are especially vulnerable to physical and emotional homophobic persecution.

Queer teachers' rights are also regularly violated in Catholic schools. In Alberta, for example, item number nine from the *Declaration of the Rights and Responsibilities of Teachers*, which is part of the *Constitution* of the Alberta Teachers' Association (2004), states that teachers have the right to be protected against discrimination on the basis of prejudice as to sexual orientation. Queer Catholic teachers who have partners cannot talk openly about them, cannot bring them to work-related social events, and certainly cannot get them signed up on the employee health benefits package. Regardless of their relationship status, queer teachers in Canadian Catholic schools regularly witness the effects of homophobic Catholic doctrine in the day-to-day operations of the school, often at great costs to their emotional and psychological well-being. Like the student Marc Hall, queer teachers are expected to remain chaste and celibate and, if they do have partners, that is something to keep secret rather than celebrate.

THE PHILOSOPHICAL FOUNDATIONS OF SEPARATE SCHOOLS

Confronted by a powerful Protestant majority, 19th-century Catholicism sought to protect itself, as Morris (1997) noted, by creating a separate universe of parallel social and cultural institutions and professional organizations designed to isolate Catholics from the implicit dangers embedded in a society formed under strong Protestant influence. The church intended that this protective isolationism serve two purposes: first, ensure that Catholics strictly adhere to Catholic doctrine; and second, undermine Protestant opponents by producing citizens who had a healthy respect for authority and discipline. However, as Ognibene and Paulli (2002) pointed out, protecting Catholic schools by isolating them served to reinforce Catholic educators' distaste for the progressive education movement, which was launched by John Dewey in the 1890s and destined to become the dominant influence on educational discourse for the next 50 years. Ognibene and Paulli (2002) wrote that, in general, "Most Catholic educators wanted nothing to do with progressivism and made a point to denounce it" (p. 42). A case in point is Father William McGlucken (1934), who argued that Dewey's educational ideas (specifically, his emphasis on the natural origins of humankind, his denial of the supernatural, the soul, and original sin, and his rejection of moral absolutes) were contrary to Catholic doctrine and "infected by the Rousseau virus" (p. 7).

Protective isolationism, then, reinforced and sustained the Church's suspicion of a progressive education that contradicted traditional Catholic doctrine and practices. The Catholic schools of my experience maintain their historic distrust of the Rousseauean approach to education. Jean-Jacques Rousseau (1712–78), the controversial social philosopher and "educationalist" (Marshall, 1998), proposed philosophical views that were at odds with the Catholic faith. Rousseau conceived of education as enabling individuals to be "freely and rationally self-legislating, actively participating in the construction of the political arrangements that form our character, our sentiments and motives" (Oksenberg Rorty, 1998, p. 242). Egan (1997) observed that modern schools exhibit three distinct aims that have always been part of the development of Western education: (a) socializing the young (borrowed from Durkheim); (b) teaching knowledge that fosters a rational view of the world (borrowed from Plato); and (c) realizing the unique potential of each child (borrowed from Rousseau).

Catholic schools, however, take little from Rousseau. Rather than crediting and encouraging the spontaneous, natural creativity of the child, Catholic schools palpably privilege the Platonic respect for reason and authority. According to Egan (1997), those educational stakeholders who believe in the Platonic ideal tend to emphasize a disinterested pursuit of truth through hard academic disciplines that will make students knowledgeable, discriminating, and sceptical. This describes schooling as I experienced it within the Catholic school system. The Albertan Catholic schools in which I studied and taught honoured the God of the Enlightenment—reason. However, they combined their faith in reason with faith in the tradition and authority of the Catholic Church. Essentially, there were two Gods to worship: the God of reason and the God of creation. Disciplined deference to the authority of the teacher and religious figures as well as respect for the core academic disciplines were the norm.

Along with its preference for Platonic ideals, the Catholic system accepted Émile Durkheim's (1858–1917) understanding of school as a structure that socializes students in order to fulfill the "needs" of society. Durkheim's functionalist theory identified scientific sociology—in its joining of Enlightenment reason with capitalism and "progress"—as a solution to social problems. As Egan (1997) explained, educators who emphasize the socialization aspect of schooling primarily associate education with the production of good (i.e., moral) citizens. This was one of the primary goals in the historical establishment of a separate Catholic school system in Upper Canada: to demonstrate that a Catholic focus on moral education, respect for authority, and discipline would produce better citizens than a Protestant emphasis on progressive education. Even today, Durkheim's theory of socialization, based on the distinction between the normal and the abnormal, influences the methodological orientation in many Catholic schools in Alberta. Certainly, this was the case in the Catholic schools that I attended and at which I was employed.

Philosophical premises such as these create schools in which there is little room for sexual minority groups to express their experiences and perspectives. Taylor (1994) argued that, on a social level, identities are formed in "open dialogue" (p. 36) with others and that this process often involves a "demand for recognition" (p. 25) on the part of minority or "subaltern" groups. Minority groups in Catholic schools such as gays and lesbians are certainly demanding recognition, but the authoritative and patriarchal structure of the system does not deign to offer it. Bannerji (2000), however, pointed out Taylor's patronizing tone and exclusionary use of "us" and "them"—binaries that he fails to problematize. While conceding Taylor's claim that everyone needs to be recognized, Bannerji questioned Taylor's appeal to an "us" who are in a position to grant such recognition. Bannerji declared that Taylor "does not question why 'we' have this power to grant or withhold it"

(p. 136) and argued that the very need for recognition of some by others signals an inequitable power relationship.

In much the same way that Taylor (1994) failed to see the power dynamics implicit in his own language, the hierarchical, authoritarian, and patriarchal philosophies that underpin Catholic schools encourage an acceptance of the power imbalance inherent in the system. Stakeholders come to regard such a power imbalance as normal, natural or even the work of divine providence. Ognibene & Paulli (2002) suggested that the pervasive theme of "Catholics as model citizens" is evident in its present-day emphasis on "civic virtue, social justice and service" (p. 40) within the school. This points to one of the deep ironies of today's Catholic schools: At the same time that Catholic educators encourage students to engage in social justice issues, they are guilty of perpetrating human rights violations against some of the most vulnerable members of the Catholic school community, non-heterosexual students and staff. As the Marc Hall case attests, Catholic school districts in Canada are wilfully and actively ignoring their legal, professional, and ethical responsibilities to protect *all* students and to maintain a safe, caring, and inclusive learning environment—responsibilities that are commonly outlined in school acts across the country. In Alberta, for example, section 45(8) of the *Alberta School Act* (Alberta Government, 2004) contains the relevant legislation:

A board shall ensure that each student enrolled in a school operated by the board is provided with a safe and caring environment that fosters and maintains respectful and responsible behaviours.

A FOUCAULDIAN AND GRAMSCIAN ANALYSIS

Foucault's (1975/1995) central argument in *Discipline and Punish* is that changes in 19th-century strategies of punishment brought a new focus on the soul, rather than the body, by using far more insidious forms of domination and control. His chapter "The Means of Correct Training" traces the development of certain "disciplines," or techniques for managing people, and the way in which they transform individuals into objects for knowledge and power through controlling processes of distinction and classification. Foucault asserted "discipline 'makes' individuals" and its success in doing so comes from the use of "simple instruments," which he called "hierarchical observation," "normalizing judgement," and "the examination" (p. 170). Each of these disciplining instruments involves a form of surveillance—surveillance of the body being Foucault's motif for modernity (Delanty, 2003).

The first instrument of power, "hierarchical observation," involves linking visibility to power. According to Foucault (1975/1995), the physical school building of the *École Militaire* operated under imperatives of health, qualification, politics, and morality by creating a space organised around continuous surveillance. The military school was a mechanism for training arranged through architecture. Drawing upon ideas in vol. I of *Capital* (1867) by Karl Marx, Foucault stated, "Surveillance . . . becomes a decisive economic operator both as an internal part of the production machinery and as a specific mechanism in the disciplinary power" (p. 175). He describes hierarchical observation as being both "absolutely indiscreet, since it is everywhere and always alert . . . and absolutely 'discreet,' for it functions permanently and largely in silence" (p. 177).

"Normalizing judgement" for Foucault was a kind of "penal mechanism" that functioned "at the heart of all disciplinary systems" (p. 177). Foucault (1975/1995) described this penal mechanism as enjoying "a kind of judicial privilege with its own laws, its specific offences, [and] its particular forms of judgement" (p. 178). These disciplining systems imposed a micro penal system over almost every aspect of behaviour, notably those not included in the formal judicial system such as time, activity, speech, the body, and sexuality. Foucault described how discipline brought "a specific way of punishing," which included the "whole indefinite domain of the non-conforming" (p. 179). Normalization, coupled with surveillance, becomes "one of the great instruments of power at the end of the classical age" (p. 184).

"The examination," Foucault's third technique of power, is a ritualized process that combines the aforementioned techniques of power: "hierarchical observation" and "normalizing judgement." Foucault (1975/1995) cast the examination as a particular human science "technology" that "implements . . . power relations that make it possible to extract and constitute knowledge" (p. 185). One of the examples Foucault offered is the "examining school," which he said "marked the beginnings of a pedagogy that functions as a science" (p. 187), where the "power of writing" (p. 189) forms the basis of this new "science of the individual" (p. 191). "The examination," then, is a mechanism that links the formation of knowledge to the exercise of power through a formalized documentation process that renders an individual a file or a case.

APPLICATION OF FOUCAULT'S THEORY OF SURVEILLANCE TO HOMOPHOBIA AS A STRUCTURE

Foucault's (1975/1995) explanation of how subjects are produced through the imposition of disciplinary instruments of power can be applied to the problem of homophobia in Catholic schools. Foucault's first instrument of power, "hierarchical observation" (which involves linking visibility to power), can be readily observed in an example taken from the hiring practices of a Catholic school system. It comes in the form of the employment contract, which has a powerful clause in it requiring the new hire to agree to uphold the tenets of the Catholic faith or "Catholicity" 24 hours a day, 7 days a week. When a certain Catholic school board first hired me, representatives of that board informed me that it is the duty of each employee to report suspicious un-Catholic behaviour that he or she might have observed in a co-worker.

If the new hire is also lesbian, the message is clear that it is not acceptable to be open about being non-heterosexual, as that would be contrary to "Catholicity." According to official Catholic doctrine, homosexual acts are "intrinsically disordered," and "under no circumstances can . . . be approved" (Canadian Conference of Catholic Bishops, 1994, p. 480). If the new lesbian teacher in the Catholic system is also in a relationship, then she will have to go to great pains to hide it. In my case, the board also informed me that it would randomly check employees' e-mail. Even though a board may lack the time or personnel to actually carry out this form of surveillance, the threat itself is sufficient to keep teachers in line because one never knows whom one can trust. According to Foucault's argument, this form of "hierarchical observation" is "absolutely indiscreet" because the employee is made aware of the various forms of surveillance, and it is "absolutely discreet" in the sense that one can never know when one is being observed or reported.

Further to this example, one can recognize the second instrument of power, "normalizing judgement," (Foucault, 1975/1995, p. 177) in the way this newly hired lesbian teacher becomes subtly controlled by the homophobic structure within the institution. Normalizing judgement is a form of penal mechanism with its own particular forms of judgement that define and repress mass behaviour. When it becomes known to others that the new female teacher is not married, she will likely be drawn into conversations about eligible men and invited to social events for the primary purpose of meeting such men. In these types of social situations, she will automatically be perceived as heterosexual and will be forced to deny the truth of her own life in order to fit in, to be regarded as normal, and to avoid risking the loss of her job for violating the Catholicity clause in her employment contract.

Moreover, discussions of sexuality are not confined to the staff room; often they unfold as part of regular banter with students in the classroom. Critical pedagogue and feminist scholar, Didi Khayatt (2000), pointed out that "sexuality is present in the classroom in the wedding or commitment rings that teachers or students may wear, in talk about boyfriends, girlfriends, husbands, wives and partners, in discussions of pregnancy and family, in talk of holiday plans and in other tacit ways" (p. 267). A seemingly innocent question about marital status can send a closeted lesbian reeling. In this way, the lesbian teacher in a Catholic school system must endure a much harsher form of Foucauldian "normalizing judgement" than her heterosexual colleagues.

Foucault's (1975/1995) third instrument of power, "the examination," which is a combination of both "hierarchical observation" and "normalizing judgement," is evident in the way that the newly hired lesbian teacher must undergo several formal teacher evaluations. Although this is standard practice with any newly hired teacher, the lesbian teacher is typically more aware than her heterosexual colleagues of how the differences that set her apart—apparently single, with no mention of a boyfriend—may be perceived by her examiners. In order to distract her examiners from reflecting upon her "abnormality," she feels that she must outperform her colleagues. Then, if her "different-ness" becomes an issue, she will be able to counter the examiners' reservations with her outstanding performance record. She is keenly aware of the "power of writing" behind Foucault's "science of the individual" and knows that one oddly worded phrase in her evaluation can carry a subtextual message that may deter future employers. She will do anything to keep hints of her "abnormality" out of her file.

ANTONIO GRAMSCI'S NOTES ON EDUCATION

In the introduction to Chapter 2, titled "On Education" (*Selections From the Prison Notebooks*, 1971), Gramsci expressed a desire to create a revolutionary party of intellectuals drawn from the working class, a group he calls the "organic intellectuals." Here, in a discussion of the Mussolini/Gentile governmental reforms of education in 1923, Gramsci identified "active education" as one of the reformers' watchwords. Like the governmental reformers, Gramsci also held an "active" concept of education, but, unlike theirs, his was not one built on rhetoric and slogans. Gramsci did not associate education with the passive reception of ideas, but with the *transformative* power of ideas (Borg, Buttigieg, & Mayo, 2002). Gramsci's concept of hegemony can be understood by carefully studying educational activities and institutions, since these are one way that bourgeois civilization perpetuates itself.

As a Neo-Marxist theorist, Gramsci can be broadly associated with *critical* accounts of societal reproduction. In this way, his work can be set up in opposition to *noncritical* accounts of societal reproduction commonly associated with the structural functionalism of Émile Durkheim. More specifically, Gramsci can be placed in the conflict theory camp of Neo-Marxists, for whom "the contradictions in the capitalist mode of production, especially those between labour and capital, are taken to be decisive" (Morrow & Torres, 1995, p. 20). Neo-Marxists typically focus on the increased importance of massive cultural institutions (for example, education and the mass media), as well as the strategic role of the liberal democratic state (Morrow & Torres). As one who explores the role of education in social reproduction, Gramsci can be identified as a Neo-Marxist.

Gramsci, it seems, recognized that a Marxist theory of power fails to address adequately the subtle but pervasive forms of ideological control and manipulation that serve to perpetuate all repressive structures. He identified two distinct forms of political control: *domination*, which refers to direct physical coercion by state-armed forces, and *hegemony*, which refers to both ideological control and, more crucially, consent. Because he stressed the multidimensionality of power relations and the role of agency and social movements in social change, Gramsci's ideas would also be at home in the critical theory camp, which was influenced by both Neo-Marxist and conflict theory traditions. In addition, he can also be identified as a critic of Marxist economic determinism because he argued for the power of ideas and the potential of autonomous individuals to affect social change.

In his notes on education, Gramsci (1971) criticized the Gentile reformers for their inconsistency. The reformers identified the study of Latin as the dogmatic learning of concrete facts, and, therefore, as a practice that should be eliminated. Gramsci argued that the reformers simply substitute religious dogmatism for the "dogmatic" study of Latin: "the fact that a 'dogmatic' exposition of scientific ideas and a certain 'mythology' are necessary in the primary school does not mean that the dogma and the mythology have to be precisely those of religion" (p. 41, note 15). The introduction of the formal study of religion in Italian schools signalled to Gramsci an obstacle blocking the school's ability to foster within students the necessary moral independence and intellectual self-discipline required to become an organic intellectual, armed with the transformative power of ideas and the ability to affect social change.

APPLICATION OF GRAMSCI'S THEORY OF HEGEMONY TO HOMOPHOBIA AS A STRUCTURE

Gramsci's notion of hegemony as the manufacturing of consent fits easily into my analysis of the problem of homophobia in Catholic schools. Hegemony refers to the ideal representation of the interests of the ruling class as universal interests (Marshall, 1998). For Gramsci, the major vehicle for bourgeois hegemony was civil society, that dynamic element of citizenship or public life that exists within the framework of the rule of law (Marshall). Cultural hegemony, the most powerful element of hegemonic manipulation, involves the production of certain ways of thinking and seeing, and the necessary exclusion of alternative visions and discourses. Nowhere is the manipulative power of hegemony more readily observable than in faith-based schools.

When one examines how the subject of human sexuality is broached in Catholic schools in the courses simply called religion, it is easy to see that what the students are receiving is not education, but rather dogma or indoctrination. While students in Alberta's non-Catholic schools learn about human sexuality in a provincially mandated course called "Career and Life Management," students in Catholic schools engage with the sexuality component of this curriculum within the sole context of religion class where Catholic doctrine infuses all aspects of learning. Provincially developed separate school curricula for these religion classes have traditionally relied heavily upon the Catechism of the Catholic Church, as well as the many encyclicals and other declarative statements from the Vatican on the topic of homosexuality. As a result, students must contend with a great deal of misinformation about sexuality. Alongside lessons that promote the rhythm method as an effective means of contraception, students learn that homosexual acts are "intrinsically disordered . . . contrary to the natural law . . . [and] do not proceed from a genuine affective and sexual complementarity [sic]" (Canadian Conference of Catholic Bishops, 1994, p. 480). Through such teachings they come to believe that "Under no circumstances can they [homosexual acts] be approved" (p. 480). It is this form of religious dogmatism that Gramsci was warning against in his critique of the Gentile educational reforms of 1923. In the human sexuality component of religion classes in Catholic schools, homophobia is manufactured, legitimized, and packaged for mass consumption.

CONCLUSION

Thus, the historical and philosophical foundations of Catholic schools have been instrumental in contributing to the institutionalization of homophobia, which continues to be maintained today through subtle, and sometimes not so subtle, forms of hegemonic surveillance. Catholic school districts manage to maintain these forms of institutionalized homophobia because of their deeply ingrained respect for tradition. Historically, Catholic schools emerged out of the politically charged climate surrounding the issue of the formation of separate schools, and the subsequent need for the Catholic Church, as a disadvantaged minority group, to prove that the religious education it promised to provide in its own system would produce respectful, orderly, and controlled citizens.

Additionally, the Catholic Church's adherence to patriarchal, hierarchical, and authoritarian philosophical ideals that would best facilitate the control of citizens established the philosophical foundation that, over time, became inextricably fused with the concept of Catholic education. One need only look to the dogmatic manner in which the subject of human sexuality is taught in Catholic schools to witness these patriarchal and authoritarian principles in action. Indeed, Catholic pedagogy in general and Catholic schooling practices in particular exemplify the Gramscian (1971) notion of hegemony: In the Catholic education system the interests of the ruling class are presented as universal interests. Moreover, each of Foucault's (1975/1995) three "simple instruments" of power (hierarchical observation, normalizing judgement, and the examination) can be seen at work in the day-to-day operations of the separate school system. These include (a) the Catholicity clause in the teaching contract, (b) the automatic assumption that teachers and students are heterosexual, and (c) the close official and unofficial examination and special scrutiny of a teacher's private life.

The persistent surveillance in Canadian Catholic schools means that queer teachers and students must engage in a constant process of self-monitoring in terms of how much information they reveal about themselves to colleagues or peers. This type of injustice would not easily escape young adults, however, who often have high expectations of fairness and justice in their surroundings. Issues related to sexual orientation, behaviour, and identity are very much a part of an adolescent's world, largely due to the formidable task of identity formation that characterizes this stage of life. As students grapple with their own sexual identity, they may want to broach the topic of diversity and equity, and some young human rights advocates in Canadian Catholic schools may risk raising the topic of homophobia whenever social justice and diversity issues are touched upon in English, social studies, or religion classes. Despite the formidable risks they face, it is conceivable that queer teachers in Canadian Catholic schools may respond favourably to these types of student challenges and seize upon these rare teachable moments to begin reversing the institutionalization of homophobia in Canadian Catholic schools one lesson at a time.

REFERENCES

Alberta Government. (2004, November 1). *Alberta school act.* Retrieved April 27, 2005, from http://www.qp.gov.ab.ca/documents/Acts/S03.cfm?frm_isbn=0779733290

Alberta Teachers' Association. (2004, May 22). *Declaration of the rights and responsibilities of teachers.* Retrieved April 27, 2005, from http://www.teachers.ab.ca/Teaching+in+Alberta/Rights+and+Responsibilities/

Bannerji, H. (2000). Charles Taylor's politics of recognition: A critique. In *The dark side of the nation: Essays on multiculturalism, nationalism, and gender* (pp. 125–150). Toronto, ON: Canadian Scholars' Press.

Borg, C., Buttigieg, J., & Mayo, P. (2002). *Gramsci and education.* Oxford, UK: Rowman & Littlefield.

Canadian Conference of Catholic Bishops. (1994). *Catechism of the Catholic Church*. Ottawa, ON: Author.

Carney, R. (1992). "Hostility unmasked": Catholic schooling in Territorial Alberta. In N. Kach & K. Mazurek (Eds.), *Exploring our educational past: Schooling in the North-West Territories and Alberta* (pp. 17–37). Calgary, AB: Detselig Enterprises.

Curtis, B. (1988). *Building the educational state: Canada west, 1836–1871*. London, ON: The Falmer Press.

Delanty, G. (2003). Michel Foucault. In A. Elliott & L. Ray (Eds.), *Key contemporary social theorists* (pp. 123–134). Oxford: Blackwell.

Egan, K. (1997). *The educated mind: How cognitive tools shape our understanding*. Chicago: University of Chicago Press.

Foucault, M. (1995). *Discipline and punish: The birth of the prison* (A. M. Sheridan Smith, Trans.). New York: Vintage Books. (Original work published 1975).

Grace, A. P., & Wells, K. (2005). The Marc Hall prom predicament: Queer individual rights v. institutional church rights in Canadian public education. *Canadian Journal of Education, 28*(3), 237–270.

Gramsci, A. (1971). *Selections from the prison notebooks*. New York: International.

Green, A. (1990). Education and state formation. In A. Green (Ed.), *Education and state formation: The rise of education systems in England, France, and the USA* (pp. 76–99). Hampshire, UK: Macmillan Press.

Hodgins, J. G. (1897). *The legislation and history of separate schools in Upper Canada*. Toronto, ON: William Priggs.

Katz, M. (1976). The origins of public education: A reassessment. *History of Education Quarterly, 16*(4), 381–406.

Khayatt, D. (2000). Talking equity. In C. E. James (Ed.), *Experiencing difference* (pp. 258–270). Halifax, NS: Fernwood.

Marshall, G. (1998). *Oxford dictionary of sociology*. New York: Oxford University Press.

McGlucken, W. (1934). *The Catholic way in education*. Milwaukee, WI: Bruce Publishing.

Morris, C. (1997). *American Catholic*. New York: Times Books.

Morrow, R., & Torres, C. (1995). *Social theory and education: A critique of theories of social and cultural reproduction*. New York: State University of New York Press.

Ognibene, R., & Paulli, K. (2002). Civic virtue, social justice, and Catholic schools: Modern pedagogy and social justice become part of American Catholic school philosophy. *Momentum, 33*(3), 40–44.

Oksenberg Rorty, A. (1998). Rousseau's educational experiments. In A. Oksenberg Rorty (Ed.), *Philosophers on education: New historical perspectives* (pp. 238–255). London: Routledge.

Rabinow, P., & Niklas, R. (Eds.). (2003). *The essential Foucault: Selections from the essential works of Foucault 1954–1984*. New York: New Press.

Taylor, C. (1994). The politics of recognition. In A. Gutmann (Ed.), *Multiculturalism: Examining the politics of recognition* (pp. 25–73). Princeton, NJ: Princeton University Press.

Tonya D. Callaghan
University of Toronto

ROBERT CHRISTOPHER NELLIS

7. A CLEANLINESS FAR FROM "GODLINESS": *FAREWELL OAK STREET*, TORONTO'S REGENT PARK PUBLIC HOUSING PROJECT, AND A SPACE'S HAUNTINGLY PERSISTENT CURRICULUM OF HYGIENIC MODERNIZATION

Keeping clean was a daily battle and a lost cause. Dirt always won out on Oak Street. –Narrator in *Farewell Oak Street* (McLean, Burwash, & Glover, 1953)

May 10th. Thank God for the rain, which has helped wash away the garbage and the trash off the sidewalks . . . Some day a real rain will come and wash all this scum off the streets. –Travis Bickle in *Taxi Driver* (Scorsese, Phillips, & Phillips, 1976)

(From *Farewell Oak Street*)

J. Nahachewsky and I. Johnston (eds.), Beyond 'Presentism': Re-Imagining the Historical, Personal, and Social Places of Curriculum, 73–85.

Nineteen fifty three's *Farewell Oak Street* (McLean, Burwash, & Glover, 1953) announces the development of Canada's first major public housing project, Toronto's Regent Park. The film depicts 19 people who had lived in one house in Toronto's Cabbagetown before its buildings fell to demolition and in their place was built the shining, modern development. I came to the film. I believe I found it speaking to me because it resonated with stories I recall from my mother about growing up in and around Toronto in the 1940s and 50s. She was 10 years old when her father, a carpenter, died of cancer. He left five girls—my mother the eldest among them—and one boy, the youngest child, still only an infant. My grandmother found herself alone with six children and only modest government relief to support them. She lived the rest of her life in Toronto Public Housing. My family history reverberates with the struggles represented in the film. *Farewell Oak Street*, a touching, well-made film, has often been reviled. It provides an opening into haunting narratives of a Toronto space of persistent, if evolving, notions of modernizing hygiene and architectural/public policy interventions into social problems.

What is "hygiene?" What does it mean to be "hygienic"? Certainly, the concept relates to health. One needs to be hygienic. One needs to remove dirt and germs from oneself. After all, such factors can contribute to ill health. Cleanliness, then, is a virtue. It can mean the difference between living well, and, in its extreme failure, not living at all. Cleanliness is a life-or-death virtue, but it is also more. The Book of Revelation (XXI, 27) states, "And there shall in no wise enter into [the Kingdom of God] any thing that defileth." The sentiment is more popularly conveyed as "Cleanliness is next to godliness." According to this thinking, the further we move away from good hygiene, the further we move away from God. As Augustine (2001) writes in reflecting upon the nature of evil, evil is *privatio boni*—privation of good—therefore, distance from God. How can we know such distance in this world? How can we know we are near or close to God in a world where divine markers are, to say the least, hermeneutically elusive? Calvinism tells us that we can know our virtue by the presence or lack of God's favour upon us—by the good fortune we have in our lives. Another way of knowing exists. If cleanliness is next to godliness, cleanliness can provide a clue. Logically, it does not necessarily follow that uncleanliness is far from God (and, thereby, according to the Augustinian formulation, evil). After all, Jesus is said to have been a carpenter, a man who got his hands dirty. Cleanliness itself, then, guarantees no proximity to godly virtue. Nonetheless, a virtuous role seems to beckon for those who help others toward cleanliness, or toward hygiene. Recall that when Jesus washed the disciples' feet (John, XIII, 5), he modeled a way toward God and virtue by washing the dirt from others. A similar, if dubious, implication haunts *Farewell Oak Street* and public interventions into the depicted neighbourhood's social problems.

FAREWELL OAK STREET

The film was a project initiated by National Film Board of Canada (NFB) Commissioner W. Arthur Irvin but completed after his tenure. Indeed, the project was inherited by incoming Commissioner Albert W. Trueman and, in some respects, turned out to be an unwelcome legacy. The film was controversial. Many viewers loathed it, especially those who saw themselves represented in the film, the new residents of Regent Park. The Member of Parliament for this area took exception to the film, likely because of its unflattering portrayal of his constituency. Evans (1991), in describing the film as "Marxless," takes note especially of the film's apparent central premise, that "no old possessions or attitudes" (pp. 37–38) would be brought from the old Oak Street to the new, shining apartments of Regent Park.

Despite the controversies surrounding the film's release, *Farewell Oak Street* was very much in keeping with a strand of tradition within the NFB, one reflecting founding Commissioner John Grierson's views of documentary as a form of "progressive," "democratic," public education (Blais & Bairstow, 1973). Admittedly, his vision privileged a certain educated elite as the purveyor of wisdom and saw in this model of public education a means to reduce structural antagonisms, specifically between labour and management/ownership and between the poor and the vision of a cohesively functioning society. Grierson's early allegiance with the Rockefeller Foundation very much set him on the course of this direction (Nelson, 1988), and *Farewell Oak Street* bears similarities to a number of early Grierson-produced films in Britain, especially 1936's *Housing Problems* (Low, 2002).

The 17-minute film is comprised of six acts. The first opens with everyday life in the modern Regent Park. We are introduced to the residents of the new development. We tour suites, and are introduced to the sparkling homes and their sparkling residents, with much attention paid to their clean practices. Indeed, the narrator in the film comments not only upon the homes but also upon the cleanliness and character of the people: "Everything is sparkling and new and tidy, and kept that way. The Bennett floors for instance and the Bennett children . . . . the Tweeds are great washers and scrubbers . . . . the McLean kitchen has a new modern look, as do the McLean ladies."

The film brackets an imaginary space and begins by declaring, "This was the western end of Oak Street" and "not a trace of it remains, except its people." Later on, in the last act of the film, the narration picks up at the same space: "This was the western end of Oak Street" and "not a trace of it remains, except its people." A hygienic clearing out occurred: a removal of all the dirt, all the architectural filth, and all the ways in which, in opposition to the dictum that "the scent of the rose lingers on the hand that gives it," a removal of the architectural filth touched those who had inhabited it.

The neighbourhood children play outside, and Mrs. Brown calls her son, Nick, in for supper. He enters the home to find his father in the living room, trying to hang some curtains. Father wonders if the curtains are straight, so Nick goes outside, stands in front of the house, and estimates the level of the curtains. The voiceover narration by the CBC's and *Bonanza*'s Lorne Greene declares that life was not always this pleasant on Oak Street. The shot dissolves and reemerges with Nick crawling over a pile of rubble on the old Oak Street, on what somewhat resembles the bombed-out debris of wartime London.

Indeed, the second act of *Farewell Oak Street* depicts life back in the tenements before they were demolished to make way for the modern Regent Park project, and in a sense they are depicted as a war zone. The enemy is dirt, filth, and a general problem with hygiene. We see Mrs. Brown waging an unending and hopeless battle with filth: "Dirt always won out on Oak Street." "The children got dirty. All children do anywhere, at school, at play, but Oak Street children suffered a dirtiness, which it seemed impossible even to fight against." A social worker or teacher or some other clean and well-dressed professional woman brings the son home from school, saying he has lice. The clearly distraught Mrs. Brown replies, "Oh, I wash his head every week. Where do they come from?" The professional woman sympathetically states, "It's these old places." The whole family feels shame, both public and private. A highly controversial scene in the film depicts "other kinds of filth": "Sometimes, the vermin was human, and the shame was secret." This comment is the first representation of its kind of a pedophile. The Browns and the other 19 people who share this building all use the same bathroom and have very tenuous privacy. The Brown's daughter lives under the watchful eye of a pedophile living in the next suite. He accosts her—"You want a candy, Jenny? Ah, come on. Don't be scared"; they grapple; she runs home and cries. She feels oppressed by both his advances and her shame. Another boy living nearby costumes himself prior to leaving his house and the dirty environs of Oak Street. The young boy makes himself impeccably clean but then rejects the overtures of his parents, clearly ashamed of his felt need to dress up and leave in order to be someone. Immaculately dressed, he walks into the foreboding, melancholy darkness, past lovers lurking in the shadows. Where he goes or what he does, we do not know.

The third act turns to the economic conditions framing the lived realities of these 19 people residing on Oak Street, discussing market conditions and how these contribute to the kind of squalid circumstances that exist there. However, it does so in such a way that it naturalizes the market and the alienation of "wage-earners" like Jim Brown: "His working hours are spent helping to erect modern little bungalows, which he can't afford. The most modest new home is out of his reach—to buy or rent. He'd consider himself a lucky man to live in one of these." During this narration, we see what we used to call "wartime houses" dotting the dirt of a new subdivision. The examination of these macroeconomic conditions, while not fundamentally questioning them, does question public priorities within them:

> Most houses, newly built, cost more today than much larger houses cost a few years back. Costs have soared, prices have soared, apartment rents are high, too high for Jim Brown. Homebuilders must compete with industry builders for cement, and glass, and steel, and labour. We're an expanding nation. We build fabulous structures to house machines, and motors, and assembly lines. We raise up mountainous shelters for commerce and finance, but we can't give Jim Brown a good home he can afford . . . that is to say, we couldn't.

The film announces that Canada's ability to build immaculate buildings to house equipment, capital, while people live in squalor, is a gross misuse of resources and a perversion of priorities.

Indeed, the city will rebuild the slums as Canada's first large-scale public housing project—Regent Park. The development will consist of 1,300 homes. The narration accompanies footage of the demolition: "Down came Oak Street, down came the verminous walls, the unclean, unhealthy rooms, and down came the fire hazards, the juvenile delinquency, the drunkenness, the broken marriages, and up rose something new—the nation's first large-scale public housing project." This fourth act of the film lays out some principal tenets of the postwar liberal welfare state in Canada. Noting that all will pay a share, the following narration proceeds over footage of the construction: "Rents based on income: Kelly the pensioner, 29 dollars a month; Brown the truck driver, 45 dollars a month; Jakes the toolmaker, 75 dollars a month; Brown paying a little for Kelly; Jakes paying a little for them both; and the people of the city and the rest of the country putting in a share."

The fifth act of the film shows the Browns coming back to their new home after the razing and reconstruction. The family arrives: "Though it seemed it never would happen, the day finally came when they could move in, a raw spring day, but sunny. They were a sight when they arrived with their bags, and boxes, and bundles, like refugees on the road instead of the new tenants of number 640 Regent Park." Awe-struck, they enter their new dwelling. The scene is admittedly emotional. Gentle strains of flute, violin, and soft piano are heard as the Browns come in and cannot believe what they behold. The walls shine to an almost blinding sheen. They go through each room dumbfounded by the beauty of the new home. The little daughter puts her hands on the walls, but her mother comes along and scolds her, frantically wiping any fingerprints off the wall. The family moves through the main floor of the house, up the stairs, and to the bathroom where they hear a strange noise—but where's Nick? They come in to see him already stripped to the waist, getting into a hot bath.

The final act brings us back to where we started, back to everyday life in Regent Park. After helping his father hang the drapes levelly, Nick comes back into the house for dinner. Unlike a dinner scene back in the old Oak Street, this scene shows the Browns singing, talking, and being a "good family." Indeed, life in Regent Park is much better than it had been on Oak Street. It is much cleaner. Mrs. Brown comments upon the new curtains: "I must say, I'm glad to get them up; those other old things were terrible rags. Nothing from the old place is any good here"; the narrator adds, "Old possessions, old attitudes, not a trace remains." The film ends by reaffirming the principles of public housing and Canada's postwar liberal welfare state. A prosperous nation like Canada has a responsibility to provide clean, proper housing for the poor and the not-so-poor. The film concludes by contending "[There are] too many Oak Streets for a rich resourceful nation, but one has gone for good!"

The narrative of modernizing hygiene implicit in the end of Oak Street, in its razing, and the building of Regent Park is clear from the foregoing description of the film. However, a sly implication accompanies the proposition of hygiene: The film subtly suggests that the residents of the former Oak Street are to blame for their poor hygiene and, by extension, for their poverty and attendant social problems. The opening act of the film makes a celebration of everyone's clean practices, their clean homes, and their clean persons. The film suggests that as the architecture changes, something of the people also changes. Clearly, their standard of living improves, but something else happens as well. The film observes, "The face may be the same, but the expression is different. It's brighter, and more interested, and friendlier. Life has changed along the quarter mile that was Oak Street." The film does not deal with how the buildings of Oak Street came to be so decrepit and run-down and how they contributed to a substandard life. The hidden proposition, obviously, is that the inhabitants allowed the buildings to become run down. On some level, the filmmakers must be aware of this accusation, for the film speaks to it by noting that with the new buildings of Regent Park comes a new attitude. Thus, the new buildings initiate the new attitude, one of cleanliness, one that will not allow social problems to reemerge. However, this proposition is complex. By noting that the new buildings initiated the new attitude, the film implicates the attitudes of the inhabitants of Oak Street in their poor living conditions. At one time, the structures of Oak Street were brand new. How did they become so decrepit, and how did the presumably parallel attitudes of the original inhabitants take a turn for the worse? How is the new attitude at Regent Park qualitatively different and how will this attitude never allow decrepitude or social problems to creep in again? Some implications of that question may be found in the historic and current discourse around Regent Park and its contemporary plan for redevelopment.

CABBAGETOWN

Before I examine life in Regent Park and the contemporary plan for its re-development, I will touch upon broader narratives of Oak Street. Oak Street was in a Toronto neighbourhood that used to be known as "Cabbagetown," named for the vegetables grown on the front lawns of the houses occupied by Irish immigrants who settled there (Bébout, 2002). It was an Anglo Saxon neighbourhood, described by Canadian writer Hugh Garner as the "largest Anglo Saxon slum in North America" (Garner, 1968, p. v). Garner wrote of the area in his novel *Cabbagetown*, released in an abridged version in 1950 and in its entirety in 1968.

The novel depicts the lives of a number of characters in Cabbagetown over a period of 8 years, focusing on Ken Tilling. The characters all try to make their way in the world, travelling down the path toward what they will become. As they engage in their journey, they come face to face with dominant issues, especially those concerning moral conduct and sexuality. They find their journeys and what they want to become increasingly difficult to attain as they find themselves put into subject positions to which they may not have originally aspired. Specifically, a girlfriend of Tilling's, Myrla Patson, finds herself pregnant and slowly but surely, though obviously not in a premeditated fashion, becomes a prostitute. Ken Tilling undergoes a kind of intellectual journey or transformation. Through his challenges of authority and his difficulty as a worker, he eventually attains a socialist consciousness and then leaves Cabbagetown to fight in the Spanish Civil War for the republican cause in the Communist-led brigades. Garner shows some of the humanity and tragedy of young lives in the area. However, he is careful to balance over-romanticization with some negative views of the area and its people. He writes, "Nobody should get eulogistic over a slum" (p. vi). He allows himself to criticize the area—he himself is from the place—but he resists licensing moralistic observers from without.

After Oak Street was levelled and the new Regent Park built, Garner commented upon the lingering resentments, which outsiders/the general public held toward the people even after they had settled in their new homes. He wrote, "Contrary to uninformed and malicious public opinion at the time, there were no substantial instances of rehabilitated slum-dwellers storing their coal in their new unaccustomed-to bathtubs" (p. vi). Apparently, one can take people out of slums, but according to persistent negative imaginaries, removing the slum from the people is somewhat more difficult. A moralistic code governed even the early days of Regent Park. For example, the strict admission criteria even stipulated that single-parent families were not allowed ("About Regent Park," n.d.).

As visitors to and residents of Toronto will note, a neighbourhood called "Cabbagetown" still exists in the city. However, the new neighbourhood of that name lies just north of the original Cabbagetown and bears practically no resemblance to the original. Today's Cabbagetown is an upscale, gentrified neighbourhood, standing in contrast to its preexisting neighbour, Regent Park. Hugh Garner wrote about the new Cabbagetown in *The Intruders* (1976), noting its similarity in name only.

The old Cabbagetown, which Oak Street transected, was seen to have engendered a stain upon the city of Toronto and that corner of Canada. The issue may be thought of as a hygienic problem. When what Garner called a slum was removed, scrubbed away, and replaced with the new Regent Park, the area carried on, at least in terms of its name. However, the new Cabbagetown was one that caused no shame. The new, hygienic version carried with it a fiction and imaginary of quaint city living, without the unpleasant, unhygienic aspects of the old Cabbagetown.

LIFE IN REGENT PARK

The haunting narrative of hygiene surrounding Oak Street and Regent Park goes back over 50 years. Sometimes the textual manifestations of the discourse suggest some curious ironies. In a 1954 *CBC Newsmagazine* documentary on the demolition of Oak Street and building of Regent Park, the film treats the "substandard housing's" dangers and the filth of the old Oak Street area, yet curiously refers to the new development not as Regent Park, but as "Regent's Park" ("Rebuilding Regent," n.d.). This reference provides an interesting variation on the development's name because, as many are aware, Regent's Park is the name of a college at Oxford University, traditionally training Baptist ministers.

This inadvertent invocation of Regent's Park and its concomitant association with Baptist Protestantism is noteworthy. In the broadest terms, what sets the Baptists apart from other sects, specifically Roman Catholicism with its practice of pedobaptism, is the mature profession of faith prior to receiving baptism by water. The believer, typically an adult, must consciously choose a life of faith and thereby renounce her or his previously unclean life. The water washes away the indiscretions of nonbelief. Blessedness and God's favour wash over the erstwhile sinner so that she or he may continue on the path toward the Kingdom of God. The documentary's slip of signification, exchanging Regent Park for Regent's Park, interestingly opens up the space, the people, and the unwashedness of Oak Street to the cleanliness and conscious moral conviction evident in *Farewell Oak Street*'s emphasis on the clean practices of the new residents. That the old ways are no good, that everything in Regent Park is clean, including the people, nicely opens the space and its discourse to a narrative of hygiene combined with moralistic practice and, even, to Divine benevolence.

Indeed, for at least a decade and a half following the development's 1949 construction, Regent Park occupied a position of pride within the imaginary of Toronto. Media reports extolled the new residents' love of the place. The May 2, 1950, *Globe and Mail* ran a headline on page 2, "New Apartment Called Heaven" ("About Regent Park," n.d.), again invoking the theme of divine absolution, and Hugh Garner himself praised the development in a 1957 edition of *Saturday Night*: "When you ask a person living in Regent Park what his reaction is to his new home over his old, he looks at you as if you're either crazy or joking" ("About Regent Park," n.d.). Regent Park functioned as a kind of symbolic repository for a postwar Toronto, brimming with optimism and new opportunity. The fact that the development came in $6 million over budget did not seem to matter ("About Regent Park," n.d.). These were heady times, and Regent Park represented the kind of goodwill project that prosperous Toronto and Canada admired in those heydays of Canada's liberal welfare state. The official institutions and their statistics agreed. Police reported far fewer arrests in the area, and the government collected far more taxation revenues as well ("About Regent Park," n.d.).

However, when *Farewell Oak Street*, itself a text brimming with postwar optimism, was released in 1954, many of the residents resented their depiction as slum dwellers. Their resentment seems fair, even today. People did not want to see the old Oak Street; people did not want to see themselves in the old district or it in them. These images were not what people wanted to see. People liked Regent Park, though. They liked seeing themselves in it and it in them.

However, the honeymoon of this marriage of optimism, prosperity, goodwill, and modernizing hygiene soon ended. By the 1960s, media accounts began to reflect a shifting mood. By this time, support for such large-scale projects had begun to dwindle. Property owners in surrounding areas no longer wanted new public-housing neighbours, and thinking about planning for public housing began to evolve concomitantly ("About Regent Park," n.d.). In the 1960s, the perception emerged that Regent Park was a repository for social problems. At first, public accounts criticized the institutional nature of the development and how it was not a genuine community. A movement of resident activism emerged in a number of resident groups in order to press the administration to develop more community and recreation facilities, as well as to take a more active role in maintenance and upkeep. However, the shifting imaginary of Regent Park changed even more. In particular, it began to be seen as a place of crime.

The imaginary of Regent Park is a space and site of contestation. Debates about the development occur regularly in Toronto's editorial pages. Some see the development, as it stands today, as little more than a site of crime, drugs, and other social problems. Yet, Regent Park has a very active and vibrant community. Many residents declare that the place is not nearly as bad as media accounts portray, and that, in fact, it is the perpetuation of such stereotypes that causes negative impressions ("Rebuilding Regent," n.d.).

In some respects, Regent Park is a small town set in the middle of Toronto. As home to numerous and active multicultural communities, it has a rich tradition and strong network of community activism and leadership and is quite vocal in articulating its interests. Granted, problems do exist in Regent Park, as they do in any city neighbourhood. However, here people are working actively to create positive opportunities for children and youth as well as a rich culture. Regent Park has developed a strong tradition of community centres, sports teams, recreation facilities, as well as a newspaper, radio station, and website.

THE REGENT PARK REDEVELOPMENT PLAN

Notwithstanding the positive aspects and rich community life of Regent Park, a growing discourse around the development is creating a narrative plotted from the admittedly negative aspects of life in Regent Park today. Years of neglect have allowed problems such as cockroaches to creep in. Ironically, Regent Park has come to occupy a narrative space similar to that of the old Oak Street. Regent Park is now seen as a hygienic problem for the civic body of Toronto. This problem must be cleansed. Like the previous Oak Street, today, more than 60 years after initial construction began on Regent Park and 55 years after the release of the proudly exalting *Farewell Oak Street*, Regent Park is slated for the same fate as the old Cabbagetown. Regent Park is to be razed and a new development built on the land.

This solution sounds familiar. Back in 1949, when the problems of Cabbagetown and Oak Street came to be too much to ignore, the city endeavoured to solve the problem by embarking upon the same course of action. The discourse of the Regent Park redevelopment bears some similar aspects. As Lorne Greene said in *Farewell Oak Street*, the housing was substandard, as was life on Oak Street. A strong aspect of the narrative surrounding the razing of Oak Street and building of Regent Park was the implication of the physical environment in the substandard life for the residents of the area.

On Oak Street, the problems had two aspects. The first concerned the general decrepitude of the structures. There were holes in windows and verminous contamination everywhere. Both Regent Park and the narratives informing the call to redevelop it recall this aspect of Oak Street. Granted, the modern Regent Park has structural problems as well. The causes of the decrepitude and infestations stem from years of neglect. (Logically, a similar problem caused the decline of the old Oak Street.) This relationship between decrepitude and neglect reveals an important theme in the discourse: accountability. Who is to blame, who is responsible, who shirked their duties? A critical view would blame the landlord; another would blame the tenants. In *Farewell Oak Street*, this type of blame is not assigned explicitly to either landlords or tenants. Implicitly, however, the film blames the tenants. The major focus on the clean attitudes, the clean persons, and the clean apartments, suggesting new attitudes and practices coming with the new buildings, begs the question, What *were* the attitudes and practices on Oak Street? The implication is that the tenants themselves were responsible for Oak Street's decrepit conditions. The film does not mention absentee or neglectful landlords shirking their responsibility for maintaining housing fit for human habitation. Moreover, nothing is said of the responsibility of the civic authorities to ensure that landlords maintain liveable housing conditions. The entire enterprise is framed—after the implication of the CBC journalist's misidentification of Regent Park as "Regent's Park" ("Rebuilding Regent," n.d.), the Oxford centre for training Baptist ministers—in terms of a washing away of past sins and a fresh start, a clean slate, the state of morally being born again.

In addition, the enterprise is framed in terms of architectural modernization. The problems on the street are framed as a hygienic problem, one subtly implicating the residents themselves, whom the film suggests were responsible for their own dirtiness. However, the problems on Oak Street were more complex than simple hygiene. After all, the film frames Oak Street in terms of all its attendant social problems: "Down came Oak Street, down came the verminous walls, the unclean, unhealthy rooms, and down came the fire hazards, the juvenile delinquency, the drunkenness, the broken marriages." Thus, hygiene signifies the social problems. Moreover, if the tenants are responsible for their hygiene shortcomings, they are also responsible for their other social problems: suggesting an alternative explanation for the problems—the poverty and general inequality in Canada—is not a radical leap. The film itself raises the spectre of such an explanation: "We're an expanding nation. We build fabulous structures to house machines, and motors, and assembly lines. We raise up mountainous shelters for commerce and finance, but we can't give Jim Brown a good home he can afford . . . that is to say, we couldn't." Indeed, the discourse collapses into one of architectural modernization, into one of the improper use of residential space. After all, according to the film's logic, the fundamental problem of life on Oak Street was a misuse of design/use scenarios. The house that the 19 people lived in on *Farewell Oak Street* was never designed for six families. Clearly, the problem was one of improper use; therefore, the solution will be to bridge that gap, redesign the space, and thereby, according to the logic, eliminate the problems.

This connection between design and use is evident in today's discourse about the Regent Park redevelopment plan. The planners cite the incidence of crime in Regent Park as informing the need to raze the entire development and rebuild it into something new ("Rebuilding Regent," n.d.). Regent Park was designed in 1949 by the brightest architects of the time, who built it according to the British "garden city model." Here, the design moves away from traditional street grids. Instead, it distributes homes throughout a flowing green space, like a park or urban garden. Modern critics contend that this design contributes to the crime that occurs here. Regent Park resists surveillance because it is off the street. Many have argued that the area became a magnet for drug dealers and other purveyors of criminal activity because of these tucked-away corners and the lack of building security common at the time. Here, unsavoury elements could ply their trade without the encumbrances caused by police surveillance. Thus, as the argument suggests, a culture of crime developed in Regent Park in no small part due to its design and the disconnection between that design and the lived realities of the inhabitants.

This line of thinking does not consider other possible causes, such as poverty, for the social problems in Regent Park. Design and urban-design solutions become a repository for solution-oriented thinking and a site for public policy intervention into social problems. This pattern was evident in 1949 during the initial construction of Regent Park and is still evident today in the discourse about its redevelopment. In a persistent narrative of architecturally mediated hygienic modernization, these social problems become cast as hygiene problems; the proposed solution is to wash them all away, allowing the community to begin again, freshly washed of its filth, clean, and ready to begin anew. This type of architectural intervention has occurred elsewhere in Canada. In the fall of 2000 ("Sheshatshiu," 2000), when young people in Davis Inlet reached the national consciousness because of inhalant abuse and suicide, the public outrage was pervasive. The solution, as we have seen before, involved building an entirely new community, entirely new structures, costing 152 million dollars and moving the people into them for a clean, fresh start ("Warm House," 2002). However, in 2002, the long-term prognosis for the solution was uncertain ("Innu Fear," 2002), and, by 2005, many of the old problems were again evident ("New Homes," 2005).

For now in Toronto, however, the persistent narrative of modernizing hygiene, of washing away the old and creating something new, remains a powerful repository for Canadian dreams of a New Day. This narrative is doubly haunted, first by the desirable and second by the undesirable. On April 6, 2004, Her Excellency, the Right Honourable Adrienne Clarkson, then Governor General of Canada, visited Regent Park. Interviewed by the community radio station, she commented that Regent Park is a blueprint for the potential of a modern multicultural Canada: "Regent Park as a model is the way we have to understand Canada is going to become" (Clarkson, 2004). Even as Regent Park itself is being cleaned, it presents an example of vibrant diversity. Certain racist Canadian imaginaries would consider Regent Park's mixture of cultures and languages "unclean." However, Regent Park's contemporary unhygienic nature, itself, haunts with the potential to wash away the filth of such intolerance and misunderstanding in the broader Canada.

CONCLUSION

The classic NFB film 1953's *Farewell Oak Street* gives an account of the razing of a part of old Cabbagetown and its rebuilding as the first major modern public housing project in Canada. The film, generally informed by a persistent, if evolving, modernizing concept of hygiene, provides an opening into haunting narratives surrounding the old Oak Street and Cabbagetown. The narrative, viewing social problems as a kind of hygienic filth, holds the people themselves directly culpable. The narrative does not implicate broader societal causes such as economic market failure. Moreover, the public policy intervention aligned with the narrative is that of design and architecture. In 1949, the old Oak Street was demolished and in its place was built the new Regent Park. The structures themselves were seen to be the cause of the inhabitants' inability to break out of a nonhygienic squalor and live clean lives. Today, design is also implicated in social problems in Regent Park. Its lack of street grids, for example, is seen to be the cause of violence, crime, and drug use. A similar solution emerges from the narrative, namely, that the entire network of structures should be demolished in order to build something new. Such thinking holds that new buildings will bring a new way of social being, for as the old buildings go down, so will the old social problems disappear. This bringing together of the disconnection between design and use will supposedly eliminate the social problems (while eliding any blame of broader social and economic factors). What will happen? What will be the state of things 50 years from now, a half-century hence? Obviously, no one today has the answer to that question. We hope that the community will have fewer problems, but of course only time will tell if the narrative of modernizing hygiene will persist and perhaps evolve into a new form with a new, if similar, set of problems, manifesting once again, a cleanliness far from godliness.

(From *Farewell Oak Street*)

REFERENCES

About Regent Park. (n.d.). *Catch da flava.* Retrieved June 30, 2004, from http://www.catchdaflava.com/History_5fof_5fRegent_5fPark

Augustine. (2001). *The confessions* (P. Burton, Trans.). New York: A. A. Knopf.

Bébout, R. (2002). *Queen street: Thematic preview.* Retrieved June 30, 2004, from http://www.rbebout.com/queen/mtc/2pparl.htm

Blais, R. (Director & Producer), & Bairstow, D. (Producer). (1973). *Grierson.* [Film].

Clarkson, A. (2004, April 6). *Interview. Catch da flava radio archive.* Retrieved July 5, 2004, from http://www.catchdaflava.com/Radio_20show_20Archive

Evans, G. (1991). *In the national interest: A chronicle of the National Film Board of Canada from 1949 to 1989*. Toronto, ON: University of Toronto.

Garner, H. (1968). *Cabbagetown*. Toronto, ON: McGraw-Hill Ryerson.

Garner, H. (1976). *The intruders: A novel*. Toronto, ON: McGraw-Hill Ryerson.

Innu fear problems may follow them to new home. (2002, December 13). *CBC News*. Retrieved July 5, 2004, from http://www.cbc.ca/stories/2002/12/13/innu_move021213

Low, B. (2002). *NFB kids: Portrayals of children by the National Film Board of Canada, 1939–1989*. Waterloo, ON: Wilfred Laurier University Press.

McLean, G. (Director), Burwash, G. (Producer), & Glover, G. (Producer). (1953). *Farewell Oak Street* [Film]. National Film Board of Canada. Retrieved December 2, 2005, from http://www.nfb.ca/trouverunfilm/fichefilm.php?id=10603&v=h&lg=en&exp=$ {farewell}%20AND%20${oak}%20AND%20${street}#

Nelson, J. (1988). *The colonized eye: Rethinking the Grierson legend*. Toronto, ON: Between the Lines.

New homes, same old problems. (2005). *CBC archives*. Retrieved December 2, 2005, from http://archives.cbc.ca/IDC-1-70-1671-11511/disasters_tragedies/davis_inlet/

Rebuilding Regent. (n.d.). *CBC – Web One—Regent Park*. Retrieved June 30, 2004, from http://www.cbc.ca/webone/regentpark/

Scorsese, M. (Director), Phillips, J. (Producer), & Phillips, M. (Producer). (1976). *Taxi driver*. [Film].

Sheshatshiu—An Innu community addicted. (2000, November). *CBC News*. Retrieved July 5, 2004, from http://www.cbc.ca/news/indepth/firstnations/sheshatshiu.html

Warm house, running water a change for Natuashish Innu. (2002, December 16). *CBC News*. Retrieved July 5, 2004, from http://www.cbc.ca/stories/2002/12/15/canada/davis_inlet021215

Robert Christopher Nellis
Red Deer College

Madeline Grumet
& William Pinar
→ reconceptualist
movement - early 70s on →
(no SOL)

Aim was to understand — not just implement or
evaluate the curriculum for the
eg not only preparing students for the
workplace & university, but also for
social & psych purposes.

Currere — the intuitive form ob
curriculum autobiographical suggests
* implies educational experiences shape
or shape one's self — understanding
This method/reconceptualized curriculum to
from course objectives
complicated conversation
with oneself

NICHOLAS NG-A-FOOK

8. INHABITING THE HYPHENATED SPACES OF ALIENATION AND APPROPRIATION: CURRERE, LANGUAGE, AND POSTCOLONIAL MIGRANT SUBJECTIVITIES

> I feel lost outside the French language. The other languages which, more or less clumsily, I read, decode, or sometimes speak, are languages I shall never inhabit. . . . But the "untranslatable" remains—should remain, as my law tells me—the poetic economy of the idiom. (Derrida, 1996/1998, p. 56)

Our narrative, and its *currere*, this regressive autobiographical moment, begins in the past, where the cicadas chant the deafening memories of a southern landscape among the old magnolia trees where I once fell behind and delayed any headings toward a final destination.

I originally experienced the intellectual difficulties of studying and translating the philosophies and autobiographical writing of Derrida (1990/2002) during my doctoral studies in curriculum theorising at Louisiana State University (LSU). Within the Curriculum Theory Project at LSU, I looked at the relationships among academic institutions and their housed systems of interdisciplinary knowledge for understanding our place in this universe we call language, whether it is French, English, or other. I sought to utilize the method of *currere* to study Derrida's texts in relation to my past, present and future lived experiences within the "third space" of being able to speak two different languages, French and English, differently (Wang, 2004). In a sense, this chapter seeks to understand how I might (re)read my lived experiences with, in, and of the French language as a child schooled in Canada's French Catholic schooling system in relation to Derrida's experiences of with the French language among other things. The chapter also looks at how such lived experiences might inform our understandings of philosophical and curricular concepts like language appropriation, alienation, and ex-appropriation within various instituted contexts such as the school curriculum here in Canada.

My work now at the University of Ottawa as a curriculum theorist in a bilingual institution has helped me to reconceptualise my initial study of these theoretical concepts. This cotextual moment is a response to questions raised in previous scholarly texts and in other interdisciplinary landscapes, now mapped within the vertical and horizontal temporal limits of this autobiographical writing, as I search for a method to understand Derrida's curriculum on inhabiting and being inhabited by the languages of the other (see Pinar, 1975/2000; Pinar, 2007; and Pinar, Reynolds, Slattery, & Taubman 1995). Verticality, Pinar (2007) tells us, is the

J. Nahachewsky and I. Johnston (eds.), Beyond 'Presentism': Re-Imagining the Historical, Personal, and Social Places of Curriculum, 87–103.

[handwritten annotations in margins: "he's explaining method - Pinar's"; "study verticality + horizontality of inter/disciplinary structures"; "What is he trying to do?"; "Deconstructing Colonialism."; "post-structuralism"]

intellectual history of a discipline, whereas horizontality refers to analyses of present circumstances, both in terms of internal intellectual trends as well as the external social and political milieus influencing our field. Studying the verticality and horizontality of inter/disciplinary structures, Pinar (2007) suggests opportunities to understand a series of scholarly moves both outside and within the field of curriculum studies. Consequently, this chapter draws on autobiographical examples and primarily on the intellectual work of Jacques Derrida to understand the vertical and horizontal temporal migrations of transnational lived experiences in the language of the other through a genealogical study of various historical, philosophical, and postcolonial curricular narratives.

How does a migratory subject appropriate the language of the other when the subject is a citizen of Canada and Britain, an immigrant with an ex-appropriate proper name, Ng-A-Fook, traced to Guyana's indentured Chinese cane reapers, and thus an imperialized postcolonial subject with identity disorders in America, Canada, and elsewhere? More specifically, how might one learn, via the autobiographical method of *currere*, from a migrant subject's lived experiences of appropriation and alienation in the language of the other? To study these curricular and theoretical questions, I examine Derrida's concept of deconstruction and its relationships to deconstructing the subject of colonialism. I seek to approximate an understanding of the impossible colonial politics of properly appropriating the language of the other and attempt to understand a curriculum of hospitality within the liminal third space of alienation and appropriation. But first, let us turn toward the textual margins of deconstruction with a letter—Derrida's "Letter to a Japanese Friend."

ADDRESSING A LETTER: THE SUBJECT OF DECONSTRUCTION

I would say that the difficulty of *defining* and therefore also of *translating* the word "deconstruction" stems from the fact that all the predicates, all the defining concepts, all the lexical significations, and even syntactic articulations, which seem at one moment to lend themselves to this definition or to that translation, are also deconstructed or deconstructible, directly or otherwise, etc. (Derrida, 1983a/1991, p. 274)

Yesterday's reading, thinking, and writing experiences a certain temporal death. However, the temporality of a yesterday—the writing and understanding of Derrida's concept of deconstruction and its immediacy—is suspended between the lines of the pages, dawn and dusk, life and death. Meanwhile, my thoughts continue to inscribe their particular traces on these pages with a particular universal energy situated between the liminal spaces of its margins. Nonetheless, today this chapter opens with a returning, to the subject of deconstruction in the letter. Within the margins, Derrida (1983a/1991) cautions professor Izutsu,

It goes without saying that if all the significations [on deconstruction] enumerated by the *Littré* interested me because of their affinity with what I "meant" [*voulais dire*] they concerned, metaphorically, so to say, only models

or regions of meaning and not the totality of what deconstruction aspires to at
its most ambitious. (p. 271)

These curricular models themselves, Derrida (1983a/1991) maintains, must be
submitted to "deconstructive questioning" (p. 271). Derrida (1992a/2001) reminds
us, asks us, demands of us in the name of responsibility for the other, to free
"deconstruction," the "subject," and "its human rights" from the "word" and its
assumed logo-centric or phono-centric idiomatic forms. Deconstructive work
involves tracing genealogies across academic borderlands and uncovering the
historical layers from which such concepts and their translations emerge, and thus
are promised and made possible through the universe of language—its disciplinary
constellations. In this movement of deconstructing the subject, which Derrida
(1992a/2001) doubts is yet possible, the subject of deconstruction is "taking into
account all the determinations and trying . . . to *improve* the concept of the human
subject" (Derrida, 1992a/2001, p. 179). Let us consider the following hypothetical
autobiographical genealogy of a postcolonial Chinese subject.

A gift of death-instituting slavery and its judicial language created a historical
space for Chinese indentured labourers, known as Cane Reapers, to birth their
existence without origin into the margins of Guyana's narratives of nationhood and
the psychological and material colonization of its indigenous people and landscape.
Britain abolished the slavery of African subjects during the 1830s. However, West
Indies plantation owners' demands for cheap labour did not diminish. Chinese subjects
subjected to persecution and famine, or wanting to escape a feudal system in search
of "common" wealth, migrated to British Guiana (see Sue-A-Quan, 1999). China
prohibited such emigration, fearing the possible political revolution caused by
those who returned from "foreign" places. One subject, his surname not yet
hyphenated, travelled the tumultuous seas without the possibility of return to
become an indentured labourer cutting cane along the tributaries of the Demerara
River. No longer with rights as a Chinese subject or protected by rights as a British
subject, Fook Ng, my great-great-grandfather, was now a colonial subject who had
to learn how to negotiate the judicial language and respective power of British rule.

Some time after the 1850s, the first ships from China made the arduous journey
to the land of many rivers, which the local Amerindians named Guiana. Upon Fook
Ng's arrival at the gates of the colonial port, a British magistrate translated and
reinscribed this foreign subject's first and last names with the unfamiliar anglicized
marks of John and Cyril, respectively, much like they renamed the symbolic
markers of the indigenous landscape. His son later reappropriated his Chinese
name, and with the addition of hyphens to his father's former Chinese title, the
family surname became Cyril Ng-A-Fook. The descendents of John Cyril Ng-A-
Fook Jr. learned how to embrace the inscription and father the language of
colonization under the guise of this new title. Although his title was translated, the
subject of Fook Ng's history continues to survive and surf the postcolonial hyphens
between self, other, language, and culture.

How does this postcolonial migrant subject of a nation negotiate his or her
understanding of the subject of translating and in turn appropriate the cultural
idioms of language, within the subject of English or French, for example? The

concept of the subject, like those of deconstruction, colonization, and their translations, can be traced, through Greek, Latin, German, French, and English universal systems, each with its own particularities for producing and instituting such languages. Derrida (1992a/2001) maintains that we must first translate the words philosophy, deconstruction, or subject for example "into a different idiom, and finally in *all* the possible idioms," to make, the "word subject understandable in other cultures" (p. 178). To approximate an understanding of deconstruction, or to deconstruct the subject of and subject within autobiography, one is also faced first with the problem of translation.

The "first thing you have to do," Derrida (1992a/2001) reminds us, "is a universal translation" of what "the subject" *is* and *is not* (p. 178). Deconstruction of the word "subject" is then first for Derrida (1992a/2001), among other things, "the genealogical analysis of the trajectory through which the concept has been built, used, legitimized, and so on" (pp. 177–178). Pinar (2008) has referred to such genealogical study (or deconstruction) as the verticality of a curricular concept within the field of curriculum studies. How might we then deconstruct the historical and intellectual dimensions to what is or is not Canadian curriculum theory for example—its various codisciplinary constellations of curricular language? Derrida (1983a/1991) makes it clear that to deconstruct the subject is not to destroy, dissolve, or cancel the legitimacy of what you are deconstructing. Furthermore, the language of which Derrida (1992a/2001) speaks is not used the same way in the Anglo-American tradition as it is in continental philosophy.

Beyond a dogmatic critique of pure reason, Derrida (1990/2002, 1991a/1992, 1992a/2001) asks us to recall, with care and rigor, our double duty, our inheritance of concepts, and the language that conceives the subject of deconstruction to reaffirm the limitless possibilities illuminated by the philosophical heritage of Husserl, Heidegger, Kant, Descartes, Aristotle, and so on, while also critiquing such heritage—what Pinar (2008) has aptly called, within the international field of curriculum studies, *The Canon Project*. Derrida (1991a/1992) explains that it is our national and individual duty to criticize, both in theory and in practice, a totalitarian dogmatism which in turn works to destroy democracy and its European, American, and Canadian heritages. Such a duty also involves criticizing institutions which institute dogmatism under new guises. Yet this same duty, Derrida stresses, "dictates cultivating the virtue of such critique, of the critical idea, the critical tradition" and submits it "beyond critique and questioning, to a deconstructive genealogy that thinks and exceeds it without compromising it" (p. 77). Therefore, this double duty, according to Derrida, asks us, in the name of responsibility, to affirm our philosophical heritage while also submitting it to a deconstructive questioning.

The "subject was first," Derrida (1992a/2001) explains, "in the Aristotelian tradition the *hypocheimenon*, something which is underneath, identical to itself, and different from its different properties, qualities, attributes; it is *the* center of an identity" (p. 178). The speaking subject performs certain representations of cultural and national identities through language using his or her mother tongue (see Derrida 1996/1998). In turn, Butler (1990/1999) stresses that "the domains of political and linguistic 'representation' set out in advance the criterion by which subjects themselves are formed, with the result that representation is extended only to what can be acknowledged as a subject" (p. 4). How might one then reaffirm the structure of the subject, within autobiography for example, while questioning the limits of its canonized representations (e.g., a white European male bourgeoisie)? How might we take on this double duty (*devoir*)? In the name of God, king, queen, country, state, or the metropolis, institutions such as the university often guard and discipline consciously and unconsciously the legitimacy of who is (which subjects are) entitled and granted access to the universal systems of Euro-, Ameri-, and/or Can-centric knowledge. And, as Butler stresses, such universal systems work in turn to shape the subject.

The American State, albeit not globally alone, continues to invest in a cultural, linguistic, and economic capital in an attempt to reproduce a common subject with a common curriculum, and thus disseminates its empire through ideological apparatuses—juridical, educational, medical, religious, media, etc.—making the subject of deconstruction, and the deconstruction of the subject, all the more pressing today. In "Privilege," Derrida (1990/2002) continues to work, without settling for a resolution, through the oppositions, paradoxes, and aporias of *what is* and *what is not* philosophy. Who has the rights to such philosophical institutions? In following such lines of questioning, *what are* and *what are not* the rights of a migrant subject? As a migrant, an indentured labourer, and a postcolonial subject, what were John Cyril Ng-A-Fook's rights of access to the institutions that house a knowledge of citizenship, its language, and in turn his en-title-ment to the *right* to name, and to *naming* his rights? Derrida makes it clear that

> the title given (or refused) someone always supposes, and this is a circle, the title of a work, that is, an institution, which alone is entitled to give (or refuse) it. Only an institution (the title of the body entitled to confer titles) can give *someone* his or her title. (1990/2002, p. 4)

But who, then, entitles an (colonizing) institution? Derrida (1990/2002) explains such institutional entitlement is presupposed, for institutions (philosophical, juridical, medical, educational, etc.) are already entitled to give someone his or her title. Institutions entitle themselves through an exemplary system, a system of circular examples (which, through a tradition of Western logo-centrism, proves its logic) originated, established, and privileged by an instituted foundation of *what is* and *what is not*.

Deconstruction, therefore, is a "questioning in the sense of search, exploration, reflectivity, rejection of all assumptions, not as an act of demolition, but as striving for awareness" of alterity, heading toward the possibility of otherness which resides within the interstitial disciplinary spaces—between the marginal limits—of such institutions (Egéa-Kuehne, 1995, p. 299). Derrida (1992a/2001) suggests that if you call deconstruction "an ethics of affirmation, it implies that you are attentive to [language of] otherness, to the alterity of the other, to something new and other" (p. 180). How does the subject of deconstruction negotiate his or her (human) rights to name his or her rights of otherness, his or her citizenship in the language of a colonizing other? How do the institutions of schooling and their respective curricularists' languages work in the configurations of such entitlements? What

91

knowledges are privileged and presupposed in (colonizing) educational institutions? Writing toward the impossible terrain of properly understanding the answers to such questions is where this narrative migrates next.

RETURNING TO THE POSTCOLONIAL SHORES OF A FOREIGN LANGUAGE

Every culture institutes itself through the unilateral imposition of some "politics" of language. (Derrida, 1996/1998, p. 39)

Once again, night time overshadows a place of thinking, reading, and writing. Meanwhile, I entangle myself with the textual body of an interview with Derrida in *Le Monde* titled "I am at War Against Myself." I continue to intellectually play with the various performative linguistic acts of translating this interview in its entirety from French to English, giving birth to a certain amount of erasure, to death of original meaning. Can one ever translate without loss, without such linguistic interpretive violence? In deconstructive fashion, Derrida avoids his interviewer's initial question about his war with pancreatic cancer. Instead, Derrida moves through the interview to recount his past work and share his current thoughts on various topics and concepts such as the conflict in Iraq, same-sex marriages, heritage, and the question of how one learns to live life.

I struggle to translate, always with a certain amount of violence and death toward the languages of the other. How might I then whisper and breathe life, a curriculum of disciplinary otherness, into the words of Derrida? Under the alienating light of darkness and solitude and its respective linguistic shadows, I remember a time when Derrida's breathing and his suspension between life and death was still shrinking, shortening, slowly ceasing. He is suffering with pancreatic cancer. I am reminded of the parallels between his and my father's colonial births, their shared encounters with institutional discrimination, exclusions, separations, and entitled ties to national citizenships and their alienating institutions. To be an alien worker is to live without title (of citizenship), without the human rights afforded under the language of en-title-ment.

Through the process of translating Derrida's interview in *Le Monde*, I stumble across words for which translation and their immediate understanding are not ready-at-hand. Are they ever? But I am suspended in the cultural web of the French language. The following sentence, "Le temps du sursis se rétrécit de façon accélérée," eludes my present comprehension. The words "sursis" and "rétrécit" are alien, and alienate, my ephemeral moment of understanding. My memories of a language, the only language we had in the French Catholic School system I attended and a language that was never mine, eludes a proper appropriation. Although I find some reprieve keeping a French-English dictionary close at hand, I continue to struggle while trying to negotiate the violence of universal translation, of poaching a singular meaning, of excluding and reducing all possible meanings of the other, to a proper English idiom (Lewkowich, 2008). I settle with the following phrase, "The time, suspended in reprieve, shrinks ever faster." At the end of this process of translating French writing into language, its inscriptions into thoughts, thoughts back into English language, and its inscriptions into writing, I learn that Derrida's time suspended between life and death shrinks ever faster.

Alienation is a certain death of the subject, and yet one's own death is an alien moment in autobiographical writing; its lived curriculum remains foreign, yet to come. Can Derrida, can each of us, write a *currere* of death, when death precedes such writing? Can one write autobiographically about the curricular death of one's language and its lived curriculum? One remains, Derrida (2004) suggests, uneducable with regards to the knowledge of knowing how to die. Yet, can one write auto-iographically about a certain death of yesterday, of who I was autobiographically speaking of yesterday, while still alive today? There is a certain kind of linguistic death between the hyphenated spaces of alienation and appropriation, a violence, a loss of meaning, involved in first, and second, and third, and fourth, …and…and…and, translations. There are appropriations of a French language that was never mine, or an English language that never was Fook Ng's, or a Chinese language that ceases to breathe life across the idiomatic lived experiences of what Greene (1978) aptly calls our household's present *landscapes of learning*. But, there is also a birthing of a language and its idiomatic otherness in such hyphenated "third space" of death, of who I was yesterday (Wang, 2004). Therefore, how does one learn to live within the aporias—a language of undecidability—of such a hyphenated third space, between appropriation and alienation, life and death?

In response to this question, Derrida (1996/1998) shares the following double postulation:

– We only ever speak one language—or rather one idiom only.
– We never speak only one language—or rather there is no pure idiom. (p. 8)

In *Monolingualism of the Other*, Derrida works to situate our lived experiences in/with/against a language, which in turn moves beyond the hyphenated spaces of appropriation and alienation. For some of us, we only speak one language, English or French. But this language does not have a pure idiomatic representation or one singular enunciated aesthetic performance. We might consider here the enunciated performances of, for example, Glaswegian or Acadian English and/or northern rural Franco-Ontarian and Parisian French. Consequently, we only ever speak one language, and we never only speak or perform one language.

Within another context, we can think in terms of curriculum theorists speaking only one language, and in turn never only speaking one language. "Many curricularists are flies caught," Huebner (1975/1999) reminds us, "in the web of someone else's language. Some are spiders, weaving webs as a consequence of their inherited ability" (p. 214). Here is where Derrida's concept of deconstructing and affirming genealogical work might push international curricularists to think beyond the temporal limits of appropriation and alienation within a certain poetic form of curriculum language. Huebner tells us that the unique characteristic of a curriculum theorist is that as a human being he or she is able to be caught in someone else's disciplinary web of language, to appropriate it as their own, to stand back and understand the complexities of its idiomatic forms, to study its structure and function, and to generate new weblike patterns. Let us then study some of Derrida's lived experiences with the colonial instituted politics of language. How might it inform this current moment of curriculum theorising of inhabiting and/or

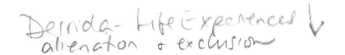

being inhabited by the international, philosophical, curricular, disciplinary, and autobiographical language of the other?

Derrida migrated from Algeria to study in Paris. But even before leaving the shores of Africa in 1949, Derrida spoke in the language of a country where he had never been himself. "My language, the only one I hear myself speak and agree to speak," Derrida (1996/1998) tells us, "is the language of the other" (p. 25). Elsewhere Derrida (1997/2001) explains,

> French is the only mother tongue I have, but while still a child I had a vague sensation that this language was not really my own. . . . So I had the feeling that this language, which was the only one I had, came from somewhere else. (p. 38)

His family migrated to Algeria from Spain before enduring the curricular processes of French colonization. The Crémieux Decree in 1870 granted French citizenship to the Jews of Algeria. Less than a century later in October of 1940, during WWII and the German persecution of Jews, Henri Philippe Pétain's administration abolished the Crémieux Decree.

Soon after the initial invasion of France in 1940, and in the absence of the official French government, the National Assembly voted in Henri Philippe Pétain as the head of what was later known as the Vichy administration which controlled the remaining two-fifths of unoccupied France. He then signed an armistice that gave Germany control over the northern landscape of France. During his administration, the language of the French constitution was changed from "freedom, equality, brotherhood," to "labour, family, country." Not all French citizens supported the newly established government. Charles de Gaulle led France Libre (Free France), the French government in exile, from London. In the southern unoccupied terrain and elsewhere in France, the French Resistance continued to fight the Germans and help Jewish subjects escape the genocide of the Holocaust. After France's liberation by the allies from the German occupation in 1945, Pétain was sentenced to death and expulsed from the Academie Française. The following year his sentence was commuted to life in prison due to his old age.

Two years later Derrida was expelled from elementary school. "Here we have a 12-year old boy," Derrida (1997/2001) writes, "who, without anyone explaining to him what anti-Semitism is, or what is happening politically, is kicked out of school" (pp. 37–38). Yet, Derrida (1996/1998) stresses, the denial of French citizenship did not prevent an unprecedented assimilation of the State official and institutionally privileged language. Derrida (1997/2001) continues, "a crack is opened in the relative security of the school, the place where culture is offered to him, where languages are taught—especially the dominant models of the French language" (p. 38). As a result of his expulsion, Derrida's parents enrolled him in a Jewish school. But he still experienced anti-Semitism outside the school, in the streets, and among his circle of peers. The lived experience of not belonging and alienation affected his relationship with the Jewish community. Derrida's (1997/2001) childhood trauma caused him to cultivate "a sort of not-belonging to French culture and to France in general, but also, in some way, to reject" his belonging to Judaism (p. 39).

In reading Derrida's account of exclusions due to his paternal and genealogical ties to Judaism, I try to imagine how exclusion emerged and emerges under the proper surname of Ng-A-Fook and its traces of Chinese-ness, or how it erases symbolically the idiomatic representation associated to the Gaelic-ness of my mother's family name, Gray. When the surname Ng-A-Fook announces itself in places as a foreigner, before a linguistic embodied arrival, before an "I" physically addresses an audience, before performing its appropriations of an English language, often racial, monolingual, mono-racial responses are evoked in relation to the absence of enunciating and performing a hybridization of such foreshadowed identities.

My father gained and lost his British citizenship in the land of many rivers. When Guyana was granted liberation in 1966, many former colonial subjects who where not born on the Queen's crown land now occupied a postcolonial status of not belonging and lost their inalienable rights granted under the title of British citizenship and its respective judicial entitlements. Nonetheless, "citizenship," Derrida (1996/1998) tells us, "does not define a cultural, linguistic, or, in general, historical participation" (p. 15). Consequently, my father, now living in Glasgow and married by judicial law to a British national citizen, was reduced to the instituted title of resident alien, a postcolonial foreigner now living at the edges of a former Empire's metropolis.

During the institutionalized mirage of global decolonization during the 1950s and 1960s, institutions in France and Britain continued to negotiate, reconceptualise, and redefine the geopolitical territories of its Empire's (lack of) national identity by the racialized groups they did not belong to—Chinese, Irish, Jewish, Black, Indian, migrants. During the 1970s, my father's associations to, and situated appropriations and performances of, a Chinese-Guyanese national and cultural identity in Britain did not enunciate a legitimized being of British-ness. Consequently, his application to become a British citizen was denied.

In "Privilege," Derrida (1990/2002) writes,

> The surface of its [the institutions'] archive is then marked by what it keeps outside, expels, or does not tolerate. It takes the inverted shape of that which is rejected. It lets itself be delineated by the very thing that threatens it or that it feels to be a threat. In order to *identify itself*, to be what it is, to delimit itself and recognize itself in its own name, it must espouse the very outlines of its adversary, if I can put it thus. (p. 5)

During different historical eras, the French and British institutional apparatuses have had to react and redefine their cultural identities and respective national narratives in the face of a certain masked otherness, by declaring with a politics of language, of ethnographically translating a curriculum of *what they were not* (see Fanon, 1967/1991) "by employing certain modes of representing the other—which thereby also brings into being translation reinforces hegemonic versions of the colonized" (Niranjana, 1992, p. 3). This universal system of exclusionary logic, of translating and defining philosophically *what the other is* and what one *is not*, of deferral, différence and displacement, worked and still works today to privilege certain national identities associated to the metropolises of a colonial motherland or

Privilege of Colonial motherland [handwritten annotation]

fatherland. Thus the acts of translation itself reify, as Niranjana (1992) makes clear, the colonial strategies and their respective epistemic violence of containing and reducing multiple meanings and performances of curriculum and language.

Therefore, in the name of responsibility for the other, Derrida (1990/2002) asks us to question recursively the essences, functions, and translations of language which privilege the foundations of our (educational and colonizing) philosophical institutions. "It is the apparent firmness, hardness, durability, or resistance of philosophical institutions," Derrida (1990/2002) suggests, which "betrays, first of all, the fragility of a foundation. It is on the ground of this (theoretical and practical) 'deconstructability,' it is against it, that the institution institutes itself" (p. 10). Cane reapers, former colonial subjects, eventually learned the hard secrets, now no longer secrets, about the frailty of colonizing institutions and its respective colonial instituted language. Consequently, some postcolonial subjects like my father, alien in foreign lands, appropriated the languages of the other and learned to navigate the polyglot, hybrid, and hyphenated spaces between an appropriation of *what is* and an alienation of *what is not* colonial culture—an appropriation of colonial cultural and economic capital. In 1975, my father left Britain perhaps not as a citizen, but still with all the credentials and in turn capital associated with being trained as a physician at a British institution when he immigrated with our family to Canada. Yet, how does a colonial or postcolonial subject negotiate between the hyphenated spaces of sameness and otherness, alienation and appropriation, the colonizer's institutional language and one's alter/native language, the schoolmaster's tongue and one's mother tongue, which in turn is always already occupied by the language of the other? What are the limits or situations of such (re)appropriations? Might we turn this migratory narrative toward inhabiting the hospital spaces of such inhospitable questions next?

ALIENATION AND APPROPRIATION WITHIN THE LANGUAGE
OF THE OTHER

> This mother language with which we are at home is the language belonging to a community—a language of sharing, a language of familiarity, a vernacular language of daily conversation, a language with a profound respect of the other and self. (Aoki, 1987/2005, p. 239)

> Language is for the other, coming from the other, *the* coming of the other. (Derrida, 1996/1998, p. 68)

Dawn and dusk, self and other, two strangers in the same sky, share a universal terrain of such unseasonal language. Language is our invisible prosthesis for moving between the shifting terrain of self and other. A spoken language with its promise of a universal terrain has no visible material body. Self and other, however, are able to perform their accents, intonations, and rhythms—of gender, class, race, culture, and differences—through the invisible bodies of language. And therefore, the invisible universal landscape of language eludes both a master's material ownership and a colonial subject's (re)appropriations of what Derrida (1996/1998) calls the terrain of *homo-hegemonic meaning*.

In Monolingualism of the Other, Derrida (1996/1998) maintains the colonial master, the teacher, "wants to make others believe" in his ownership of a language, of a universal terrain called *homo-hegemonic meaning*, "as they do a miracle, through rhetoric, the school, or the army" (p. 23). A first trick, he continues, is thus played: a master's ownership of the invisible places, which in turn host and repute language. You are welcome to my national house of curriculum studies, unconditionally welcomed, as long as you agree that I own all appropriations of meanings associated to the word curriculum for example. "Mastery begins," Derrida stresses, "through the power of naming, of imposing and legitimating appellations. . . . It always follows or precedes culture like its shadows" (p. 39). Therefore, like a shadow and its visible absence of light, the colonial master's lack of proper appropriation, his ownership of invisibility, moves him to impose his fantasies of possessing the alchemy of a mono-language onto the linguistic landscape of a colonized other.

Upon arriving to foreign lands and during their colonization, it was common practice for Europeans to systematically reinscribe the landscape itself, and the animals, insects, plants, and indigenous people who inhabited it, with anglicized remarks. The colonizer, the master, demonstrated his fantasies of ownership through renaming the land, and thus appropriating the indigenous terrain of meaning. (For a further discussion that complicates colonial power, naming, and ownership of land, see Smith's (1999) *Decolonizing Methodologies: Research and Indigenous Peoples*.) As a result, the possibility of translation, its fluidity and its migrations cease to exist in such a master's house. Instead, its movements, disruptions, displacement, and excesses fix colonized cultures, or the designs of "curriculum" language, for that matter, to static interpretations devoid of alter/native idiomatic representations or of the possibilities of hosting a language of otherness.

Moreover, the colonial master's language of liberation, emancipation, revolution, and decolonization then plays a second trick. "It will provide freedom," Derrida (1996/1998) asserts, "from the first while confirming a heritage by internalizing it, by reappropriating it—but only up to a certain point, for, as my hypothesis shows, there is never any such thing as absolute appropriation or reappropriating" (p. 24). A master's performed ownership, proper appropriation of a monolanguage, an institutional language, and the invisibility of its otherness cannot be fully promised or assimilated by the other.

This lack of promise, the unattainable terrain of *homo-hegemonic meaning*, is the uncanny madness of language. Nonetheless, "the language, the only one I hear myself speak, and agree to speak, is the language of the other" (Derrida, 1996/1998, p. 25). Therefore, our responsibility for the other, in the face of a sovereign other, requires hospitality for the other's inalienable alienable rights to the landscape of a universal language that is never mine. Language is a structure, Derrida writes, of alienation without alienation. The practices of colonial alienation and of being othered by its language, Derrida maintains, is language. In a sense, even when we speak to each other in one language, even when we share the universality of one language, we still risk the possibilities of alienating one another. The professional language of the curricularist, Huebner (1975/1999) tells us, often pulls them away from their feelings and respective language, thus alienating them from their biographies. For example, how might we create pedagogical and curricular spaces that are unconditionally open to such alienation, such pulling away, without alienating a student and/or a colleague who inhabits curriculum language from an alter/native philosophical and national standpoint on multicultural and/or antiracist education? Curricular discourse or the language utilized, whether it is in Australia, Canada, the United States, and/or Guyana, is inhabited by an institutionalized mother tongue, which in turn is already inhabited by the language of the other. In Canada, the two officially instituted colonial languages are French and English. Therefore, to be at home with the French or the English language, to inhabit each one as a second skin, I must be in some ways at home with welcoming the excesses of each other's otherness.

At Immaculé Conception, I remember for the first time hearing the teacher pronounce the accentuated strangeness of the name Ng-A-Fook in the language of the other. Or learning with difficulty to differentiate between the grave, acute, circumflex, and dieresis accentuated sounds of é, à, è, ê, û, ë, au, eu, ou, and où. I have flashbacks of flashcards. French was my language of learning at the elementary and secondary schools. For 6 hours a day, the language of the other and its culture attempted to teach me. Each day, we mastered a model that promised good speech and good writing. As a child, there was always a certain amount of unconditional hospitality toward the language of the other. My attempts to appropriate the impossible purity of its idioms were not, however, without a certain sense of accentuated alienation. English is my mother tongue. But there were few places of hospitality to receive its utterance at school. I was forbidden to practice the alchemy of the only language I spoke, never only spoke, and which never was mine, inside and outside the school walls. For me, French was the schoolmaster's language. Because of my alien responses to experiencing the accentuation of a second language, or my refusal to utter in the language of the other, I often found myself sitting in the silent refuges of the hallway shadows, lost in translation, between the hyphenated spaces of appropriation and alienation.

Derrida (1996/1998) stresses that the very conditions of unconditional hospitality toward the language of the other "relies upon a foundation, whose sovereign essence is always colonial, which tends, repressively and irrepressively, to reduce language to the One" (p. 40). "This homo-hegemony," Derrida adds, "remains at work in the culture, effacing the fold and flattening the text" (p. 40). Here, the host and the other's language we receive, house, and feed have the dual possibilities of being a guest and an enemy, a promise and a terror.

After immigrating to Canada, like many other immigrant families from the West Indies, we briefly lived in Scarborough, Toronto. A few months later upon a friend's advice, my father travelled up to northern Ontario, to a small rural logging town called Kapuskasing (which means "bend in the river" in Cree), where the tributaries of its river migrate north bending back and forth across the landscape. Once there, Father was able to call upon the language of his British credentials to negotiate and secure the necessary economic capital to purchase a house, appropriate local aboriginal land, and set up a medical practice. We soon joined him. The majority of the population in Kapuskasing was and still is Franco-Ontarian, which is a linguistic minority within Ontario itself. Mother and Father knew the importance of appropriating the institutional languages of the other. Although our mother tongue and spoken language was an Irish-Guyanese postcolonial form of the English language within our household, and the spiritual hands of an Anglican Church baptized my two brothers and me, our parents enrolled us in the local French Catholic schooling system. As foreigners, we were welcomed unconditionally while expected to live within the institutional conditions of French Catholic schooling—its explicit, implicit, and hidden curriculum—set up by this foreign institution's administration and teachers. We soon learned how to listen, how to learn, how to get along, how to enunciate, how to hear each other, and how to translate, not without negotiation and/or difficulty within the instituted spiritual, curricular, written, and spoken languages of a northern rural Franco-Ontarian Catholic culture of schooling.

We lived as Anglophones within the broader provincial linguistic politics of this geographically isolated northern Canadian culture, within its institution for teaching and maintaining an appropriation of the French language and its respective genealogical ties to Franco-Ontarian cultural identities. We were both a guest and a potential internal colonizing and assimilating enemy, caught between the historical margins of two colonial languages. French Second Language students like me were a linguistic minority within another linguistic cultural minority. There was an emphasis to learn how to speak and enunciate *proper* French, without any accentuated differences, without translation and/or Anglophone appropriations. My attempts to properly appropriate the written, spoken, and accentuated language of the other caused a certain amount of biographic alienation from the professional languages of the school curriculum.

If then each of us is born into the concrete language of our mother tongue, as Aoki (1987/2005) suggests, how then does one negotiate a curriculum that inhabits the hyphenated spaces between the conceptual margins of colonizer and colonized, appropriation and alienation, conditional and unconditionally hospitality, the alter/native language of the other, of their particular mother tongue, and a universal language reduced to the One? In response to this last question, of a yesterday, today, and tomorrow, there are many strategic codisciplinary turns. One of the strategic moves Derrida introduces to provoke our understandings of the concept of appropriation, our reduction of an institutional language enunciating explicit curricular laws, proper and thus irreducibly open only to themselves, is to introduce us to the concept of ex-appropriation. In this deconstructive double movement, "'exap-' marks the sense of '-propriation' with an irreducible discordance or dissociation between its two directions" (Kamuf, 1991, p. xxiii). "Whereas the proper movement of the proper," Kamuf explains, "can only be in an appropriative direction back to itself, the circle of return cannot complete itself without also tracing the contrary movement of expropriation" (p. xxiii). The more a schoolmaster, a colonial subject, or a second language learner seeks to appropriate and jealously own a language that is proper to itself and thus uncontaminated by the other, the more "-propriation" loses itself in relation to the "ex-" of an exteriority to itself. Ex-appropriation, Derrida and Stiegler (2002) explain, is this double movement of heading toward meaning while trying to appropriate it, "while knowing at the same time that it remains— and while desiring, whether I realize it or not, that it remain—foreign, transcendent, other, that it stay where there is alterity" (p. 111). But, as dusk marks the death of another day and the specters of Derrida return and whisper, language must be a place of hospitality for the invisible movements of understanding between self and other to occur.

Concepts such as deconstruction, subject, colonial, colonizer, postcolonial, alienation, appropriation, and mono-language, and their proper place of *homo-hegemonic meaning*, remain in a perpetual movement. They are a migration of unfinished promises, of ex-appropriation, caught between the liminal spaces of translation, always on the verge of untranslatability. Therefore mono-lingualism of the other, learning language and its translation is a promise, Derrida (1996/1998) suggests, which no longer expects what it waits for. And thus, learning the only language I speak, the only language I never speak, unconditionally hosting the invisible language of the other and its landscape of universal translation, welcoming him or her as a friend or enemy remains veiled by the promise of an understanding which can never properly be attained.

FALLING BEHIND: ANOTHER HEADING TOWARD UNFINISHED GOODBYES

It is this language that holds us, as both hostage and support. (Chambers, 1994, p. 33)

Wouldn't this mother tongue be a sort of second skin you wear on yourself, a mobile home? But also an immobile home since it moves with us? (Derrida, 1997/2000, p. 89)

The language of spring is here in Canada. It is now March, 2009. I witness another season shrinking, shortening, and changing ever faster. At dusk, during this time of curriculum theorising, the cracks of my windows and doors are now open to host a different kind of invisibility which floats over this northern urban landscape. A language of unions and of differences on this terrain called *homo-hegemonic meaning*, between self and other, Derrida's texts and my translations, have made their historical and always situated singularities present within these margins.

Through death, Derrida gives life to another language, a heritage of deconstruction, now suspended within the translation of these pages and the universal landscape of the English and French languages. Is it memories or the nostalgia of experiencing the language of the other within the margins of this textual body and its alienation, appropriation, and ex-appropriation always temporally migrating with us, that faithfully keep Derrida's philosophical inheritance alive?

A responsible inheritance of Derrida's deconstruction asks us in the name of the other to recursively question the subject's rights to *name* for example, and to name the *rights* of his or her institutional language. Responsibilities of stewardship over this heritage of deconstruction by keeping it alive, also involve questioning any institutional language that presupposes its foundations with universal systems of exclusionary logic. Deconstruction as a method for reading, learning, and/or theorising, Derrida (1991/1992, 2004) tells us, performs a double duty which is faithful to a disciplinary, cultural, and philosophical heritage while also disrupting Euro-, Ameri-, and/or Can-centric reductions of properly appropriating a language of the other and its respective translations.

The autobiographical examples presented in this paper provide an exemplarity of singularities that challenges universal claims to an essential narrative representation, homo-hegemonic meaning. The value of exemplarity, Derrida (1991/1992) writes, is that it

> inscribes the universal in the proper body of a singularity, of an idiom or a culture, whether this singularity be individual, social, national, state, federal, confederal, or not. Whether it takes a national form or not, a refined, hospitality or aggressively xenophobia form or not, the self-affirmation of an identity always claims to be responding to the call or assignation of the universal. (p. 72)

Each time that Fook Ng, John Cyril Ng-A-Fook, and I utter our differences, the disorder of our cultural and postcolonial identities, and our situated and partial autobiographical narratives, we must call upon the universal terrain of language and inscribe its universality within the singularities of our historical and educational experiences with alienation and appropriation. In such examples, a migrant postcolonial subject does not settle for a proper cultural and national identity, but remains unsettled, perpetually migrating within the hyphenated curricular and liminal spaces of colonizer and colonized, alienation and appropriation, the language of the other and a language reduced to the One.

In *Monolingualism of the Other*, Derrida teaches us the impossibility of properly appropriating the schoolmaster's language. Self and other are caught in the double movement of ex-appropriation, a hyphenated space of understanding that verges on untranslatability. However, Derrida ask us to learn how to listen carefully, and open ourselves toward hosting unconditionally the language of the other as both a potential host and enemy. To do so, you and I must be open to a possible alienation *double* without alienation caused by receiving the excesses of otherness—to the terror of *move-* not knowing what is to come. This double movement of teaching and learning involves *ment of* a listening, a curricular movement of heading unconditionally and conditionally *teaching +* toward each other. *learning*

The suspension of daytime across the landscape foreshadows this autobiographical narrative. Canadian geese are returning to take their refuge in the vanishing wetlands of southern and northern Ontario. Meanwhile, the French language that was only mine, never only mine, the language of the other, held hostage inside me, the language I only ever speak, never only speak, is perpetually migrating within a liminal space of appropriation and alienation, of living and dying. How might I teach a dying language to survive, and in turn, learn to support a language that perpetually says goodbye? What landscape of language did Derrida long for in the face of death? How does one host the language of death? And, how might its invisible universal terrain greet you and me? Let us now say farewell to such unfinished goodbyes.

REFERENCES

Aoki, T. T. (1987/2005). The dialect of mother language and second language: A curriculum exploration. In W. F. Pinar & R. L. Irwin (Eds.), *Curriculum in a new key* (pp. 235–246). Mahwah, NJ: Lawrence Erlbaum Associates.

Boehmer, E. (1995). *Colonial and post-colonial literature.* New York and Oxford: Oxford University Press.

Butler, J. (1990/1999). *Gender trouble: Feminism and the subversion of identity.* New York: Routledge.

Chambers, D. (1994). *Migration, culture, identity.* New York and London: Routledge.

Derrida, J. (1972/1982). *Margins of philosophy* (A. Bass, Trans.). Chicago: The University of Chicago Press.

Derrida, J. (1983a/1991). Letter to a Japanese friend (D. Wood & A. Benjamin, Trans.). In P. Kamuf (Ed.), *A Derrida reader: Between the blinds* (pp. 270–276). New York: Columbia University Press.

Derrida, J. (1983b/1995). There is no one narcissism (P. Kamuf et al., Trans.). In E. Weber (Ed.), *Points... interviews, 1974–1994* (pp. 196–215). Stanford, CA: Stanford University Press.

Derrida, J. (1989/1995). "Eating well," or the calculation of the subject (P. Kamuf et al., Trans.). In E. Weber (Ed.), *Points... interviews, 1974–1994* (pp. 255–287). Stanford, CA: Stanford University Press.

Derrida, J. (1990/2002). *Who is afraid of philosophy?* (J. Plug, Trans.). Stanford, CA: Stanford University Press.

Derrida, J. (1991a/1992). *The other heading. Reflections on today's Europe* (P. A. Brault & M. B. Naas, Trans.). Bloomington, IN: Indiana University Press.

Derrida, J. (1991b/2002). *Negotiations... Interventions and interviews, 1971–2001* (E. Rottenberg, Trans.). Stanford, CA: Stanford University Press.

Derrida, J. (1992a/2001). Talking liberties. In G. J. J. Biesta Denise & Egéa-Kuehne (Eds.), *Derrida and education* (pp. 177–185). New York and London: Routledge.

Derrida, J. (1992b/1995). *Points... Interviews, 1974–1994* (P. Kamuf et al., Trans.). Stanford, CA: Stanford University Press.

Derrida, J. (1996/1998). *Monolingualism of the other, or the prosthesis of origin* (P. Mensah, Trans.). Stanford, CA: Stanford University Press.

Derrida, J. (1997/2000). *Of hospitality* (R. Bowlby, Trans.). Stanford, CA: Stanford University Press.

Derrida, J. (2004). *I am at war with myself.* Le Monde. Retrieved from http://www.lemonde.fr/web/recherche_articleweb/1,13-0,36-375883,0.html

Derrida, J., & Ferraris, M. (1997/2001). *A taste for the secret* (G. Donis, Trans.). Oxford, UK and Cambridge, UK: Blackwell.

Derrida, J., & Stiegler, B. (2002). *Echographies of television: Filmed interview* (J. Bajorek, Trans.). Cambridge, UK: Polity Press.

Egéa-Kuehne, D. (1995). Deconstruction revisited and Derrida's call for academic responsibility. *Educational Theory, 45*(3), 293–309.

Egéa-Kuehne, D. (2001). Derrida's ethics of affirmation. In G. J. J. Biesta & D. Egéa-Kuehne (Eds.), *Derrida and education* (pp. 186–208). New York and London: Routledge.

Fanon, F. (1967/1991). *Black skin, White masks* (C. L. Markmann, Trans.). New York: Grove Press.

Greene, M. (1978). *Landscapes of learning.* New York: Teachers College Press.

Huebner, D. (1975/1999). The task of the curriculum theorist. In V. Hilli (Ed.), *The lure of the transcendent* (pp. 212–230). Mahwah, NJ: Lawrence Erlbaum Associates.

Kamuf, P. (1991). *A Derrida reader: Between the blinds.* New York: Columbia University Press.

Kohák, E. (1984). *The embers and the stars: A philosophical inquiry into the moral sense of nature.* Chicago and London: University of Chicago Press.

Lewkowich, D. (2008). *Poaching in the landwash: An interrogation of cultural meaning in a St. John's, NL collective reading group.* Master's thesis. Ottawa, ON: University of Ottawa.

Niranjana, T. (1992). *Siting translation: History, post-structuralism, and the colonial context.* Los Angeles: University of California Press.

Pinar, W. F. (1975/2000). Search for a method. In W. Pinar (Ed.), *Curriculum studies: The reconceptualization* (pp. 415–424). Troy, NY: Educator's International Press.

Pinar, W. F. (2004). *What is curriculum theory?* Mahwah, NJ: Lawrence Erlbaum Associates.

Pinar, W. F. (2007). *Intellectual advancement through disciplinarity: Verticality and horizontality in curriculum studies*. Rotterdam, The Netherlands: Sense.

Pinar, W. F., Reynolds, W., Slattery, P., & Taubman, P. (1995). *Understanding curriculum*. New York: Peter Lang.

Smith, L. T. (1999). *Decolonizing methodologies: Research and indigenous peoples*. New York and London: Zed Books.

Sue-A-Quan, T. (1999). *Cane reapers: Chinese indentured immigrants in Guyana*. Vancouver BC: Riftswood.

Wang, H. (2004). *The call from the stranger on a journey home*. New York: Peter Lang.

Nicholas Ng-A-Fook
University of Ottawa

G. H. RICHARDSON

9. IMAGINED COMMUNITIES, REAL BORDERS: CURRICULUM AND THE COMPLEX POLITICS OF NATIONAL IDENTITY CONSTRUCTION IN WESTERN CANADA

INTRODUCTION: EDUCATION AND NATIONAL IDENTITY CONSTRUCTION

Among scholars who examine nationalism and national identity, there is widespread agreement that nations use their educational systems to construct and maintain national identities. For example, Eugen Weber notes that the production of patriotism and national sentiment has been the "greatest function of the modern school" (Weber, 1976, p. 332), and Benedict Anderson refers to the role of the state in constructing a "common imagining" of the nation (Anderson, 1995. Similarly, Eric Hobsbawm and Terrance Ranger comment on national identity as a "manipulated and manufactured phenomenon" (Hobsbawm & Ranger, 1983, p. 1), and Ernest Gellner speaks of national identities as the product of "education-dependent high cultures" (Gellner, 1983). More recently, educational philosopher Walter Feinberg has identified the central role schools play "in creating a national identity and a shared loyalty" (Feinberg, 1998, p. 3).

In attempting to understand the complex ways in which the process of national identity formation plays itself out in education, a striking example can be seen in the *Western Canada Protocol for Social Studies Education*. A collaborative project of the four western provinces and three northern territories, the Protocol was released in the spring of 1999. In view of its ambitious goal, "to ultimately contribute to a Canadian spirit – a spirit that will be fundamental in creating a sense of belonging for each one of our students as he or she engages in active and responsible citizenship locally, nationally, and globally" (Government of Alberta, 1999b), and in light of current concerns over the need for public policy initiatives that preserve some sense of national or regional identity as a socially cohesive force in the face of globalization and accelerating pluralism (Barber, 1996; Jusdanis, 2001), the Protocol merits close examination.

CONTEXT

Beginning in 1993, Canada's four western provinces and three territories embarked on an unprecedented and extensive collaborative process called the Western Canada Protocol for Basic Education. Their collective aim was to create common curriculum frameworks for the core academic subjects. By 2000, this work was

J. Nahachewsky and I. Johnston (eds.), Beyond 'Presentism': Re-Imagining the Historical,
Personal, and Social Places of Curriculum, 105–114.
© *2009 Sense Publishers. All rights reserved.*

essentially complete, and regional curricula had been produced for all grade levels in mathematics, English language arts, and social studies. Of these core areas, social studies was the last to be dealt with and proved, by far, the most controversial. During the consultative process that followed the release of a draft document for the Social Studies Protocol, widespread opposition to the document emerged. In fact, this collective protest had sufficient force to result in the complete abandonment of the program in the fall of 2001 despite the immense commitment of resources, time, and money that completion of the Protocol had necessitated.

Such widespread opposition to public policy initiatives is generally rare in a Canadian context and particularly so in regards to educational reform. While it might be seen that the ambitious scope of the Protocol itself (taken together, Western Canada accounts for more than 30% of Canada's population) could have had the potential to generate a proportionately large and possibly negative response, the production of regional mathematics and English language arts curriculum had produced no comparable reaction.

From response data collected during the public consultation phase, the main source of opposition to the draft version of the Social Studies Protocol was easily identifiable. Less than 35% of respondents agreed with the Vision Statement for Social Studies presented by the draft document, and only 52% of respondents agreed with the description of the Role of Social Studies the draft document set forth (Government of Alberta, 1999b). At the heart of both the Vision Statement and Role of Social Studies was a conception of national identity that prescribed distinctive curricular outcomes for Francophones and First Nations communities in terms that many of the respondents found difficult to accept. As one respondent noted,

> The issue of "distinctive outcomes for Aboriginal and Francophone students" is extremely problematic in a number of ways. It is important to recognize the needs of these two groups, but to do so by providing distinctive outcomes creates far more problems that it solves. How can the objective of common educational goals for social studies be reconciled with the call for distinctive outcomes for Aboriginal and Francophone students? (Government of Alberta, 1999b)

In a more general sense, respondents also expressed the concern that narrowing the focus of national identity formation to specific groups was a retrograde step that ignored the fluidity and complexity of national identity formation in plural societies. As another respondent suggested,

> what is needed [in the Protocol] is a far more sophisticated understanding of what identity means, of the fact that in Canadian society individuals increasingly have multiple and layered identities, and of how our identities are socially and historically constructed as well as relational. (Government of Alberta, 1999b)

Using the example of the Western Canada Protocol for Social Studies Education, this paper will present a case study of the complexities inherent in attempting to define national identity in Canadian contexts. In addition, from an examination of the collapse of the Protocol, it will be suggested that there are lessons to be drawn for all plural nations whose education systems are engaged in similar attempts to design curricula of national identity.

Fundamentally, in terms of national identity construction, the Protocol illustrates the attempt to design a regionally based curriculum of national identity that was reflective of cultural diversity rather than cultural uniformity. In place of previous social studies curricula that tended to present national identity in more narrowly essentialist terms, the Protocol opted to speak in the plural rather than in the singular. As the draft document clearly indicated, the intent of the proposed social studies curriculum was to enable students to "appreciate and respect Aboriginal, Francophone, English language, and multiple cultural perspectives" (Government of Alberta, 1999a). And although in doing so the document performed an invaluable service in redeeming the important role Aboriginal and Francophone Canadians played in the formation of Canada's national identity, the Protocol performed a significant disservice in effectively drawing lines between identity communities in such a way that it marginalized a large and growing number of "other" Canadians (non-Anglophone ethnic minorities) who did not enjoy constitutional protection of their cultural and linguistic identities. And who, by virtue of their assigned "otherness," assumed the status of decentered peoples (Said, 1979) on the fringes of the curricular map.

THE PROTOCOL AND THE CREATION OF NATIONAL HIERARCHIES

In plural states, and especially in plural states whose demographic balance is rapidly shifting, the attempt to create Benedict Anderson's "common imagining" of the nation too easily resolves itself into a process of privilege and exclusion (Chaterjee, 1993; Laclau, 1996; Willinsky, 1998; Richardson, 2004). Or to put it more directly, into a question of whether naming the "official" constituents of national identity, creates asymmetrical power relationships between different classes of citizens (Duara, 1996). Although the Protocol attempted to address the issue of respecting diversity, it only did so in a partial and, from the responses to the draft document made during the consultative process, wholly unsatisfactory manner. In this regard, I think the Protocol must be held at fault. Effectively, it created four categories of "named" identities, but the terms under which these identities were described created their own national hierarchy that appeared to leave little doubt about the order of cultural precedence.

The initial draft document for the Protocol spoke of the need to be reflective of "Aboriginal, English language, Francophone, and multiple cultural perspectives . . . in creating a sense of belonging for each one of our students" (Government of Alberta, 1999a). In stressing the need to acknowledge Aboriginal and Francophone perspectives, the Protocol performed an act of cultural redemption that retrieved the vital role that First Nations and Francophone groups played and continue play in Canada's West and North. The nature of this redemptive function was quite clear in the section of the Protocol that described the role of Social Studies. Thus:

> Social Studies will enable Francophone students to assert their rights and responsibilities as fully participating French citizens of Canada . . .

> Social Studies will enable Aboriginal students to understand their roles and responsibilities as citizens of Aboriginal Nations and of Canada . . .

and again, later

> Social Studies will enable Francophone students to develop a sense of legitimacy and pride in their *francité* (language, identity and culture), and to participate in building a dynamic community. . . .

and

> Social Studies will enable Aboriginal students to become grounded in, and proud of their Aboriginal identity, and to participate in living and renewing their culture. (Government of Alberta, 1999a)

Canadians in all four identity categories were encouraged more generally to "thrive in their cultural and Canadian identity with a legitimate sense of belonging to their communities and to Canada" (Government of Alberta, 1999a)

In terms of the special attention accorded First Nations and Francophone Canadians, it could easily be argued that these educational intents were the legitimate and logical extension of the constitutional guarantees both groups enjoy under the Canada Act. The right of self-determination (and this clearly includes educational control) is a constitutionally sanctioned entitlement of First Nations citizens, and Francophones have linguistic and cultural rights (again, with clear implications for educational control) enshrined in the act. But for the two groups not named in the same terms, and particularly for non-Anglophone ethnic minorities, rather vaguely described as groups representing *multiple cultural perspectives*, effective relegation to the status of unspecified other resulted in widespread criticism of the Protocol when it was presented at consultation forums.

As already indicated, in plural states, the attempt to create what Benedict Anderson (1995) has called "a deep horizontal comradeship" of national affiliation is troubled by difficult questions. For example, is it possible to establish a commonly held identity in the midst of accelerating diversity (Soysal, 1994; Castles & Davidson, 2000; Richardson, 2002)? In choosing an overarching set of *national* characteristics on which to base the nation, whose identities are to be included and whose identities left out (Feinberg, 1998)? And as a result of choices that are made in this regard, are symbolic boundaries created between those groups whose identities carry with them the legitimizing sanction of being named as official constituents of the nation as opposed to those who remained unnamed (Mitchell & Russell, 1996)?

In plural states, there are no easy answers to these questions; they remain, instead, the contested ground on which such notions as national identity, social cohesion, and, ultimately, democracy itself, are played out (Mouffe, 1995; Brown, 2000; Richardson, 2006). If questions about the viability, form, and content of national identity are troublesome in plural nations, in states such as Canada that

Kymlicka (1995, 2001) typifies as both multinational and polyethnic, they assume a particular complexity.

For political philosopher Will Kymlicka, the terms "polyethnicity" and "multi-nationalism" indicate the degree to which modern states have complex politico-demographic structures that are no longer easily subsumed under the term "multiculturalism." By polyethnicity, Kymlicka means those ethno-cultural minorities that have resisted assimilation and that wish to preserve their linguistic and cultural identities *without* demanding the rights of self-government or territorial recognition (Kymlicka, 1995, p. 14). Multinationalism, on the other hand, implies that specific ethno-cultural minorities (and in Canada this specifically means Francophones and First Nations groups) have achieved the right to a degree of self-government and territorial recognition that Kymlicka notes are both "inherent" and "permanent" (Kymlicka, 1995, p. 30).

In response to the complexity generated by Canada's multinational, polyethnic structure, Charles Taylor (1993) has speculated that the only way to create a sustainable sense of national identity in Canada is the through acknowledgement of what he terms the "deep diversity" that binds us all together in a common national project. By "deep diversity" Taylor means that

> a plurality of ways of belonging would also be acknowledged and accepted. Someone of, say, Italian extraction in Toronto or Ukrainian extraction in Edmonton might indeed feel Canadian as a bearer of individual rights in a multicultural mosaic . . . . But this person might nevertheless accept that a Québecois or a Cree or a Dene might belong in a very different way, that these persons were Canadian through being members of their national communities. (Taylor, 1993, p. 183)

And while Taylor acknowledges that such a diffusion of the more traditional structures of national identity may violate the Western (and modernist) vision of the liberal state, he concludes that states such as Canada can only survive by adopting the "pluralist mould" (p. 184).

Accepting Taylor's "plurality of ways of belonging" as a structure around which national identity can be constructed is not an easy task—Taylor himself has acknowledged Canada's "unresolvable national identity" (p. 111). But any attempt to formulate a curriculum of national identity in plural cultures that ignores this notion risks situating national identity in a modernist paradigm that would tend to portray minority cultures (and particularly those polyethnic communities not protected by constitutional guarantees) solely in terms of their contribution to the health and development of the dominant culture (McCarthy, Crichlow, Dimitriadis & Dolby, 2005).

In opting to privilege multinationalism over polyethnicity, the Protocol failed to take into account the notion that national identity in plural societies such as Canada is fluid, hybrid, and evolving. As Douglass (1998) indicates, "*how* as opposed to *where* [identity communities meet] is subject to constant negotiation" (p. 88). For example, the ethno-cultural composition of the population varies significantly throughout Canada's West and is in rapid transition. As a consequence, the

Protocol's consignment of non-Anglophone minorities to the vague status of "multiple cultural perspectives" flies in the face of the evolving demographics of the region. Using recent census data in British Columbia, for example, it emerges that 9.8% of the population is either Francophone or has some association with *francité*, while those with Asian origins account for 19.4% of the population. In Alberta, the same data reveals that 5.31% of the population is of aboriginal descent, while 28.4% of the population is of non-British, non-French European origin (Government of Canada, 2001). It must be emphasized here that atonement for past injustices done to First Nations and Francophone minorities in terms of their virtual exclusion from various regional curricula is clearly much more than a numbers game; in the case of the Protocol it represented a genuine (and much needed) attempt at cultural redress, but, in the context of Taylor's notion of deep diversity and the increasingly plural context of schooling in Canada, questions emerge about whether cultural redress justified the Protocol's relegation of non-Anglophone minorities to subordinate or subaltern status.

Historically, this move was of particular concern not merely because it ignored the significant (and growing) proportion non-Anglophone cultural minorities make up of the West's population, but because it effectively represented a substantial retreat from previous curricula that acknowledged the officially multicultural nature of Canada. For example, in the 1987 Grade 10 Manitoba social studies curriculum, a 3-week study of multiculturalism was mandated around the statement that "Canada is a multicultural society [in which] the changing dynamics of the makeup of the population and cross cultural interaction poses many challenges" (Government of Manitoba, 1987). The same acknowledgement of the role pluralism plays in national identity can be seen in the student learning expectations of the 2001 Grade 11 British Columbia social studies curriculum which specifies that students will "identify elements that contribute to the regional, cultural, and ethnic diversity of Canadian society" and "describe the role of cultural pluralism in shaping Canadian identity" (Government of British Columbia, 2001).

The Protocol's retreat from acceptance of the reality of cultural pluralism was all the more curious when one examines the region's history. Since Confederation, successive immigrations of non-Anglophone minorities (Ukrainians, Japanese, Germans, Chinese, to name a few) have played a significant role in developing the resource-based economy of the West and in giving the region its vibrant cultural identity (Friesen, 1987; Cavanaugh & Mouat, 1996). Their treatment in the Protocol, their effective relegation to *second-class citizen* status, must be viewed a serious shortcoming of a document that attempted, in its own words, to "have the concept of Canadian citizenship at its heart" (Government of Alberta, 1999a).

THE PROTOCOL AND CULTURAL DIFFERENCE

In plural nations, the emergent conception of national identity as the "unstable, never-secured effect of a process of enunciation of cultural difference" (Scott, 1995, p. 11) has not yet achieved wide acceptance. As Roger Collins notes, "That both cultural differences and social conflict are inherent features of any pluralistic society is a perspective that remains at odds with the mainstream perspective that treats social conflict as social disease" (1993, p. 202). This equation is founded on the modernist idea that social harmony is the ideal in pluralistic states, but as Chantal Mouffe (1995) reminds us, harmony can easily be a mask for assimilation and repression:

> Instead of trying to reduce the existing plurality through devices like the veil of ignorance . . . we need to develop a positive attitude toward differences, even if they lead to conflict and impede the realization of harmony. Any understanding of pluralism whose objective is to reach harmony is ultimately a negation of the positive value of diversity and difference. (p. 44)

Mouffe's warning about the dangers of subsuming difference under the drive to create social cohesion is echoed in recent curriculum scholarship that suggests the need to reconceptualize curriculum as fundamentally plural and multi-vocal. In Yatta Kanu's terms, such a reconceptualization implies both a rigorous deconstruction of the cultural (and colonial) biases of existing curricula as well as a creative imagining of a curriculum open to "multiple discourses, and plural assumptions and strategies" (Kanu, 2003, p. 79)

To the degree that the draft version of the Protocol emphasized the harmonious and consensual nature of constructing Canadian identity around an all-encompassing sense of cultural diversity—for example, the document reminds us that one of the roles of social studies is to enable students to "celebrate and strengthen the Canadian identity" (Government of Alberta, 1999a)—it fell prey to the assimilationist and repressive tendencies Mouffe and Collins warn of and significantly short of Kanu's generous vision of a more open, discursive curriculum. What is more, to the degree that it created a named national hierarchy, the Protocol fell prey to a reductionist approach to national identity formation that has deep roots in modernism and that acts at once as a privileging and exclusionary mechanism (Richardson, 2006).

As postcolonial scholar Homi K. Bhabha notes, "the first duty of the state is to 'give' the nation its cultural identity and above all to develop it" (Bhabha, 1990, p. 178). But this process necessarily involves the naming of the constituent groups making up the nation and, as Hobsbawm and Ranger (1983) remind us, the construction of a sustaining mythic identity structure—or invented tradition—around those constituent groups. It then follows that symbolic borders are created between those groups who are named as constituting the "core" elements of the nation and those groups who are not named in the same terms. The difficulty the Protocol had in naming non-Anglophone ethno-cultural minorities as constituent elements of Canadian identity—they are variously referred to [in lower case] as groups representing "multiple cultural perspectives" (Government of Alberta, 1999a), or "diverse cultural perspectives" (Government of Alberta, 2000)—suggests an implied national ranking structure when compared directness of language when the document refers to "Aboriginal, Francophone, [and] English language perspectives" (Government of Alberta, 1999a).

The existence of subtle, yet nonetheless undeniable, borders that separate and delineate the power and position of named from unnamed groups can perhaps best be seen in anecdotal accounts that highlight the boundaries between identity communities in plural states such as Canada. For example, in her investigation of the closure of a multicultural school in Ontario, Bonny Norton-Peirce cites the poignant comments of Maria, an Italian Canadian student: "A lot of commercials you see are about ethnic people. They show commercials about Canada and different ethnic people. And it's like they're trying to say, 'This is an ethnic country, be proud.' But then you get the people themselves in Canada who just don't look at Canada that way" (Norton-Peirce, 1995, p. 175). Such observations suggest a more problematic and ambivalent understanding of pluralism, both in terms of how it affects Canadian identity and of how it might be presented in the curriculum.

CONCLUSION

The effort to design a viable Western Canadian Protocol for Social Studies can be seen as a kind of cautionary tale that illustrates the difficulties that education systems in all plural societies face as they attempt to construct national identity across what postcolonial scholar Homi Bhabha has called "a bar of difference" (Bhabha, 1990). What is more, the failure of the Protocol to establish any kind of consensus view of national identity suggests the complexities of implementing social studies curricula, even those limited to regionally based identities, that do not respect local or provincial realities. And finally, questions about official perceptions of cultural difference and the impact those perceptions had on the design of the Protocol must be raised. If the intent was to create a regionally based curriculum of national identity around the acknowledgement of cultural difference, of different ways of expressing "Canadianness," then such a curriculum should have genuinely recognized the open-ended and ambiguous process of national identity formation in diverse societies rather than have narrowed it to particular acts of cultural redemption and preservation. To have done otherwise was to have risked the construction of significant boundaries of privilege and recognition between identity communities in Canada and, ironically, to have reproduced some of the same exclusionary processes the Protocol was designed to remedy in the first place.

REFERENCES

Anderson, B. (1995). *Imagined communities: Reflections on the origin and spread of nationalism*. London: Verso.

Barber, G. (1996). *Jihad vs. McWorld: How globalism and tribalism are reshaping the world*. New York: Ballantine Books.

Bhabha, H. K. (1990). *Narrating the nation*. In H. K. Bhabha (Ed.), *The nation and narration* (pp. 1–7). London: Routledge.

Brown, D. (2000). *Contemporary nationalism: Civic, ethnocultural and multicultural politics*. London: Routledge.

Castles, S., & Davidson, A. (2000). *Citizenship and migration: Globalization and the politics of belonging*. New York: Routledge.

Cavanaugh, C., & Mouat, J. (Eds.). (1996). *Making Western Canada: Essays on European colonization and settlement*. Toronto, ON: Garamond Press.

Chaterjee, P. (1993). *The nation and its fragments: Colonial and postcolonial histories*. Princeton, NJ: Princeton University Press.

Cochrane, C. N., & Wallace, W. S. (1926). *This Canada of ours.* Toronto, ON: National Council on Education.

Collins, R. (1993). Responding to cultural diversity in our schools. In L. Castenell & W. F. Pinar (Eds.), *Understanding curriculum as racial text: Representations of identity and difference in education* (pp. 195–208). Albany, NY: State University of New York Press.

Douglass, W. A. (1998). A western perspective on an eastern interpretation of where north meets south: Pyrenean borderland cultures. In T. M. Wilson & H. Donnan (Eds.), *Border identities: Nation and state at international frontiers* (pp. 74–91). Cambridge, UK: Cambridge University Press.

Duara, P. (1996). Historicizing national identity, or who imagines what and when. In G. Eley & R. G. Suny (Eds.), *Becoming national: A reader* (pp. 53–71). Oxford, UK: Oxford University Press.

Feinberg, W. (1998). *Common schools/uncommon identities: National unity and cultural difference.* London: Yale University Press.

Friesen, G. (1987). *The Canadian prairies: A history.* Toronto, ON: University of Toronto Press.

Gellner, E. (1983). *Nations and nationalism.* Oxford, UK: Blackwell.

Government of Alberta. (1999a). *Foundation document for the western protocol for social studies.* Edmonton, AB: Alberta Learning.

Government of Alberta. (1999b). *Response document to the Western Canada protocol for social studies.* Edmonton, AB: Alberta Learning.

Government of Alberta. (2000). *Foundation document for the development of the common curriculum framework for social studies kindergarten to grade 12.* Edmonton, AB: Alberta Learning.

Government of British Columbia. (2001). *Social studies 11.* Victoria, BC: Ministry of Education.

Government of Manitoba. (1987). *Social studies senior 1: Canada today.* Winnipeg, ON: Department of Education Training and Youth.

Government of Canada. (2002). *2001 census data.* Ottawa, ON: Queen's Printer.

Hobsbawm, E., & Ranger, T. (1983). *The invention of tradition.* Cambridge, UK: Cambridge University Press.

Jusdanis, G. (2001). *The necessary nation.* Princeton, NJ: Princeton University Press.

Kanu, Y. (2003). Curriculum as cultural practice: Postcolonial imagination. *Journal of the Canadian Association for Curriculum Studies, 1*(1), 67–81.

Kymlicka, W. (1995). *Multicultural citizenship: A liberal theory of minority rights.* Oxford, UK: Clarendon Press.

Kymlicka, W. (2001). *Politics in the vernacular: Nationalism, multiculturalism and citizenship.* Oxford, UK: Oxford University Press.

Laclau, E. (1996). Universalism, particularism, and the question of identity. In E. Wilmsen & P. McAllister (Eds.), *The making of political identities* (pp. 71–83). Chicago: University of Chicago Press.

McCarthy, C., Crichlow, W., Dimitriadis, G., & Dolby, N. (Eds.). (2005). *Race identity and representation in education* (2nd ed.). New York: RoutledgeFalmer.

Mitchell, M., & Russell, D. (1996). Immigration, citizenship and the nation-state in the new Europe. In B. Jenkins & S. Sofos (Eds.), *Nation and identity in contemporary Europe* (pp. 65–84). London: Routledge.

Mouffe, C. (1995). Democratic politics and the question of identity. In J. Rajchman (Ed.), *The identity in question* (pp. 33–46). London: Routledge.

Peirce, B. N. (1995). Learning the hard way: Maria's story. In B. Kanpol & P. McLaren (Eds.), *Critical multiculturalism: Uncommon voices in a common struggle* (pp. 165–196). Westport, CN: Bergin and Garvey.

Richardson, G. H. (2002). *The death of the good Canadian: Teachers, national identities and the social studies curriculum.* New York: Peter Lang.

Richardson, G. H. (2004). Nostalgia and national identity: The history and social studies curriculum of Alberta and Ontario at the end of empire. In P. Buckner (Ed.), *Canada and the end of empire* (pp. 249–267). Vancouver, BC: UBC Press.

Richardson, G. H. (2006). Singular nation, plural possibilities: Reimagining curriculum as third space. In Y. Kanu (Ed.), *Curriculum as cultural practice: Postcolonial imaginations* (pp. 283–301). Toronto, ON: University of Toronto Press.

Said, E. (1979). *Orientalism*. New York: Vintage Books.

Scott, J. (1995). Multiculturalism and the politics of identity. In J. Rajchman (Ed.), *The identity in question* (pp. 9–18). London: Routledge.

Soysal, Y. (1994). *Limits of citizenship: Migrants and postnational membership in Europe*. Chicago: University of Chicago Press.

Taylor, C. (1993). *Reconciling the solitudes: Essays on Canadian federalism and nationalism*. Montreal, QC: McGill-Queen's University Press.

Weber, E. (1976). *Peasants into Frenchmen: The modernization of rural France 1870–1914*. Stanford, CA: Stanford University Press.

Willinsky, J. (1998). *Learning to divide the world: Education at empire's end*. Minneapolis, MN: University of Minnesota Press.

Dr. G. H. Richardson
University of Alberta

SUZANNE DE FROY

10. USING IMAGE AS A WAY INTO A KNOWLEDGE DOMAIN

INTRODUCTION

Lave and Wenger's (1991, 1998) notion of Communities of Practice is a powerful construct to assist curriculum designers in answering the question, How does one establish movement from the periphery to the center of the literacy domain? My model illustrates how the concept of image promotes the ability to develop deeper understanding. Two approaches show how adolescents are assisted in creating and interpreting images that promote higher levels of engagement for them in the written word.

– External images provided by videos, graphics, or art assist students' efforts to enter the realm of deeper understanding.
– Internal images through guided imagery based on students' life experiences provides a context to connect content to curriculum objectives.

Critical components in this model are knowledge forms, self-reflection, and shared discourse. Students come to realize how different words or scenes can be interpreted, which ultimately establishes meaning for them and a way into a knowledge domain that was previously inaccessible.

BACKGROUND

As a classroom teacher and researcher working in an alternative high school setting for more than 5 years, I listened to struggling adolescents and realized decoding or encoding while constructing meaning can be extremely difficult for them, confirming the challenges identified by Bereiter (2002) and Willows (1987). The journey toward this realization began on a day I was using the traditional instructional strategy of reading aloud. I noticed one of my students had her eyes closed with her head on the desk, and I tried to calmly encourage her engagement by saying, "Come on, you know it's important to learn how to read by following along." She replied, "I'm listening to you, Miss. It's just too much work to get the pictures in my head at the same time I'm trying to figure out the words."

Her comments marked the beginning of an inquiry for me that recognizes how important it is for many students to have an opportunity to access an image based on personal understanding before entering into the symbolic world of words. As a doctoral candidate and teacher researcher, my unpublished manuscript, *Developing Literacy With Adolescents* (2005), positioned my role as a curriculum designer

J. Nahachewsky and I. Johnston (eds.), Beyond 'Presentism': Re-Imagining the Historical, Personal, and Social Places of Curriculum, 115–121.

attempting to improve student learning by understanding the philosophy, psychology, and epistemology of sound learning theory.

THE GENERAL STRUGGLE

Literacy refers to the ability to read and write while establishing meaning for oneself and others. Recent research has acknowledged that acquiring fluency is a complex process involving the coordination of multiple internal and external attributes (Jetton & Dole, 2004). For students who demonstrate difficulties, many intervention resources have been designed for a younger audience but not appropriate to engage or sustain a teenager's interest. Therefore, classroom instruction has an opportunity to significantly influence outcomes, as suggested by Guthrie and Wigfield (2000) and Alvermann (2002).

With the dearth of curriculum materials promoting literacy development for the adolescent, high school teachers have been required to seek answers beyond the traditional resources available in their immediate school communities. As a curriculum designer, I assumed the responsibility of developing units informed by the knowledge of my students and by current research that reflects an interlinked cycle of analysis, design, development, implementation, and evaluation.

Analysis requires positioning individual students while establishing a class baseline at varying levels of competence, interest, attitudes, and confidence to engage. Teenagers attending our alternative facility face a wide range of ability and/or motivation issues. Generally, they have a history that reflects a lack of success in the regular secondary program, so learning has been disrupted or they are at risk of dropping out.

A primary and challenging goal of the school's program is to rebuild confidence and self-esteem by providing opportunities that allow for success. Recent research suggests that motivation to engage in learning is related to a student's ability to read and write (Alvermann, 2002). Completed diagnostics indicate that over 80% of our students read at Grade 6 level or below. Observations of willingness factors determined that many struggling adolescents would take extreme measures not to reveal the fact that they have reading and writing difficulties. For example, avoidance or noncompliant behaviours would often surface when learning required engagement in a literacy activity.

Drawing on the Knowledge Building research of the Bereiter and Scardamalia (1998), I approached curriculum design with the intent to create conditions that would encourage a willingness among the students to accept a legitimate position as both learner and teacher of others to develop literacy skills and negotiate meaning. Wenger (1998) described negotiated meaning as a dynamic interaction that is historical, contextual, and unique, leading to a gradual achievement. I hoped that once the students had secured the image of learner and teacher as a valid conception for themselves, they would be able to legitimately engage in various forms of inquiry to advance their knowledge and resolve problems of understanding.

I brought these ideas and concerns to the attention of reading specialist, Dr. Dale Willows, who suggested using a multisensory approach as a theoretical perspective to inform pedagogical decisions and provide a balanced and flexible "literacy diet."

COLLECTIVE IMAGINATION AND IMAGE INTERPRETATION

Wenger (1998) suggested that learning has to do with the development of our Communities of Practices and our "ability to negotiate meaning" (p. 96). Interpreting everyday life experiences organizes our thinking and creates points of focus through the combined action of reification and participation. The concept of reification refers to understanding given a congealed form, which reflects various representations of literacy and becoming a product or a point of focus around which the negotiation of meaning becomes organized. The effort of creating a new idea or knowledge involves an active process and may be illustrated in our attempts to formulate understanding through discursive activities such as perceiving, reflecting, interpreting, explaining, describing, and representing. Process and product always imply one another, so congealed forms such as concepts, theories, narratives, stories, and tools will be created in both the written or oral tradition. Participation is considered action in relation to others as an active process of mutual engagement or belonging that represents community membership. Wenger has advanced the notion that negotiation of meaning is the interplay of the duality of reification and participation, and that identity as form of competence is formed through the combined action. For the struggling student, creating the conditions for participation was viewed as the key to learning and entry into the literacy domain.

Adopting a multisensory approach, I introduced students to the foundational knowledge of a number of curriculum disciplines by using images from various mediums, including videos, documentaries, art, and graphics. As a first approach in the design and development of a unit, I sidestepped the demanding cognitive effort of initially decoding traditional textbook information and explanations. Another consideration was the form of personal knowledge to be advanced.

Bereiter (2002) identified six forms of personal knowledge that characterize how we relate to the outside world. These forms, which deserve special attention from an educational point of view, include the following:

- Skills (as forms of procedural knowledge or "knowing-how" to decode or encode the written language).
- Statable knowledge (that is communicable to others, based on facts and information that can be discussed, evaluated, or reflected on).
- Episodic knowledge (as memory of events experienced or stories encountered, allowing for the accumulation of episodes to aid in making connections that are both factual and fictional).
- Regulative knowledge (to get yourself to function in an activity and be able to summarize, review, and raise questions including thinking critically about one's favoured ideas).
- Impressionistic knowledge (refers to the realm of positive or negative feelings and impressions that also influence our actions—in reading it may influence our interpretations, and in our writing it may influence our creative effort).
- Implicit understanding (refers to those aspects of informal knowledge that characterize relationships, such as the knowledge necessary to tie things together, make predictions, make connections to other domain experiences, to

other moments in history, and to our own life experiences, leading to the generation of new ideas).

By considering this multidimensional perspective, teachers can go beyond focusing on developing a student's basic set of skills and abilities.

The implementation phase of curriculum planning depended on my creating conditions that allowed students and teacher together to stop, think, and talk about the relative content of the discipline. Images captured the students' interest and drew on their visual and auditory capabilities to help them in interpreting the images. I routinely used conversational language in giving meaning to key foundational facts and information. Misconceptions became opportunities for clarification and further explanations by others. In a short period of time, students felt comfortable that they could contribute to the learning process and became willing to "talk aloud" in the oral tradition prior to engaging in the written word.

As meaning was being established through discussions, I incorporated fundamental literacy elements of phonology and morphology as explicit tools to assist students in the symbol coding process. Key vocabulary was made explicit by having students create their personal graphic representations for a community "word wall." To clarify key concepts, I prepared an initial bank of questions about the images based on a continuum, with a range of difficulty proceeding from making simple direct or indirect questions to making critical connections between the discipline and society, culture, and history. With flexibility thus incorporated, the "I wonder why" questions supported creativity and a willingness to further investigate problems that the students themselves genuinely cared about. In this way, success was possible and expected, and movement was evidenced as students shifted from the periphery toward the center of the literacy domain, refining their knowledge at deeper levels.

CREATING INTERNAL IMAGES THROUGH GUIDED IMAGERY

Guided visualizations built on the initial findings of image interpretation as a way into a domain offered another venue for me with students who struggled with literacy. As I encouraged them to move from the periphery of the literacy domain into the center, students were able to create their own internal images so that meaning was constructed prior to engaging in symbol coding processes. The *Journal of Mental Imagery* recognizes that the use of imagery is growing in a variety of disciplines, including education and special education, creative arts, behavioural studies, sociology, psycholinguistics, literature, clinical psychology, and philosophy. Drawing on the work of David E. Hunt (1987, 1992), students' life experiences were used to represent episodic knowledge, as suggested by Bereiter (2002), and served as a valuable resource to bring out self-perceptions, implicit theories, and personal images.

A distinctive space is critical to ease student participation into guided imagery. From a postcultural perspective, the roles and expectations inherent in human relationships will be expressed as values, beliefs, behaviours, rules, products, and symbols that bind teachers and their students together. Struggling adolescent students often need to overcome the perceived shame associated with their difficulties and must feel safe before they will attempt to express how they are interpreting their personal image. Therefore, the resulting interactions on personal and community levels must reflect a desired form of discourse that is achievable through mutual agreements.

Participation in guided imagery has to be voluntary so that each individual is as open as possible to the experience. Teachers situate various scenes so that students imagine themselves partaking in historical or imagined events. In each scene, students close their eyes and listen to the teacher's voice calmly outlining various sensory details designed to focus their attention. After a brief pause to collect their thoughts, the students write an account of the image they have pictured, without worrying about spelling or punctuation. Then they sit quietly as others process and describe their personal images. Integrity is demonstrated as each individual respects the privacy of others by staying in their own space while connecting to the collective effort. This courtesy promotes freedom of expression, and personal dignity is honoured by respecting the unique way others understand the world.

Content for guided imagery is derived from the curriculum while ensuring relevancy to the students' lives. Acknowledging that an adolescent's life is filled with indecision and choices that are made on a day-to-day basis, it is easy for us to recognize that presentation of alternatives is at the heart of numerous literacy sources. A favourite for the students, which eased participation into this personal experience, is based on Robert Frost's poem "The Road Not Taken." For example, the teacher might situate the imagined opening scene with the following:

> It is a Saturday morning in the Fall, and you realize you are free to do whatever you would like for the entire day. You decide to return to the woods. It is a place you have been to many times before, a safe place. So you finish your breakfast and put on your coat, and as you step outside you notice a difference in the air as compared to the inside of your home. After a few seconds, you set out for your walk. As you make your way towards the woods, you look for the old familiar path, but as you approach the opening, you notice another path off in the distance, a path you have never before explored. You notice that it has hardly been traveled, and you pause for a moment to decide which way you are going to go. Which path do you choose?

After a brief pause, students are asked to explain their decision in writing, all the while keeping their thoughts to themselves. Cascading images are generated through a series of additional questions, each designed to guide their experience of the forest so the students can visualize possible surroundings, picture the movement of birds or small animals, hear imaginary streams, feel the fresh air against their skin, and smell the earth beneath their feet. Closing thoughts ask the students to describe how the experiences made them feel. Descriptions about their special place, often expressed a sense of peace or calm spoke, with hopes of returning once again. As words capture initial impressions, the resulting text is considered a first draft, ideal in the form produced. Robert Frost's poem is then read and discussed as a literary form designed to express a moment of indecision, choice, and consequence.

By connecting the concrete to the abstract, the students are able to further explore this common human condition by considering whether the different road was the right one for Frost. It is common for students to suggest that for Frost, it was the only one that he could have taken. As there is no right or wrong decision, students willingly share their decision and experiences. A number of writing activities are also designed to extend the activity, such as elaborating, using adjectives and adverbs to further describe their experiences, or revising their initial draft into the past tense so they could construct a letter to a childhood friend who might have understood this personal trip into the woods.

Interestingly, my teacher colleagues have read some students' work, noting the change in engagement. At times, these colleagues asked about details of the field trip or location of the woods that generated such prolific accounts of their experience, not realizing that the students simply took the journey into their own imaginations.

CONCLUSION

Imagery provides the opportunity for teachers who assume the role of curriculum designers to consider numerous forms of student knowledge while determining a performance level along a developmental continuum. Through thoughtful planning, students may realize how different words or scenes can be interpreted, ultimately establishing meaning and a way into a knowledge domain that was previously inaccessible. Bereiter (2002) suggests that adolescents' personal knowledge is richly varied in ways that reflect the differences in their lives and backgrounds. As curriculum designers, teachers need to consider elements of knowledge and incorporate opportunities for self-reflection and community discourse to further levels of personal confidence and competence in the domain of literacy. Teaching students to revise their own writing so the underlying image is clear is accomplished by helping them to be better listeners, writers, and readers—this is teaching thinking. Imagery as a way into a knowledge domain holds considerable promise for an intellectually passive student who is introduced to the possibility of actively directing his or her own thoughts, thereby creating movement from the periphery of a knowledge domain toward the center.

REFERENCES

Alvermann, D. (2002). Effective literacy instruction for adolescents. *Journal of Literacy Research.* Retrieved April 2, 2009, from http://www.coe.uga.edu/lle/faculty/alvermann/effective2.pdf

Bereiter, C. (2002). *Education and mind in the knowledge age.* Mahwah, NJ: Lawrence Erlbaum Associates.

Bereiter, C., & Scardamalia, M. (1998). Beyond bloom's taxonomy: Rethinking knowledge for the knowledge age. In A. Hargreaves, A. Lieberman, M. Fullan, & D. Hopkins (Eds.), *International handbook of educational change* (Part 2, pp. 675–692). Dordrecht, The Netherlands: Kluwer Academic.

De Froy, S. (2005). *Developing literacy with adolescents.* Unpublished manuscript. Department of Human Development and Applied Psychology, OISE/UT.

Frost, R. (1930). *A pocket book of Robert Frost's poems.* New York: Washington Square Press.

Guthrie, J. T., & Wigfield, A. (2000). Engagement and motivation in reading. In M. L. Kamil, P. B. Mosenthal, P. D. Pearson, & R. Barr (Eds.), *Handbook of reading research* (Vol. 3, pp. 403–422). Mahwah, NJ: Erlbaum.

Hunt, D. E. (1987). *Beginning with ourselves.* Toronto, ON: OISE Press.

Hunt, D. E. (1992). *The renewal of personal energy.* Toronto, ON: OISE Press.

Jetton, T. L., & Dole, J. A. (2004). *Adolescent literacy research and practice.* New York: Guilford Press.

Lave, J., & Wenger, E. (1991). *Situated learning: Legitimate peripheral participation.* Cambridge, MA: Cambridge University Press.

Scardamalia, M., & Bereiter, C. (2003). Knowledge building. In *Encyclopedia in education* (2nd ed., pp. 1370–1373). New York: Macmillan Reference.

Wenger, E. (1998). *Communities of practice: Learning, meaning, and identity.* Cambridge, MA: Cambridge University Press.

Willows, D. (1987). *The psychology of illustration: Basic research.* New York: Springer-Verlag.

Wyatt-Smith, C., & Cumming, J. (2000). Examining the literacy-curriculum relationship. *Linguistics and Education, 11*(4), 295–312.

Suzanne De Froy, Ed. D.
University of Windsor, N9B 3P4

KUMARI V. BECK

11. SEEKING THE "INTER": CONTEXTUALIZING, CONTESTING AND RECONCEPTUALIZING INTERNATIONALIZATION OF CURRICULUM

SEEKING

My particular inquiry into the historical and cultural spaces of curriculum is located in the terrain of internationalization of higher education in North America. The exploration of the internationalization of postsecondary curriculum was prompted by my experience of teaching in international teacher education programs in a Canadian university. Our students came seeking a Canadian or North American content, while we instructors were encouraged to internationalize our curriculum so that it became relevant to our learners. What does it mean to internationalize curriculum, when is it useful to do so, and how can it be implemented?

These and other questions regarding international education face practitioners as the internationalization of higher education in Canada becomes more prevalent. A majority of Canadian postsecondary institutions agree that internationalization is a high priority for their institutions (Association of Universities and Colleges of Canada [AUCC], 2007). Indeed, it seems that today almost every postsecondary institution "does" international education. While international activities and programs proliferate, however, the research is barely catching up. Mestenhauser's (1998) observation that the literature in the field "though rich and plentiful— remains . . . accidental, occasional, and random" (p. xviii) holds true of the current situation. It is not surprising, then, that many describe the internationalization of higher education as a site of conceptual confusion for practitioners, students, and scholars alike (Bond, 2006; Knight, 2000; Mestenhauser, 1998).

The experience of fragmentation is reflected not only in the divide between theory and practice, but also within the very practices themselves. Internationalization has been defined as a "process" that integrates "an international, intercultural or global dimension into the purpose, functions or delivery of postsecondary education" (Knight, 2004, p. 11). Although frequently defined as process, internationalization continues to be commonly understood and measured in terms of activities (Beck, 2001), and issues related to intercultural understanding, difference, and diversity rank low in interest and/or activity (Knight, 2000). Although curricular issues have been identified as high priorities in Canadian internationalization, activity in matters relating to internationalizing the curriculum remains sporadic (AUCC, 2007; Knight, 2000). In brief, there appears to be little understanding of the value of, and necessity for, attending to these issues (Beck, 2001).

J. Nahachewsky and I. Johnston (eds.), Beyond 'Presentism': Re-Imagining the Historical, Personal, and Social Places of Curriculum, 123–137.
© *2009 Sense Publishers. All rights reserved.*

The emergence of a worldwide field of curriculum studies that engages in cross-border and cross-disciplinary conversations provides opportunities to explore "theoretical and practical possibilities for building new transnational and transcultural solidarities in postcolonial curriculum inquiry" (Gough, 2004, p. 1). As Gough further explained, "building such solidarities requires a rethinking of the ways in which we perform and represent curriculum inquiry, so that curriculum work within a global knowledge economy does not merely assimilate national (local) curriculum discourses/practices into an imperial (global) archive" (p. 1). This "building of solidarities" exemplifies the notion of curriculum as complicated conversation (Pinar, 2004).

These conversations have not, unfortunately, penetrated the instructional spaces or academic theorising in the internationalization of the postsecondary classrooms. I am proposing that the notion of the internationalization of curriculum as presently conceived in the field of international education be reconceptualized so that it aligns more closely to developments in the field of curriculum studies, or, at the very least, is more open to its influences. This is a complex task given the paradigm tensions and rationales within the internationalization process, which have been acknowledged but hardly explored. I contend that the tendency in such a climate is to address curriculum with simplistic definitions and to avoid complicated conversation. My hope is that explorations such as the present one, and similar lines of questioning, will interrupt and create new spaces that will provide opportunities for these conversations to occur. How might this dialogue move the field past the fragmentation of curriculum as a particular product of a specific discipline? In what ways will this conversation influence the cultural space of curriculum? And how can the spaces of internationalization be transformed and reimagined?

The search must begin, I argue, by contextualizing the notion of internationalization. I will provide a brief overview of how internationalization of higher education and the internationalization of curriculum are understood. In order to contest present approaches to the task of internationalizing curriculum, it will be necessary to further contextualize by showing the connection between globalization and higher education. I will argue that present practices of internationalization are heavily influenced, even driven, by globalization and a market ideology. This has resulted in a particular view of curriculum—curriculum-as-product—a view that promotes the commodification of knowledge. I begin the process of reconceptualizing the "internationalization of curriculum" by borrowing from parallel conversations within globalization theory (Arjun Appadurai's concept of "scapes"), postcolonial thought (Homi Bhabha and "third space") and the internationalization of curriculum studies (William Pinar, Ted Aoki, and others). In the process, I transform isolated strains of thought into a complicated conversation, a conversation that will reside in the "between." Understanding the complexity of our present condition must become part of our task for curriculum, for it is this understanding that will make possible the seeking of the "inter" in "international."

CONTEXTUALIZING/CONTESTING

Although the university itself has long been considered international in its fundamental mandate for research and scholarly activity, academics acknowledge that the actual phenomenon of internationalization is a recent one (Lemasson, 1999). Used loosely and often interchangeably with "globalization," the term is understood differently by practitioners, scholars, administrators, and staff, depending on their location and the particular activities of their program.

The lack of understanding of the terms and the focus on activities and practice reflects the absence of scholarly attention to, and lack of discussion regarding, the notion of internationalization. While some references link internationalization with multiculturalism and interdependency (Francis, 1993), and more recently there has been a "recognition and valuing of diversity, especially cognitive diversity which develops in different cultural contexts" (Bond, 2006, p. 2), the popular route has been to adopt Jane Knight's definition of internationalization as "the process of integrating an international, intercultural or global dimension into the purpose, functions or delivery of post-secondary education" (Knight, 2003, p. 2). There are many references to the "complexity" and "confusion" of the field (e.g., Knight, 2004, p. 9), yet few scholars concern themselves with the theoretical distinctions among, and the problems associated with, this complexity and confusion. While advocating for a common definition and for parameters that will help to advance internationalization, de Wit (2002) commented, "While one can understand this happening, it is not helpful for internationalization to become a catchall phrase for everything and anything international" (p. 114).

Internationalization of curriculum has been identified as a key strategy of internationalization of higher education in Canada (AUCC, 2007; Knight, 2000), and the support for internationalized curricula in the literature on international education is extensive (see Harari, 1981; Francis, 1993; Knight, 1994; Maidstone, 1995; Mestenhauser, 1998; Raby, 1995; Scott, 1993; van der Wende, 1995). Raby (1995), for example, argued that "internationalization ideals predict a holistic, transcultural environment that allows individuals to surpass ethnocentric perceptions, perspectives and behaviour and permits inculcation of international literacy" (p. 1), and that this is achieved primarily through the internationalized curriculum. Scholars tend to understand the internationalization of curriculum as a process of infusion (Francis, 1993; Knight, 2000, 2004; McKellin, 1998). Yet, evidence of internationalized curriculum reported in the literature amounts to little more than course offerings with international content such as area studies, comparative and international studies, development studies, international business, communications and so on. There has been little interest in exploring the notion of internationalized curriculum as a process of infusion.

Aoki (2004) has described three views or models of "school" that are relevant to this conversation. The first school strives to develop "rational thinking" skills; here, "the curriculum" is understood as "a thinking curriculum" that emphasizes "intellectual skills" (p. 361). Aoki's second kind of school is all about "doing"; it is a school that emphasizes and nurtures practical skills for productive purposes (p. 361). This school is utilitarian oriented; here, usefulness in the post-school workplace is the guide to curriculum building. In other words, this type of school prepares students for the marketplace and, ultimately, moulds students into "marketable products" (p. 361). Aoki compares this model to professional schools at universities. I contend that this perspective of the role and function of the school reflects the predominant orientation to postsecondary "schooling," in which notions of global citizenship, participation in a global village, intercultural competencies—all popular buzz words for university plans and visions for the future—are tied to the "usefulness" for the competitive postuniversity job market. Influences of this approach and its impact on curriculum development for international education are rarely discussed in the internationalization literature. This paper is an exception. Yet, before I proceed to address these issues, I would like to consider Aoki's third type of school, which offers an alternative to the "thinking" and "doing" models discussed above.

Aoki's (2004) model school is "given primarily to being and becoming, a school that emphasizes and nurtures the becoming of human beings. Such a school will not neglect 'doing' but asserts the togetherness of 'doing' and 'being' enfolded in 'becoming.' Here, it is understood that to do something, one has to be somebody" (p. 361). I shall return to this point later, for it will serve to guide our conversation on reconceptualizing internationalized curriculum. Aoki's approach is nothing new, but we need to revisit it given the increasing commodification of international education in the postsecondary sector. At this point, however, I will continue to contest and contextualize and argue that doing so will provide the opportunity for the complexity that conversations on internationalization often avoid. As Bond (2006) warned, "In spite of changes that have already occurred in some universities and in some fields of study, the internationalization of the curriculum has the potential to remain symbolic, an unfulfilled promise" (p. 9). To move beyond the symbolic, it is necessary to examine what influences have shaped the present views on internationalization and the notion of internationalization of curriculum in postsecondary institutions.

CONTESTING/CONTEXTUALIZING

While there is some recognition that internationalization is a response to, and even a product of, globalization, in the internationalization literature there has been little analysis of the implications of this on international education internationalization of higher education. This may be the result of the popular response to globalization: One is either for it or against it. Academics acknowledge that this unprecedented movement of people, ideas, goods, and knowledge is creating a set of conditions that are vastly different from those we have known, but the prevailing unwillingness within international education to engage in its materiality will result in the continuance of simplistic, and hence, ineffective, approaches to internationalization in general, and curriculum in particular.

The literature on the connections between globalization and education supports the argument that economic globalization is making its mark on education (Bartell, 2003; Bond & Lemasson, 1999; Cambridge, 2002; Edwards & Usher, 2000; Levin, 2003; Rizvi & Lingard, 2000; Smith, 2000). The research alludes to common themes across several countries: Most educational reform is promoted through changes in governance; change is formulated in economic terms; institutions are encouraged to be run in business-oriented managerial styles; student outcomes are aligned to employment-related skills and competencies; and there are attempts to control and initiate national curricula (Bartell, 2003; Edwards & Usher, 2000; Smith, 2000). This trend has been noted in higher education as well. Universities are becoming more corporate and less collegial, more consumer oriented, and more concerned with accountability and excellence (Edwards & Usher, 2000, p. 79). Indeed, "The borders of universities have opened in new ways for their services and products" (Gumport and Sporn, as cited in Bartell, 2003, p. 48). Edwards and Usher (2000, pp. 76–81), citing Lyotard's analysis of knowledge production in post modernity, describe this in terms of "performativity," which they define as performing to external demands. Here, performativity of the institution is

> located within wider discourses of economic globalization and competitiveness. Education becomes the means of attaining and maintaining the flexibility that is considered necessary in the face of the technological and socio-economic change required by these conditions. (p. 76)

Education is viewed as part of the economy and as an investment in human resource development that will ensure national competitiveness on the global stage.

As universities respond to the needs generated by globalized conditions, internal tensions arise (Scott, 1998). On the one hand, universities are "local" institutions, expected to take care of the needs of local communities. This "inward-looking" orientation includes providing marginalized people with access to all university programs and structures. On the other hand, competition, national pressures, and opportunities created by globalization impel the university to look outwards. This prompts universities to widen the scope of the institution, enhance networks, and enter into the competitive positioning for prestige and status. Scott identified this as the global/local tension of the times, characterizing it as the tension between the "massification" of higher education and internationalization (p. 109).

In this era of globalization, the nation state is becoming increasingly insignificant; hence, the state seeks to strengthen its position by tightening its connection to higher education. At the same time, the university sees advantages in linking itself to state power. It looks to the government to augment its budget, and, in turn, governments increasingly look to universities to fulfill a national purpose. Although governments fund higher education for reasons besides making the nation more internationally competitive, they are applying increasingly more pressure on universities to play a role in aligning with national policy in the training of graduates in specific competencies. Hence, it seems that government's apparent and overarching goal is to maintain national competitiveness and national identity.

Ironically, as governments seek to align themselves with the university, they are also cutting back on university funding and resources for postsecondary institutions because of increased public and corporate pressure to direct funds to other projects. This has encouraged educational institutions to develop a more entrepreneurial approach in order to ensure survival, with strategies such as the marketing of educational products and services (Aoki's View 2 school). Cambridge (2002) compared international education to product branding: International education "may be compared with other globally marketed goods and services such as soft drinks and hamburgers; a reliable product conforming to consistent quality standards throughout the world" (p. 230).

While it is important to situate internationalization within contemporary realities, it is equally significant that one engage in "the recovery of memory and history" (Pinar, 2004, p. 240) and examine the history that has propelled it to the present. The escalation of globalization began about the time that decolonization was taking place, making way for "the new corporate colonialism" (Mander and Goldsmith, as cited in Smith, 1999b, p. 97) to take hold. The "beginnings" of international education in its contemporary form can be traced to development aid offered soon after World War II to "underdeveloped" countries that were struggling to reestablish themselves. As Bond and Thayer Scott (1999) have noted,

> Educated people were needed to build a country and to help others to build their nations abroad. Because in the minds of most Canadians the university defined what it means to be educated, education in general and universities in particular were at the heart of development." (p. 48)

During this time of development contracts and expanded activity, the meaning of the term "international education" as internationally oriented courses (such as international relations) has widened to include interactions and exchanges between educational institutions and their teachers, scholars, administrators, and students. The concept of curriculum in these programs appears to be related to the goals of development—improving, helping, and advising in situations that are largely considered deficit. Thus, a conversation concerning curriculum must include the critiques of the discourses, the ethics of development, and in particular the notion of improving different others to conform to standards set by western/northern countries.

In the marketplace of international education, the flow has been generally from east/south to west/north. As international students from eastern/southern states move to attend institutions in western/northern states, there is a growing trend among these institutions to encourage further enrolments by establishing satellite campuses and off shore delivery of programs (Knight, 2004). "Receiving" nations are predominantly rich countries of the OECD (Organization for Economic Co-operation and Development) who compete in the marketplace for a larger share of the lucrative business of international students. Internationalization, viewed from this perspective, is hardly a mutual experience or phenomenon, and access to these new forms of capital is restricted to a mobile elite. In effect, globalization creates the market for Western education, while colonial dependency creates the desire. Unfortunately, the widespread acceptance of the ideology of globalization as universal and a natural advancement or progress, has established a hegemonic educational "world order." Under such circumstances, how do educators create conditions conducive to the equitable internationalization of education and appropriate program standards?

It would appear that, unless recognized and named, international education might run the risk of reproducing and maintaining those very power relations that create and maintain debilitating dependencies. In this context, as Ghandi (1998) argued, postcolonial critique offers us "the possibility of thinking our way through, and therefore out, of the historical imbalances and cultural inequalities produced by the colonial encounter" (p. 176).[1] These considerations, the influences of globalization and the parallels with the colonial, are foundational to the task of reconceptualizing the internationalized curriculum. I will now illustrate how these theories, along with others from curriculum inquiry, can become an integral part of moving the complicated conversation of internationalization of curriculum forward.

RECONCEPTUALIZING/CONTESTING/CONTEXTUALIZING

Before we proceed, we must take a brief look at the role played by "complicated conversation." Aoki (2004) understood conversation as an open encounter: Conversation, he claimed, is "not empty," "not and neither" is it "chit-chat," but a mutual activity wherein participants "engage in a reciprocity of perspectives" (p. 228). In other words, conversation goes beyond instrumental functionality to include recognition of deeper levels of complexity.

> If East-West conversation in curriculum is to be authentically East-West dialogue, if North-South conversation is to be authentically North-South dialogue, I contend that such conversation must be guided by an interest in understanding more fully what is not said by going beyond what is said. (Aoki, 2004, p. 227)

Earlier in this paper, I alluded to many things that remain unspoken in the internationalization conversation, and that is where I will begin this particular conversation. I start by contesting the status quo.

Internationalization as "Eduscape"

The dominant paradigm of globalization—the economic market model—has penetrated internationalization. Globalization is often depicted as a centre-periphery binary model, with a powerful West engulfing the rest. In surveying the massive inequities, exclusions, appropriations and greed perpetrated through the business practices of multinational corporations, there is no doubt that the corporate economic model has, indeed, created a corrosive and hegemonic world order. However, are we, as Smith (2000) asked, so helpless that we must stand by and witness the pervasive market model as it invades our educational (and thus curricular) practices? And if we are not, what paths of resistance are available? I suggest that the cultural dimensions of globalization, theorised in sociology, and cultural studies and postcolonial thought, offer possibilities for resistance and transformation so that we may subvert the prevalent trends in internationalization and provide a theoretical basis for the internationalization of curriculum. These possibilities are being theorised in curriculum studies, as I will illustrate. First, to sociology.

129

Giddens (1990) and Robertson (1990, 1997) described globalization as a complex process driven by a number of forces. It is a "dialectical process because it does not bring about a generalized set of changes acting in a uniform direction, but consists in mutually opposed tendencies" (Giddens, 1990, p. 64). In this series of complex interactions (in effect, the synthesis of globalizing and localizing orientations) the local is not separate from, nor a binary of the global, but part of it (Edwards & Usher, 2000).

I have been drawn to Appadurai's (1990) theory on the "dimensions of global cultural flow" as a way of both understanding and theorising internationalized curriculum. Appadurai challenges the binary centre-periphery model of world systems in which forces of Western modernity penetrate and absorb peripheral cultures. He dismisses simplistic explanations for cultural flows, positing a process of indigenization by which global ideas, activities, or objects are adapted and changed, or indigenized when assimilated into a local community. To understand these "growing disjunctures," he proposes a framework of perspectival constructs called "scapes" that flow in "increasingly non-isomorphic paths" (p. 301). The dimensions through which this occurs are five-fold: ethnoscapes, the distribution of mobile individuals; technoscapes, the distribution of technology; finanscapes, the distribution of capital; mediascapes, the distribution of information through a variety of media, and ideoscapes, the distribution of political ideas and values (pp. 296–297).

Appadurai conveys the fluidity, irregularity, and variety that is characteristic of the globalization process, as well as the ways in which these various elements influence and impact one another. It offers a useful framework for understanding the extremely complex relationships among these dimensions and the multiple ways in which flows occur among them, effectively highlighting the simultaneity of convergence and fragmentation. If we see the global-local discourse in this way, we can reframe internationalization of education as an "eduscape" allowing for the simultaneity of convergence and fragmentation, and more importantly, making opportunities for the "flows" of the various elements to move in "increasingly non-isomorphic paths" rather than in the assimilationist (or conformist) paths of centre-periphery that have become expected from a western-eastern binary.

Notably, Aoki (2004) also used images of landscapes in an essay dealing with "multiplicities" and the "curricular landscapes of practicing teachers and their students" (p. 299). Aoki referred to the tensions between curriculum-as-plan, and curriculum-as-experience. This is the "other curriculum," the lived curriculum with all of its multiplicities. Aoki reminds us that we often think of curriculum singularly as "*the* curriculum" (p. 204), meaning "curriculum-as-plan," which generates "an instrumental landscape" (p. 204). He cites Deleuze in urging us to consider multiplicity and the *between*:

> In *Dialogues*, Deleuze states: "In a multiplicity what counts are not . . . the elements, but what there is between, the between, a site of relations which are not separable from each other. Every multiplicity grows in the middle." (Aoki, 2004, p. 205)

Aoki goes on to understand this as the space (between) curriculum-as-plan, and lived curriculum, conceiving of curriculum as "an open landscape of multiplicity" (p. 207).

As I bring these topographical ideas together, internationalization is an eduscape, a space of the between, a "multiplicity that grows in the middle," the open landscape where mediascapes, ethnoscapes, financescapes, and ideoscapes influence one another in multiplicity. In yet another connotation, the eduscape of the internationalized curriculum is indeed the lived curriculum of the students. This is complicated conversation that results in complexity of practice because it requires "a living in tensionality—a tensionality that emerges, in part, from indwelling in the difference between two curricula: the curriculum-as-plan and the lived curriculum" (Aoki, 2004, p. 202). Let me illustrate this with a brief example.

Although tensions and in-between spaces are a reality for most students as they struggle to find personal relevance within the curriculum-as-plan, living in the interstices is an especially challenging and recognizable condition for international students enrolled in our universities. Our instructional team, working with an international cohort of graduate students from China, grappled with the tensions arising from "indwelling" between the institutional expectations imposed by curriculum-as-plan and our experience of the lived curriculum (Beck, Ilieva, Scholefield, & Waterstone, 2007). These students had come to Canada with the aim of taking back "profound knowledge" and a Western degree in English language teaching, acquisitions that would improve their job market prospects in their own countries. As a colleague explained, "Part of our task as educators in this International Program was to teach the practices privileged and legitimated in the particular field or marketplace of Western higher education" (Waterstone, as cited in Beck et al., 2007) and to do it in a way that enabled students to participate in scholarly activities as part of their curriculum. Among the challenges we negotiated were situations related to being positioned as the gatekeepers of desired knowledge, challenging the norms of internationalization and the promotion of Western ideas and "knowledge" as universally desirable, and creating an environment where the students could "become" rather than conform. We found ourselves experiencing and occupying the cracks and fissures that were forming between curriculum-as-plan and the eduscape that was unfolding (Beck et al., 2007). "It is," Aoki explained, a space of doubling, where we slip into the language of "both this and that, but neither this nor that. . . . The space moves and is alive" (as cited in Pinar, 2005, p. 5).

The idea of in-between spaces that influences our thinking emerges as well in Homi Bhabha's notion of the Third Space. Space becomes an especially interesting theoretical and physical terrain in globalized times. As the forces of globalization form and reinforce perceptions of a diminishing space, a compression of space and time, and a move towards "one space," there is a near preoccupation with reclaiming space and creating new space (Edwards & Usher, 2000).

Third Space

Bhabha (1994) theorised a third space in the context of cultural difference. He claimed that there is an incommensurability about cultural difference that is difficult to accommodate under one universalist framework. Bhabha described the concept of cultural translation in terms of culture functioning as a "signifying or symbolic activity" (Rutherford, 1990, p. 210). According to Bhabha, cultures are not single fixed entities; rather, they have lack an essence and are always "subject to intrinsic forms of translation" (Rutherford, 1990, p. 210). Bhabha acknowledged that translation might be interpreted as a form of imitation in which the original itself is never finished (Bhabha, 1994). Given that cultural translation denies the essentialism of a culture, cultural forms are always in a process of hybridity. For Bhabha (Rutherford, 1990), "The importance of hybridity is not to be able to trace two original moments from which the third emerges, rather, hybridity…is the "third space" which enables other positions to emerge" (p. 211). Cultural translation is about negotiating new situations from the perspective of re-formed positions and ideas rather than from a position within old paradigms. As Bhabha has noted, "A new situation may demand . . . that you should translate your principles, rethink them, extend them" (as cited in Rutherford, 1990, p. 216).

This "new situation" emerges within the action of internationalizing the curriculum, which is situated in the negotiation and conversation about and within cultural difference. Aoki (2004, chap. 21), in an essay exploring hyphenated Canadian identities, examined the experience of Ozawa, a Japanese musician/conductor living in the West and playing western music. A media article of the day described Ozawa as living in two worlds; Aoki, in contrast, understood Ozawa as living "between East and West" (p. 354). He continued:

> I see his dwelling as a dwelling in tensionality in the realm of between, in the tensionality of differences. It is the difference that really matters and for Ozawa, as for us, it is not so much the elimination of the differences, but, more so, the attunement of the quality of the tensionality of differences that makes a difference. (Aoki, 2004, p. 354)

This suggests a profound possibility for curriculum that is located in the multiplicity of cultural difference: the attunement of the quality of the tensionality of difference. As educators who find ourselves in the space between, in the "inter" of the international, we might first begin our task by understanding and acknowledging the tensionality of difference, and attending to the attunement of those tensions, or even, the facilitation that leads to personal attunement.

Writing about Aoki, Pinar (2005) observed, "This 'third space' within which we can dwell both incorporates and leads us to the world outside" (p. 5). There are parallels here with the "world" and its local-global (within and outside) implications. The third space where multiplicities grow and from which we negotiate the world emerges in-between the local and the global spaces. The emergent and diverse conversations that I have had with the international students participating in a qualitative study investigating their experiences confirm their constant negotiation between these worlds. This negotiation was both imagined and real, between the materiality of their being in a foreign place that professes to welcome diversity and the experience of having to conform and be contained. Their survival, and success, relates to whether, and how, they are able to live these tensions.

Place and Space, Local and Global

Along with space, the theme of place is predominant in globalization theory and international curriculum studies. In the former, there are accounts of the consequences of globalization including deterritorialization (Appadurai, 1996), disembedding of people from place (Giddens, 1990), and loss of "home" (Edwards & Usher, 2000). These consequences have led to vast movements of people due to various causes. Giddens (1990) explained disembedding as a "lifting out" of social relations from local contexts of interaction and their "restructuring across indefinite spaces of time-space" (p. 21). Thus, for Giddens, globalization is a stretching of worldwide social relations (p. 64) that reduces the significance of local activities and events and their impact on people's lives and autonomy, and so sets in motion a perpetual cycle of disembedding. Edwards and Usher argued that the heightened consciousness of "one place" which globalization produces results in an increased and intensified awareness of the "interconnectedness of local ecologies, economies and societies, of the significance of place and location" (p. 10). The local, accordingly, is not in opposition to the global but must be understood as a part of it.

There are parallel conversations about the local and global in curriculum studies. Pinar (2005), referring to the work of Zhang and Zhong, emphasized that "curriculum wisdom" [has a] "local character." Zhang and Zhong pointed out that in this era of globalization it is crucial to "understand the locality of curriculum wisdom." To understand "locality," Zhang and Zhong emphasized the idea of "place," suggesting a geographical—in its cultural as well as physical sense— conception of "locality" (p. 2). This move to validate and honour locality counteracts the dominance of globalization and the perceived universality of Western thought inherent within it. Yet, the notion of local, whether as place/locality or as emerging from a specific location, is complex and contestable. The anticolonial stance inherent in much local curricular wisdom is essential to the process of countering the present trend to promote (and generate a desire for) Eurocentric or Western curricula as universal knowledge. However, a local postsecondary classroom within a Canadian institution will likely include a multiplicity of learners. In a context such as this, what does the wisdom of the local mean? Whose idea of local will be adopted, and where does that locality reside? Further complications arise when we realize that there is much implicated in the local that is nonlocal. As Cresswell (as cited in Miller, 2006) argued, "Thinking of place as performed and practiced can help us think of place in radically open and nonessentialized ways where place is constantly struggled over and reimagined in practical ways" (p. 35). Wang (2006) examined these dilemmas, concluding that

> the concepts of both the local and the global are hardly stable signifiers: the interactions among the local destabilizes the global while the global affects the formation of the local. A dynamic movement between the local and the global questions both as fixed identities. (p. 3)

Wang's assessment echoes the sociological analysis of these concepts: It illustrates an understanding of "an intertwined, multilayered, and moving relationship [between local and global] to form a network with complex links" (this parallels the eduscape). Wang theorised this relationship as a "third space"—yet another synchronicity that speaks to how well this concept resonates for us as an idea that has come into its own.

SEEKING THE "INTER"

I would like to return to Aoki's conception of a "View 3" school, one that facilitates the becoming of both learner and teacher. A learning environment oriented around being encourages reflexivity about the self, the world, and the kinds of conditions that influence the lived-experience. Being with self and others is a prelude to doing and thinking (Aoki, 2004, p. 361). In a space shaped by this particular orientation toward learning, conversation becomes a powerful means by which educators can facilitate such a state of being. As Aoki explained,

> The meaningfulness of one understanding comes into view illuminated by the whole context; and the meaningfulness of the whole comes into view illuminated by a part. It is in this sense that I understand conversation as a bridging of two worlds by a bridge, which is not a bridge. (p. 228)

How might these conceptions influence the conversations around internationalizing the curriculum? The conversation, though complicated, has turned up some patterns of convergence, such as conceiving of the various connections and relationships in the internationalization process as an eduscape, and curriculum as a third space, considered as both part of the condition of, and expressive of, globalization. Miller (2006) made an important contribution when she argued "those now-unavoidable flows and mobilities point to a necessary conceptualization of a worldwide curriculum studies field as always in the making" (p. 34). I see here more patterns of convergence involving Aoki's themes of "becoming," patterns that prompt me to suggest that internationalizing curriculum itself is a task that is "always in the making."

In seeking the "inter," I am searching for a notion of curriculum that disrupts the simplistic conceptualization of internationalization as currently understood in international education, but more importantly, one that embraces curriculum's function as a bridge—that is not a bridge—between a worldwide curriculum studies field and internationalized curriculum. I fear that the conversations will not leave the bounds of curriculum studies. For those postsecondary practitioners who, subject to external demands, are already pressured to produce, the idea of curriculum-as-plan appears to be much more attractive than curriculum-as-conversation with its attendant complexity and perpetual state of becoming. To this end, I am inclined to see the current definitions for internationalizing the curriculum as part of the problem, to regard the definitions themselves as barriers that shut down the generative aspect of curriculum. Hence, as a first step on that seeking bridge, I recommend that we do away with definitions for internationalization of higher education. We can understand the condition and our task far more effectively through conversation, through attunement, and by being present in its unfolding. Gough (1999) believed that any advances made in addressing the complexity of the condition and task at hand were "more likely to emerge from a state of disequilibrium rather than stability" (p. 82). Despite the current scepticism surrounding opportunities for conversation, I am hopeful that the conversations will begin, for internationalization carries within it, metaphorically and etymologically, the possibility for "inter," if only we seek it.

NOTES

[1] I do not subscribe to the view that the term "postcolonial" signals the end of colonization. Rather, I understand it as a position for reflecting on, and being vigilant about, colonial oppression, and for advocating anticolonial resistance, and transcending the colonial condition, which manifests itself in diverse settings and forms, such as the psycho-social impacts of colonization of the mind as articulated by Nandy (1983).

REFERENCES

Aoki, T. (2004). *Curriculum in a new key: The collected works of Ted T. Aoki.* Mahwah, NJ: Lawrence Erlbaum.

Appadurai, A. (1990). Disjuncture and difference in the global cultural economy. In M. Featherstone (Ed.), *Global culture: Nationalism, globalization and modernity* (pp. 295–310). London: Sage.

Appadurai, A. (1996). *Modernity at large: Cultural dimensions of globalization.* Minneapolis, MN: University of Minnesota Press.

Association of Universities and Colleges of Canada (AUCC). (2007). *Internationalizing Canadian campuses.* Report on findings of the 2006 Survey on Internationalization. Ottawa: AUCC. Retrieved January 2008, from http://www.aucc.ca/_pdf/english/publications/aucc-scotia_web_e.pdf

Bartell, M. (2003). Internationalization of universities: A university culture-based framework. *Higher Education, 45*(1), 43–70.

Beck, K. (2001). *An ethic of inclusion for international education: A response to globalization.* Unpublished master's thesis, Simon Fraser University.

Beck, K., Ilieva, R., Scholefield, A., & Waterstone, B. (2007, February). Locating gold mountain: Cultural capital and the internationalization of teacher education. *The Journal of the American Association for the Advancement of Curriculum Studies, 3.* Retrieved March 2007, from http://www.uwstout.edu/soe/jaaacs/vol3/beck.htm

Bhabha, H. (1994). *The location of culture.* London: Routledge.

Bond, S. T. (2003). *Engaging educators—Bringing the world into the classroom. Guidelines for practice.* Ottawa, ON: Canadian Bureau for International Education.

Bond, S. T. (2006, March). *Transforming the culture of learning: Evoking the international dimension in Canadian university curriculum.* Paper presented at the conference on Internationalizing Canadian Universities. York University. Retrieved April 2006, from http://international .yorku.ca/global/conference/canada/papers.htm

Bond, S. T., & Lemasson, J.-P. (1999). *A new world of knowledge: Canadian universities and globalization.* Ottawa, ON: International Development Research Centre.

Bond, S. T., & Thayer Scott, J. (1999). From reluctant acceptance to modest embrace: Internationalization of undergraduate education. In S. Bond & J.-P. Lemasson (Eds.), *A new world of knowledge: Canadian universities and globalization* (pp. 77–98). Ottawa, ON: International Development Research Centre.

Cambridge, J. (2002). Global product branding and international education. *Journal of Research in International Education, 1*(2), 227–243.

deWit, H. (2002). *Internationalization of higher education in the United States of America and Europe: A historical, comparative and conceptual analysis.* Westport, CT: Greenwood.

Edwards, R., & Usher, R. (2000). *Globalization and pedagogy: Space, place and identity*. London and New York: Routledge.

Francis, A. (1993). *Facing the future: The internationalization of post-secondary institutions in British Columbia*. Vancouver, BC: Centre for International Education.

Gandhi, L. (1998). *Postcolonial theory: A critical introduction*. New York: Columbia University Press.

Giddens, A. (1990). *The consequences of modernity*. Stanford, CA: Stanford University Press.

Gough, N. (1999). Globalization and school curriculum change: Locating a transnational imaginary. *Journal of Educational Policy, 14*(1), 73–84.

Gough, N. (2004). A vision for transnational curriculum inquiry. *Transnational Curriculum Inquiry, 1*(1), 1–11. Retrieved May 2006, from http://nitinat.library.ubc.ca/ojs/index.php/tci

Harari, M. (1981). *Internationalizing the curriculum and the campus: Guidelines for AASCU institutions*. Washington, DC: AASCU. (ERIC Document Reproduction Service No. ED212244)

Knight, J. (1994). *Internationalization: Elements and checkpoints*. Ottawa, ON: CBIE.

Knight, J. (1995). *Internationalization at Canadian universities: The changing landscape*. Ottawa, ON: AUCC & Ryerson International.

Knight, J. (2000). *Progress and promise: The 2000 AUCC report on internationalization at Canadian universities*. Ottawa, ON: AUCC.

Knight, J. (2003, Fall). Updating the definition of internationalization. *International Higher Education, 33*, 2–3. Retrieved from http://www.bc .edu/bc_org/avp/soe/cihe/newsletter/ News33/text001.htm

Knight, J. (2004). Internationalization remodeled: Definition, approaches, and rationales. *Journal of Studies in International Education, 8*(1), 5–31.

Lemasson, J.-P. (1999). Introduction: The internationalization of Canadian universities. In S. Bond & J.-P. Lemasson (Eds.), *A new world of knowledge: Canadian universities and globalization* (pp. 1–20). Ottawa, ON: International Development Research Centre.

Levin, J. S. (2003). Two British Columbia University colleges and the process of economic globalization. *The Canadian Journal of Higher Education, 33*(1), pp. 59–86.

Maidstone, P. (1995). *International literacy. A paradigm for change*. Victoria, BC: Province of British Columbia Ministry of Skills, Training and Labour.

McKellin, K. (1996). *Maintaining the momentum: The internationalization of British Columbia's post-secondary institutions*. Victoria: British Columbia Centre for International Education.

Mestenhauser, J. (1998). Introduction. In J. Mestenhauser & B. Ellingboe (Eds.), *Reforming the higher education curriculum: Internationalizing the campus* (pp. xviii–xxvii). (Series on Higher Education). Phoenix, AZ: American Council on Education & Oryx Press.

Miller, J. L. (2006). Curriculum studies and transnational flows and mobilities: Feminist autobiographical perspectives. *Transnational Curriculum Inquiry, 3*(2), 31–50. Retrieved March 2007, from http://nitinat. library.ubc.ca/ojs/index.php/tci

Nandy, A. (1983). *The intimate enemy: Loss and recovery of self under colonialism*. New Delhi: Oxford University Press.

Pengelly, B. (1989). *The development of international education activities in British Columbia colleges 1978–1988*. Unpublished master's thesis, University of British Columbia.

Pinar, W. (2004). *What is curriculum theory?* Mahwah, NJ: Lawrence Erlbaum.

Pinar, W. F. (2005). A bridge between Chinese and North American curriculum studies. *Transnational Curriculum Inquiry, 2*(1), 1–12. Retrieved March 2006, from http://nitinat.library.ubc.ca/ojs/index.php/tci

Raby, R. (1995). *Internationalizing the curriculum: Ideals vs. reality*. Paper presented at the 19th Annual Conference of the Association of California College Administrators, San Jose, CA. (ERIC Document Reproduction Service No. ED388368)

Rizvi, F., & Lingard, B. (2000). Globalization and education: Complexities and contingencies. *Educational Theory, 50*(4), 419–426.

Robertson, R. (1990). Mapping the global condition: Globalization as the central concept. In M. Featherstone (Ed.), *Global culture: Nationalism, globalization and modernity* (pp. 15–30). London, Newbury Park and New Delhi: Sage.

Rutherford, J. (1990). Interview with Homi Bhabha. In J. Rutherford (Ed.), *Identity: Community, culture, difference* (pp. 207–221). London: Lawrence & Wishart.

Scott, P. (1998). Massification, internationalization and globalization. In P. Scott (Ed.), *The globalization of higher education.* United Kingdom: The Society for Research into Higher Education & Open University Press.

Smith, D. (1999). Economic fundamentalism, globalization and the public remains of education. *Interchange, 30*(1), 93–117.

Smith, D. (2000). The specific challenges of globalization for teaching and vice versa. *Alberta Journal of Educational Research, 46*(1).

Stanley, D., & Mason, J. (1997). *International learning outcomes.* Victoria: British Columbia Centre for International Education.

van der Wende, M. (1995). *Internationalizing the curriculum in higher education. Internationalization of higher education.* Paris: OECD.

Wang, H. (2006). Globalization and curriculum studies: Tensions, challenges, and possibilities. *Journal of the American Association for the Advancement of Curriculum Studies, 2.* Retrieved in March 2007, from http://www.uwstout.edu/soe/jaaacs/vol2/wang.htm

Whalley, T. (2000). *Internationalizing learning through linked assignments: An instructor's manual.* Victoria, BC: BCCIE.

Kumari V. Beck
Simon Fraser University

JAMES NAHACHEWSKY AND DAVID SLOMP

12. SOUND AND FURY: STUDIED RESPONSE(S) OF CURRICULUM AND CLASSROOM IN DIGITAL TIMES

INTRODUCTION

It is a tale told by an idiot full of sound and fury. Signifying nothing.
> *Enter a messenger.*

Thou com'st to use thy tongue – thy story quickly. (Shakespeare, *Macbeth*, V.v.)

In Faulkner's *Sound and Fury*, perspective is everything. Moments happen quickly and changes come slowly. The same may be stated for classrooms and curricula in a digital age, with a shift in perspective that recently has thrown many modernist educational boundaries and underlying assumptions into doubt—including constructs of learner and teacher, and schooling itself (Gee, 2004; Knobel & Lankshear, 2007). This shift is due, in part, to young people's own fluid, de-territorialized meaning-making afforded by the consumption and, perhaps more importantly, the production of digital texts. These texts often occur in social platforms such as MySpace, Twitter, YouTube, and the like, which are adapted to, and adapted by, young people in an ever-emergent cascade of screens. In online places, students' ways of knowing and representations of their meaning-making circulate widely across time and space. Digital texts, as created by young people, become sites of action and agency. Arguably, brick and mortar classrooms are not.

The implications of evolving digital platforms for educational product and process are beginning to drive curriculum theory more pointedly, particularly within the situated discourse of English language arts (ELA), or language and literacy education. Stoicheff and Taylor (2004) declared, "Today digitization has opened up endless possibilities for visual and acoustic innovation, but our understanding of what constitutes a text remains rooted in the traditions of the medieval page. The architecture of the page has not changed significantly since then, a result of its tremendous economy and functionality" (p. 8). Yet Bolter (2001) declared that we are living in the "late age of print" (p. 2). This evolution of textuality, just as changes to education as a whole, is complex. Within books themselves, Lewis (2001) has likened textual and reader relationships in a manner that we may adapt to view teacher, learner, and the text of curriculum – as an ecology: "Word and image, organism and environment, mutually shape each other but there is no reason to suppose that the dynamics of this relationship remain the same from page to page, let alone from book to book" (p. 48). Much of the contemporary textual landscape in which young people are developing their

J. Nahachewsky and I. Johnston (eds.), Beyond 'Presentism': Re-Imagining the Historical, Personal, and Social Places of Curriculum, 139–151.

"literate habitus bubbles up and flows around popular and consumer culture and emergent electronic texts, often out-manoeuvering or subverting the supervisory gaze and control of adults" (Carrington, 2005, p. 45). The spaces of classroom and educational digital texts create complex dialogic "contact zones" (Bakhtin, 1981), where we may witness the representation of learner, teacher, and curriculum in interesting, complex, and nontraditional ways.

This chapter, through its suite of three situated writings, examines the responses of curriculum and classroom to the sound and fury that informs the discourse of evolving literacy and learning in new times. These writings emerge directly from two qualitative studies, "Reading the Writer" (Nahachewsky, 2003) and "At the Edge Reason" (Nahachewsky, 2009), that inquired into the experiences of students and teachers in a virtual, and a traditional English language arts classroom in two Western Canadian Provinces. These two studies provide a situated, yet longitudinal perspective which reveal the complexity of teaching and learning in a digital age; complicating subjective "presentism" (Pinar, 2004) in theory and practice. The first section of this chapter is a critical reading of the Western and Northern Canadian Protocol (WNCP), which provides a common curricular outcomes-based English language arts framework for the two provinces in which the classroom studies were conducted. As we shall see, this common curriculum framework strives to define and perhaps limit the perspective(s) of who students and teachers are.

THE CURRICULUM

When Father gave it to me he said I give you the mausoleum of all hope and desire; it's rather excruciatingly apt that you will use it to gain the reductio ad absurdum of all human experience which can fit your individual needs no better than it fitted his or his father's. (Faulkner, 1929, p. 76)

Language–can never be neutral, it imposes a point of view not only about the world to which it refers but toward the use of mind in respect of this world. (Bruner, 1986, p. 29)

The common curriculum text we consider in this chapter is somewhat of an anomaly in a country that gives the responsibility for the education of its young people to each province and territory. In 1993, an agreement for the development of the Western and Northern Canadian Protocol for Collaboration in Basic Education was signed by the Ministers of Education from Manitoba, Saskatchewan, Alberta, British Columbia, Yukon, and the North West Territories. Nunavut signed on to the project 7 years later. In the preamble to the 1993 protocol, the Ministers of Education acknowledged that, although education is a provincial jurisdiction in Canada, common expectation and concerns regarding basic education among Canadian provinces could be addressed through a collaborative coprovincial process. Further, the ministers agreed the WNCP should establish high standards for education and ensure students access to an array of educational opportunities. The primary issue the ministers identified in the agreement was *the need to optimize the limited resources of the provinces in improving education*. To that end, the provinces agreed to collaboratively create new curricula and to work together to develop both standards of student performance and student assessment programs. Reaction panels composed of teachers, administrators, parents, postsecondary educators, business representatives, and members of community organizations provided feedback on the process and the product. This collaborative effort resulted in the identification of common educational goals and student learning outcomes designed to prepare students for present and future language requirements:

> Clear student learning outcomes and high learning standards in the ELA curriculum Framework are designed to prepare students for present and future language requirements. Changes in society and technology have affected and will continue to affect the ways in which students use language to think, to communicate, to learn. Students must be prepared to meet new literacy demands in Canada and the international community. The ability to use language effectively enhances students' opportunities to experience personal satisfaction and to become responsible, contributing citizens and lifelong learners. (WNCP, 1998, p. vii)

Foundational to a critical understanding of the WNCP is an understanding of its conception of *language*. The WNCP ELA framework grounds its understanding of language in a Vygotskian perspective. As such, it defines language as a tool. It recognizes that skill in applying this tool is developed within social contexts. The protocol links this tool directly with understandings of thought, and it acknowledges that skills needed to apply this tool are transferable across contexts. Multiple purposes are also suggested throughout the document. These purposes include the following: to facilitate thinking, define culture, develop personal identity, build interpersonal relationships, extend experience, facilitate reflection, contribute to a democratic society, construct and convey meanings, and facilitate metacognitive awareness. Each of these purposes, however, begs a larger purpose, identifiable in the question, To what end? For example, to what end do we use language to facilitate thinking or to construct meanings? This larger purpose is not clearly defined in the framework.

In *Actual Minds, Possible Worlds*, Bruner (1986) suggests that our use of language has a constitutive role in creating social reality and concepts of our *selves*. This has important implications for the culture of education and the concepts of self that teachers and students co-construct particularly through readings of and engagement with curricula in digital times. Bruner believes that much of education has lost this sense of wonder and exploration by merely transmitting culture and knowledge. Students are seen as participants in this culture but as participants who are given a role "as performing spectators who play out their canonical roles according to rule when the appropriate cues appear" (p. 123). This role causes "the child to only identify himself as owner, as user, never as creator; he does not invent the world, he uses it; there are prepared for him actions without adventure, without wonder, without joy" (p. 124). Bruner would rather that students have a role in making and remaking the culture of education, in negotiating meaning, and opening a sense of wonder.

If students are allowed, through openness in the curriculum and their teachers' language, to become part of a negotiation, facts then are created and become interpreted understandings shared by teacher and students, rather than transmitted by teachers as predisposed 'truths'. The students become "at once an agent of knowledge making as well as a recipient of knowledge transmission" (Bruner, 1986, p. 127). The role of teachers, then, in part, is to use language to negotiate meanings in relation to the texts of the students' lives, the curriculum, and educational culture. Bruner believes that only through opening curriculum's possibilities, through an understanding of the importance of language, can teachers allow students to help create that culture:

> If he [a student] fails to develop any sense of what I shall call reflective intervention in the knowledge he encounters, the young person will be operating continually from the outside in—knowledge will control and guide him. If he succeeds in developing such a sense, he will control and select knowledge as needed. If he develops a sense of self that is premised on his ability to penetrate knowledge for his own uses, and if he can share and negotiate the result of his penetrations, then he becomes a member of the culture-creating community. (Bruner, 1986, p. 132)

In Bruner's view, learning becomes a constructed experience within a community that can respond to, and perhaps transform, the challenges and changes of static curricula in a digital age. We must look to real classroom experiences to consider the response of teachers and students to the sound and fury of this digital age.

A DIGITAL CLASSROOM

> Through the fence, between the curling flower spaces, I could see them. (Faulkner, 1929, p. 3)

Our emergent digital times, through a cascade of hyper-textual and multimodal possibilities—both textual and pedagogical—challenges the authority of any one author or teacher. Educational theorists have become intrigued by these challenges and changes in relation to classroom practices and literacy curricula such as the WNCP (1998). In this section of the chapter, we visit an online senior English language arts classroom to better understand the interaction and relation of the "classroom" teacher, his students, and changing times. Through this example, one can perceive a challenge to "presentism" through a coauthoring of "curriculum" beyond the page, and "classroom" beyond walls.

Reading the Classroom in First Person

The home page of this educational Web site opens up a unique but highly structured learning environment. It combines static and dynamic text, icons, symbols, and multicolored hyper-text links on a subtly colored background. The page follows a basic left to right, up to down split that made its navigation intuitive according to culturally normative reading patterns. Yet one was not restricted by this orientation. A flashing keyhole icon, a symbolically sun-drenched "Thought for the day," and multicolored textual links suggested the reader/viewer construct their own path of experience and understanding in this educational hypertext.

Under the heading of "Homeroom for:_____" and a dynamic banner that advertised the school board's online classes, several interactive links as well as static bits of text are located. A blue-colored "English B 30" heading link the reader/viewer to a separate "ELA 30 World Literature Homepage" that consists of the school board's logo in motion, and five other dynamic iconic links titled "Cyber-orientation (read first)," "Calendar," "Course materials," "Communication tools," and "Student tools."

On the Homeroom page directly beneath the course icon, I noticed other linked textual messages such as, "There are new discussion postings," and "There are new assignment postings for you." Across from these messages sits the "Thought for the day," which on this day was somewhat appropriate: "Even if you can control nothing else in your life, you can indeed exercise powerful and effective control over the thoughts that occupy your mind."

At the bottom of the Homeroom page sit two headings, "Bookmarks" and "Personal." Each heading has supporting links for the student, such as "Participating in an e-learning community" and "Ask a homework/research question." These are part of the commercially homogenous Web CT program but could be personalized in content choice for individual reader/viewer's academic needs.

As a researcher and adapting reader, I navigated my way through the web-course and its pages. Questions and concerns kept surfacing for me: What were the students experiencing? How comfortable or uncomfortable were they in this environment? Did they find the text and graphics engaging or boring? Would they set the class up differently than it was? Would they be allowed to make changes to the structure and operation of the class, its assignments, or readings? What were the new reading experiences for them? Perhaps most importantly, I questioned how this environment and its complicated discourse affected their previous literacy practices.

Course/Coarse Expectations

I continued clicking and linking through the presented order of five icons on the home page and skimmed their content. As I continued my online observations I was able to orient myself with this online classroom environment, its structure and operation. The information located through the links was for the students' benefit. It allowed them to get a sense of the functioning of the software, appropriate classroom communication behaviours, classroom routines, as well as prescribed readings and assignments. The information consisted of a combination of policy statements, rules, lists, anecdotes, and textually-aided pictorial demonstrations that originated from the school's administration, course instructor Mr. Rosencrantz (a pseudonym), and previously enrolled students. The multimodality of these layered textual and semiotic messages was intended to create a particular classroom culture with a goal-oriented work ethic and cooperative communication environment:

The ELA B30 course will explore an exciting new delivery system with the implementation of an interactive on-line class. The course design will offer a student-centered approach to learning. Students will be able to interact with the instructor and other students on a continual basis via e-mail, chat rooms, and bulletin boards. The wealth of resources and web-sites on the internet will truly make this course a study of global literature. . . . While there is a certain degree of independence for students, interaction with other students in the class is strongly encouraged. The Bulletin Board, the Chat Room, and the E-Mail provide wonderful opportunities for the exchange of ideas among students. In addition to the assigned tasks using these tools, students are expected to communicate frequently with each other. It is hoped that students will be the lifeblood of the discussion areas. . . . Remember that you won't have all those non-verbal cues that you get in the physical classroom, and neither will your instructor...What does this mean for you? Again, that taking a class online means you won't be sitting quietly in the classroom; participation is essential for everyone involved. . . . As always, effective communication is critical to success.

The goals of this course manifested many postulated theoretical aspects of the New London Group's (1996) concept of multi-literacies. Terms such as "student-centered," "collaborative," "interactive," "exploring," and "global" in relation to "websites," "chat rooms," "e-mail," and "bulletin boards" acknowledged an evolving way of learning as well as an evolving way of communicating. The students were reminded that their literacy practices would be different as well. They would rely exclusively on lexical cues and clues for construction of self and intended meaning: "Words on the screen help the teacher 'see' you...effective communication is critical to success." Other posited multi-literate characteristics were manifest in the inclusion of past students' comments regarding their experiences in the course. These messages, obtained through Mr. Rosencrantz's online survey of students' past experiences in the class, were democratization in the learning process. The class's public bulletin board echoed this perspective. The following communications appear as they were originally posted, with inconsistencies included (pseudonyms are used throughout):

posted by Mr. Rosencrantz on Wed Jan 30 07:46
Subject Greetings Everyone
Hi Everyone. If you're reading this, then you've jumped
over one of the technological hurdles of the course—
you can find a bulletin board message. What I want
everyone to do is to post a short little introduction.
I'll start.
I am in my 15th year of teaching. I like strong coffee,
the Boston hockey team, and golf. I have 2 kids—Saul is 4,
Samantha is 2. I love to read legal thrillers in my spare
(?) time. This will be my fourth time teaching this
class on the internet. If I've learned a few things

that help students, these are the biggies: 1. Don't get
behind 2. There's no such thing as a dumb question
(well, there is, but I don't mind if you ask them). I'm
looking forward to working with you this semester. :)

posted by Alice on Mon Feb 04 20:46
Subject Hello!
Hey everyone! It took me a while to get here, cause I
couldn't figure out what to do and by some miracle I am
finally here! yaay! Anyway, apart from that, I am
really, really looking forward to cyber school although
at the beginning I was pretty iffy about the whole
thing. I am 17 years old and attend Trinity and I
enjoy listening to guitar solo's and 80's rock music (I
am not ashamed to say it either!) I hope I get to know
everyone of you guys better and enjoy your second
semester!! Alice D.

posted by Mr. Rosencrantz on Tue Feb 05 08:03
Subject Hello!
Finally!!! Someone appreciates 80's music!!! I may have
to put some sound tracks into the course for everyone to enjoy—
Dexy's Midnight Runners, Soft Cell. Tears for Fears ...
(I'm getting a little misty right now) ;)Mr. R.

posted by Sara P on Wed Feb 06 16:16
Subject Hello!
i loooooove 80's music! it's nothing to be ashamed of.
you know what else is sweet? 80's movies. The breakfast
club, pretty in pink, sixteen candles, weird
science...john hughes was a god. -sara-

posted by Rachel L. on Thu Feb 07 09:53
Subject right?
Good Morning!! I hope this is right...I slowly figuring
this all out. It sure is different. Have a great day!
~*RL*~

posted by Mr. Rosencrantz on Thu Feb 07 15:37
Subject right?
You got it. It does get easier. :)Mr. R.

posted by Rachel L.on Fri Feb 08 09:18
Subject First Three
Good Morning everyone! How is everyone doing on those

first three assignments? I'm not very good at this part
of english. Any pointers? Thanks. ~*RL*~

posted by Cara B on Mon Feb 25 22:07
Subject whats going on
hey everyone my name is cara and i was wondering how
cyberschool was going with everyone! and a little note
to sara if you read this...80's music sucks i
have no clue what you are talking about! love Cara

posted by Sharron on Mon Feb 25 23:16
Subject whats going on
cara, you're cracked. 80's music is the best!!! same
with 80's movies!! The Breakfast Club was on this
weekend, anybody catch it? sooooo good! Here's something
to think about, back in that day, Molly Ringwald, Emilio
Estevez, Judd Nelson, Ally Sheedy, and Anthony Michael
Hall were super popular actors. Now they're pretty much
unheard of. Ever think that Brad Pitt, Ben Affleck,
Jennifer Love Hewitt etc. are going to be lost in
obscurity in the next 10 years? Think about it. i'm a
dork, i know.

The above excerpted strand of writing represents one of the few strings of
communication that related to a textual topic beyond the scope of the course's
prescribed literature and topics. Although this strand mimics many of the
characteristics of synchronous online chat, the participating members, including
Mr. Rosencrantz, were writing their responses over several days. This was a high-
stakes discourse. The teacher worked to shape a culture and tone for the class
through his electronic writing. The students fluidly created their identities,
understandings, and relationships in response to Mr. Rosencrantz and other
students. One was not assured of a response to a particular posting. Rachel tried to
engage members in a discussion on the first three assignments, but no one other
than the teacher decided to respond to her. Others decidedly carried on a discourse
about 1980s (historical) texts such as music, movies, and personalities. A strong
sense of appropriation and cotextuality (Bakhtin, 1981) was established in the
public space of the bulletin board. Identities and understanding, such as Cara's,
became fluid and coauthored. Through digital spaces, learners and teacher
stretched their traditional relationships with the ELA curriculum, their idea of
classroom, and each other. The teacher and students were situated, yet they moved
through time and text in a fluent manner appropriating words and ideas in a co-
construction of understanding and identity that pushed at the edges of page, brick,
and mortar. The next section of this chapter provides another perspective—that of a
teacher and her students located within a traditional classroom space a few years
further into our digital age.

TEACHING IN A BRICK AND MORTAR CLASSROOM IN DIGITAL TIMES

> I discovered . . . then, that I had gone through all that I had ever read, from Henry James through Henty to newspaper murders, without making any distinction or digesting any of it, as a moth or a goat might . . . in a series of delayed repercussions like summer thunder. (Faulkner, 1929, p. 218)

> Teaching ELA today is like conducting an experiment with too many variables. (Kathy)

Kathy worked as department head and English specialist in a mid-sized high school in a rural community that was quickly becoming a bedroom community to a large urban centre during the recent economic boom and exponential population growth in Alberta. The location of her school meant that other local rural schools fed their middle-year students into Kathy's high school, making the student population of her classes quite homogeneous in its social, political, and religious background. This affected her perception and construction of herself as teacher:

> What you do or don't do, everybody notices and knows. The feeder schools— kids come in with a preconceived notion of who you are as a teacher, what your reputation is. So "reputation, reputation, reputation Iago"; it is everything to me and thus I've got to tread those platforms very carefully, and parents have a very strong influence on what happens in this school.

The many allusions that Kathy made during our interviews and in her written responses to the literature that she was studying with her classes revealed a teacher who possessed a strong sense of central canonical texts. She possessed a purposeful authority with literature, and literature served an explicit purpose in her classroom. Yet, her textual and pedagogical choices engaged a plurality of identity and openness to possibility that contemporary ELA teachers seem to need.

> I think as companion pieces popular culture works fine; as reference points— the kids understand that. We're doing Hamlet with the 30's and this is her first performance of her mind dissolving and as the kids said at the end "Nobody out crazies Ophelia" and that is Matt Groening, right? So they know it and there is no harm in that. I'm going to be doing *A Street Car Named Desire*. Rather than letting them know about it or showing it as an addendum at the end, I begin the play by showing them that clip from The *Simpson's*, not because it does the story but then because you can contextualize and you can say "based on this perhaps parallel, perhaps parody, perhaps slightly relevant little text, what do you now know about Blanche Dubois as Stella. Let's get your pre-thoughts out there." You know you can use the media in different ways and I don't think there is anything wrong with that but I don't think you can take away from the absolute genuine article. It is so much more profound. You can't teach *Hamlet* unless you teach *Hamlet*. A paraphrase, or a selected reading from does not cover the breadth of it. *Hamlet* scales mountains, not toboggan hills.

Kathy was very much a ripper and burner, cutter and paster of multiple texts. She did this not to build a single authoritative truth for her students in the classroom, but rather to socially construct constellations of truth through an appropriation (Bakhtin, 1981) of the myriad textual representations that orbit main canonical works. Kathy also facilitated the "textualization of self" (Richardson, 2006) that is so valued by students through many media—from digital representations to classroom chatter. But she also frequently questioned her effectiveness and identity as language and literacy teacher in digital times. The culture of the local community affected Kathy's perspective on teaching, on both the power and powerlessness of teachers. Her colleagues and students affected her evolving understandings of what a literate individual is. Her 15 years of teaching experience grounded her considerations of teaching in digital times, especially the complex nature of it. Within the changes and affordances of learning and teaching in digital times, Kathy remained aware of competing discourses and forces for her students' attention and her own energies:

> It is things—competing forces: the kids needing to go out to practice for a play when I need them here for a conversation. The kids needing, up until recently, time for CTS projects, some of which you see around the room— and now you have to teach them the technology when you don't know it yourself. The students needing to be able to access power point [*sic*] in your classroom or wanting to do exams on the computer and how do you deal with that? There're just so many details. Like the companion pieces that I needed this morning—my email file wouldn't house them, but then I opened my email to do attendance after the class had started and the file had made its way through the system and it is there and I couldn't print it and I started this process yesterday morning. So technology is wonderful but it is also terrible....The fact that I spend all weekend here and come to school at 6 in the morning seems irrelevant. What more do you need? Where does it all come from? And yet the perception of it is simplicity. Remember the science teacher who said I wish I could just pick up a book and read it to the kids. Teaching ELA is the simple and the complex.

Throughout my classroom observations, Kathy demonstrated a willingness to, and adeptness at, engaging the students in multitextual conversations. She used digital texts such as DVD movies, Photoshop representations, information from the Internet on myth and archetype, as well as canonical texts to allow for an exploration of theme. She did this in part because she believed that

> These kids are used to thinking in ways that we never were. We were taught in rote fashion, in demand fashion . . . so while they are maybe not as methodical or as organized as we would have been, they can multitask and see a variety of influences coming into a main concept. Their paradigms are different. Rather than seeing things linearly on paper they open up their computer and like a hyper text there is another window that opens up and inside that and so on; you know it is Robert Frost's poem "way leads on to way" knowing you will never come back so you lose a thread from here but

you gain another thread from there. And that's the way their brain must be hardwired—mine is not hardwired that way. I sometimes cannot follow the dynamics the way it goes—I think that's not the way I was going but okay I'll live with it. I don't know but I might be becoming perhaps a bit better at trying to house that conversation in a central stream but it's all just hit and miss. Sometimes it works and sometimes it doesn't.

Kathy's sense of her self as teacher in digital times was above all else emergent, just as her pedagogy and textual choice was. This impacted directly on her notions of literate individuals and her consideration of ELA teacher as coauthor rather than authority in the classroom.

> I feel emerging literacy. It is a perpetual quest. I hope that I'm better at it than I used to be, but I hope I'm not as good at it this morning as I will be this afternoon....I think what I author in this classroom is a platform or way to be more than the specific text itself. I publish a lot of things, I talk to them, I write to them, I write with them. But am I the author of this classroom? Absolutely not. We are co-authors—I hope so anyway....Like Lear, until I face(d) my (pedagogical) storm I remain (was) so very weak and pitifully blind; that doesn't (didn't) so much "happen" as it is perpetually happening—the verb tenses are thwarting my intentions.

The act of teaching ELA in digital times, for Kathy, was not only like conducting an experiment with too many variables; it became an ellipsis of many emergent texts and moments in a coauthoring of subject area content and self as literate and learned. What does this emergent process mean for curriculum and educational theorists?

WE TOO ARE COMPOSED OF MANY MOMENTS

> But to have the school authorities think that I have no control over her, I can't. (Faulkner, 1929, p. 180)

Can I?

We are composed of many moments, from waking through sleeping, in our personal and professional lives. Experience, memory, and theory intermingle. They provide the conglomerated aesthetic and efferent aspects of educator which alternate between very public and then cloistered stances. We are, perhaps as Kathy feels, composed of too many moments amid the binary flow of digital technologies and times. What may be most important to realize, though, is that we as educators and curricular theorists are not defined or authored during this digital age by any one moment, curriculum, or understanding of teacher and learner. As we have seen from the two studies above, teachers' and students' understandings are coauthored within the educational spaces of digital times. Perhaps curriculum, both what it contains and what it strives to constrain through presentism, can be coauthored as well.

The examples of the two classrooms, and the experiences of learners and teachers located there, clearly point to a reconsideration of individual learner and teacher, and a challenge to author(itative) knowledge as defined by curricula such as the WNCP (1998). The realm of digital spaces "makes possible—indeed, makes normal—the radical convergence of text, image, and sound in borderless ways that break down the primacy of propositional linguistic forms of 'truth bearing'" (Lankshear, 1996, p. 16). Teacher and student may be re-visioned. Understanding becomes a process engaged by many in a cascade of personal, social and historical "contact zones" (Bakhtin, 1981) rather than within one subjective individual. This perspective invites a connection to Barthes's (1977) notion of the "death of the author":

> We know now that a text is not a line of words releasing a single "theological" meaning (the "message" of the Author-God) but a multidimensional space in which a variety of writings, none of them original, blend and clash. The text is a tissue of quotations drawn from innumerable centers of culture . . . the only power is to mix writings, to counter the ones with the others, in such a way as never to rest on any one of them. (Barthes, 1977, p. 146)

This is not sound and fury. The subjectivity of "presentism" (Pinar, 2004) is challenged through an intertextual relationship of the historical past to this moment and beyond. The theorist, practitioner, and learner "contradict presentism by self-consciously cultivating the temporality of subjectivity, insisting on the simultaneity of past, present and future, a temporal complexity in which difference does not dissolve onto a flatted social surface" (p. 240). Through this deep cascade of text and experience our perspectives as educators and curricular theorists is changed. In re-visioning teacher(s) and learner(s) during these emergent digital times through a vast hypertext, skein, web, appropriation, meme, quotation, or mash-up, certain privileged texts such as mandated curricula, classroom structures, and a myopic sense of authority are relinquished to complete the sense of "self" and world so valued by teachers and students.

REFERENCES

Bakhtin, M. (1981). *The dialogic imagination*. Austin, TX: University of Texas Press.

Barthes, R. (1977). *Image, music, text*. New York: Hill.

Bolter, J. (2001). *Writing space: Computers, hypertext, and the remediation of print*. Mahwah, NJ: Lawrence Erlbaum Associates.

Bruner, J. (1986). *Actual minds, possible worlds*. Cambridge, MA: Harvard University Press.

Carrington, V. (2005). New textual landscapes, information and early literacy. In J. Marsh (Ed.), *Popular culture, new media and digital literacy in early childhood*. New York: RoutledgeFalmer.

Faulkner, W. (1929, 1984). *The sound and the fury*. New York: Random House.

Gee, J. P. (2004). *Situated language and learning: A critique of traditional schooling*. London: Routledge.

Governments of AB, BC, MN, NWT, SK, and YK. (1998). *The common curriculum framework for English language arts: Kindergarten to Grade 12*. Retrieved December 2009, from www.wncp.ca

Kermode, F., et al. (Eds.). (1997). *The riverside Shakespeare* (2nd ed.). Boston: Houghton Mifflin.

Knobel, M., & Lankshear, C. (2007). *A new literacies sampler*. New York: Peter Lang.

Lankshear, C. (1996). Critical pedagogy and cyberspace. In H. Giroux, C. Lankshear, P. McLaren, & M. Peters (Eds.), *Counternarratives: Cultural studies and critical pedagogies in postmodern spaces* (pp. 149–188). New York: Routledge.

Lewis, D. (2001). *Reading contemporary picturebooks: Picturing texts.* London: RoutledgeFalmer.

Nahachewsky, J. (2003). *Reading the writer: Multilayered literacy experiences in an online senior language arts classroom.* Unpublished master's thesis, University of Saskatchewan, Saskatoon.

Nahachewsky, J. (2009). *At the edge of reason: Teaching language and literacy in a digital age.* Unpublished doctoral dissertation, University of Alberta, Edmonton.

New London Group. (1996). A pedagogy of multi-literacies: Designing social futures. *Harvard Educational Review, 66*(1), 60–91.

Pinar, W. (2004). *What is curriculum theory?* New York: Lawrence Erlbaum Associates.

Richardson, W. (2006). *Blogs, wikis, podcasts and other powerful web tools for classrooms.* Thousand Oaks, CA: Corwin Press.

Stoicheff, P., & Taylor, A. (Eds.). (2004). *The future of the page.* Toronto, ON: University of Toronto Press.

James Nahachewsky
University of Victoria

David Slomp
University of Ottawa

AUTHOR BIOS

Kumari Beck's research interests are interdisciplinary and span international education, internationalization of higher education, globalization and postcolonial theory, social issues in education, anti-racist and multicultural education, and the ethics of care. She is an Assistant Professor in the Faculty of Education, Simon Fraser University.

David Blades is Professor of science education and curriculum studies at the University of Victoria, where he serves as Director of the Centre for Excellence in Teaching and Understanding Science. When the winds are right, he can be found pondering educational reform aboard his 27-foot sailboat, Ruach.

Tonya Callaghan is the author of the book, *That's so Gay! Homophobia in Canadian Catholic Schools.* She has over ten years teaching experience in national and international, rural and urban, Catholic and non-Catholic environments. A recipient of a Social Sciences and Humanities Research Council's Canada Graduate Scholarship, she is currently pursuing doctoral studies in education at the University of Toronto.

Suzanne De Froy is a Literacy Success Teacher at Assumption College High School and an Instructor at the University of Windsor. She works with a team of teachers and their 'at risk' students who have difficulties and disabilities in normal reading and writing processes. Her multi-sensory approach applies action research, differentiated instruction and imagery when designing individual and classroom reading and writing interventions. Her research interests include the social construction of knowledge, discourse and knowledge building, professional development, the role of technology in education, literacy development and mathematics education.

Dwayne Trevor Donald was born and raised in Edmonton and is a descendent of the Papaschase Cree. He is an Assistant Professor in the Faculty of Education at the University of Alberta. His work focuses on the curricular and pedagogical significance of Aboriginal-Canadian relationality.

Pariss Garramone is a PhD. Candidate in the Faculty of Education at York University. Her dissertation research is focused on environmental education and explores visual autobiographies of women forestry workers in Northern Ontario.

Ingrid Johnston is a Professor in the Department of Secondary Education in the Faculty of Education at the University of Alberta. Her research and teaching interests focus on postcolonial literary theories and pedagogies, curriculum studies, English education, adolescent literature and questions of cultural difference and teacher education. Her book *Re-mapping Literary Worlds: Postcolonial Pedagogy in Practice* (Peter Lang, 2003) was recently published in Chinese translation with Education Science Publishing House in Beijing.

James Nahachewsky is a member of the Faculty of Education in the Department of Curriculum and Instruction at the University of Victoria. His research interest in evolving textual ecologies and digital epistemology emerged during his time as an English language arts and media studies classroom teacher in Saskatchewan. This is his first edited book.

Rahat Naqvi is an Assistant Professor in the Faculty of Education, specializing in French and Second Language Pedagogy. She has worked in a variety of international settings that include French and Asian Studies at the National Institute of Oriental Languages, Sorbonne, Paris. Her most recent research involves examining the impact of dual language books on the bilingual development and academic achievement of primary level learners in schools across Calgary, Alberta.

Robert Christopher Nellis is a faculty member in the BEd program at Red Deer College. He has taught courses in educational psychology, media education, family studies, and English. Robert's PhD thesis from the University of Alberta's Department of Secondary Education won the 2008 Canadian Association for Curriculum Studies Dissertation Award, and his book *Haunting Inquiry: Classic NFB Documentary, Jacques Derrida, and the Curricular Otherwise* is published by Sense.

Nicholas Ng-A-Fook is an Assistant Professor of Curriculum Theory within the Faculty of Education at the University of Ottawa. He is an active member of its Developing a Global Perspective for Educators Institute. His current research focuses on provoking the interdisciplinary countenances and regional distinctions of curriculum theorizing within the field of Canadian Curriculum Studies. In turn, his research seeks to engage both the historical and intellectual dynamics of curriculum theorizing as a form of social justice through the aesthetics of life writing.

George Richardson is Associate Dean, International, and Associate Professor (Secondary Education) in the Faculty of Education at the University of Alberta. His research specializes in the role of education in national identity formation and on citizenship education in plural societies. He is co-editor of the journal "Canadian Social Studies."

David Slomp is an Assistant Professor of literacy education in the Faculty of Education at the University of Ottawa. He has published nationally and internationally on writing and assessment. His interest in curriculum theory relates to his research focus on the impact of standardized composition tests on learning and learners.

Jennifer Tupper is an Associate Professor in the Faculty of Education at the University of Regina. Her primary research interest is citizenship education. She has published in such journals as Curriculum Inquiry, Teacher Education Quarterly, Canadian Journal of Education, and Canadian Social Studies. She is co-editor with Patrick Lewis of "Challenges Bequeathed: Taking up the Challenges of Dwayne Huebner" published in 2009 by Sense Publishers.

INDEX

CPSIA information can be obtained at www.ICGtesting.com
Printed in the USA
LVOW011911011211

257431LV00002B/4/P